The Middle East Strategic Balance 2002-2003

Ephraim Kam and Yiftah Shapir, Editors

JCSS – Jaffee Center for Strategic Studies

The purpose of the Jaffee Center is, first, to conduct basic research that meets the highest academic standards on matters related to Israel's national security as well as Middle East regional and international security affairs. The Center also aims to contribute to the public debate and governmental deliberation of issues that are, or should be, at the top of Israel's national security agenda.

The Jaffee Center seeks to address the strategic community in Israel and abroad, policymakers, opinion-makers, and the general public.

The Center relates to the concept of strategy in its broadest meaning, namely the complex of processes involved in the identification, mobilization, and application of resources in peace and war, in order to solidify and strengthen national and international security.

The Middle East Strategic Balance 2002-2003

Ephraim Kam and Yiftah Shapir, Editors

 Jaffee Center for Strategic Studies
TEL AVIV UNIVERSITY

The Middle East Strategic Balance
is published with the generous assistance of
the Dr. I. B. Burnett Research Fund
for Quantitative Analysis of the Arab Israeli Conflict

This book was typeset in the Graphic Design Studio at Tel Aviv University, and printed and bound by Kedem Printing Ltd., Israel

Cover: AP photo

Contents

Tables

Charts

Preface

With this volume, the Jaffee Center for Strategic Studies launches its new publication, *The Middle East Strategic Balance 2002-2003*. It replaces what has been the Center's annual flagship publication for almost two decades: *The Middle East Military Balance*. The latter offered its readers a concise analysis of the important strategic developments in the region, together with a very detailed account of the military forces possessed by the region's states. In contrast, the new publication provides an extensive analysis of strategic developments and a brief account of the region's military forces. The change of emphasis reflects both our understanding that readers are increasingly interested in an assessment of strategic developments in the region, and modern technology, which allows us to place on line the data we collect and analyze regarding the region's military forces.

Dominating the global agenda in 2002–2003 were Middle East issues, among them events leading up to the war in Iraq, the United States war on terror that is inextricably linked to the Middle East, and the Israeli-Palestinian crisis, which in its present unresolved state looms as a major threat to regional peace and bears significant international ramifications. These issues have been debated repeatedly in Middle East affairs and thrust international attention, desired or not, on the countries in the area and the challenges they present to regional stability.

Part I of the present volume contains eight analytical chapters that focus on regional developments and issues that are particularly related to Israel's strategic options. The book opens with Ephraim Kam's strategic survey of the Middle East, which examines the principal developments in the area against the backdrop of vacillating regional trends between stability and instability, and the stability of the key states' individual regimes. In Chapter 2, Kam zooms in on two important Gulf States, Iraq, beset by the United States, and Iran, inching toward change and moderation at the same time that it appears as an increasing nuclear threat. Chapter 3, by Shlomo Brom, reviews the military balances of the Middle East, focusing on the Arab-Israeli balance, the balance in the Gulf, and the balance of non-conventional weapons. In Chapter 4, Anat Kurz analyzes the post-September 11 environment with regard to counterterrorism challenges, specifically how US efforts to construct a broad international front translated into punitive and preemptive measures.

In Chapter 5, Mark Heller examines the Arab-Israeli arena, focusing primarily on the crisis with the Palestinians in the wake of the violence that erupted following the abortive peace talks between Israel and the Palestinians, brokered by the Clinton administration. Chapter 6, written by Yehuda Ben Meir and me, surveys Israeli public opinion on issues of national security, based on the understanding that this opinion is an important determinant of Israeli strategic choices. Chapter 7, written by Imri Tov, presents a strategic assessment of Israel's economy as it struggled with the financial decline of international markets and its own burden of the Palestinian conflict. Nachman Tal's discussion of Israeli Arabs and the particular challenges that their sector presents to the State of Israel is the final chapter of the analytical portion of the book.

The second part of this volume, compiled by Yiftah Sapir, offers an overview of the region's military forces, including the major changes in the orders of battle and the key components of their force structures. The detailed data regarding the inventories of military forces that had appeared in previous volumes will now be available on line and updated on a continuous basis at the Center's website (www.tau.ac.il/jcss). Placing this data on the website and keeping it current is made possible through proceeds from the Dr. I. B. Burnett Research Fund for Quantitative Analysis of the Arab Israeli Conflict.

This book analyzes the strategic developments in the Middle East during 2002 and early 2003, up until the military campaign launched against Iraq by the United States and the United Kingdom on March 20, 2003. We at the Center deliberated extensively whether to postpone publication of this book until it would be possible to take full account of the war and its implications. In the end we decided that this would require an unacceptable delay, since these ramifications – for Iraq, the region, the Israeli-Palestinian conflict, and the international system – would take many months to unfold, especially given that the task of winning the peace in Iraq in the aftermath of the military victory was likely to prove both lengthy and difficult.

While the monumental changes expected to result from the war in Iraq are thus not covered here, we deemed it important to provide an analytical baseline for weighing these future changes. Furthermore, the Jaffee Center has also produced an initial review of the military campaign in Iraq, *After the War in Iraq: The New Strategic Balance*, published by Sussex Academic Press. A larger analysis of the ramifications of the Iraq War will be presented in the framework of the next volume of *The Middle East Strategic Balance*.

Finally, I would like to express my gratitude to the members of the Jaffee Center staff who made the publication of this volume possible: my deputy Ephraim Kam, who edited the analytical part of the volume; Yiftah Shapir, head of the JCSS Middle East Military Balance project and assisted by Tamir Magal and Avi Mor, who provided the quantitative data presented; and Moshe Grundman, assistant to the Head of JCSS, who coordinated every aspect of completing this volume. A very special thanks to our resident editor, Judith Rosen, whose sensitivity and good nature facilitated the transformation of the texts produced by our Center's research staff into a readable book. In addition, thanks go to Moshe Tlamim, principal translator of the material written in Hebrew, and Michal Semo and Tali Nov Dolinsky for the graphic design of this volume.

I hope that the book in its new format satisfies the needs and interests of readers who want to receive a comprehensive picture of recent strategic and military developments in the Middle East.

Shai Feldman, Head of JCSS
Tel Aviv, August 2003

PART I

MIDDLE EAST
STRATEGIC ASSESSMENT

CHAPTER 1

The Middle East:
The Stability Factor

Ephraim Kam

There is no doubt that the war launched in Iraq in March 2003 will prove to be the most significant development the Middle East has witnessed for more than a decade. Whatever the outcome, it will impact on critical components of the Middle East arena: the future of Iraq; the position of the US in the Middle East and on the international front; the domestic and international security of countries in the region, including Israel; the regional arms race, particularly non-conventional proliferation; and other conflicts in the Middle East, chief among them the Arab-Israeli conflict.

Along with the war in Iraq, the Middle East of 2002-2003 was heavily influenced by two additional developments whose impact will carry over into the coming years as well. One development was the war on terror, which dominated American security and foreign policy, especially in the Middle East, where it impacted on many countries in the Arab and Muslim world. The other major development was the Israeli-Palestinian crisis, which captured a leading place on the regional and international agendas, and involved the efforts of several governments to resolve the crisis, or at least limit the collateral damage. Both developments will continue to have major implications on the stability of the Middle East and the policies of some of the region's key players.

The ramifications of these developments will be examined against the general background of two dominant issues in the Middle East arena. The first issue relates to vacillating impulses between regional stability and instability, specifically the proclivity to peace process and dialogue versus the threat of war and outbreak of violence among countries and peoples. The second issue pertains to the stability of the major regimes in the Middle East, and their risk of overthrow or of collapse. The link between these two issues is obvious: peace processes and military moves will undoubtedly have an influence on regime stability; and vice versa, regime changes are likely either to contribute to dialogue and peace processes or exacerbate the risk of war.

Regional and regime stability were tied directly to the main developments of the last two years. The war in Iraq was liable to transform Iraq into the focus of regional instability, although in the long run, the fall of Saddam Hussein's regime would likely contribute to regional stability. Similarly, terrorism and the war on terror could affect the stability of Middle East regimes, as could the Arab-Israeli conflict, which has always influenced regional trends of stability. The fear existed that the current Israeli-Palestinian crisis would escalate, heighten the risk of a regional downturn, and threaten the stability of the Israeli and Palestinian leaderships, as well as the leaderships of Arab countries such as Egypt and Jordan. The opposite was also possible: a settlement of the present crisis and a return to the Israeli-Palestinian peace process could contribute to regional stability.

The following survey comprises four principal issues:

- Regional stability, especially relating to peace processes and dangers of war, which was the most important issue on the Middle East agenda. Treatment of this issue also calls for a look at long-term processes that extend beyond the last two years that are the subject of this study.
- The implications of the September 11 terror attack for the Middle East. The survey will present an overview of these implications, while the case of Iraq will be examined in detail in the chapter on the Gulf.
- The implications of the Israeli-Palestinian crisis. This issue is discussed at length in a separate chapter, and therefore the present survey will focus only on some of its main aspects, especially its regional ramifications.
- Regime stability in the Middle East. This survey will discuss the stability of the main regimes in the region, excluding Iraq and Iran, which are treated separately in the chapter on the Gulf.

The Region's Stability

Recent decades have repeatedly identified two main sources of instability and potential for war in the Middle East. One was the Arab-Israeli conflict, which implicated Israel and its neighbors, as well as more distant Arab countries, first and foremost Iraq, that were actively involved in the conflict and whose national security was influenced by it. The second source was the Persian Gulf area, where the main protagonists were Iraq, Iran, and the Gulf States, headed by Saudi Arabia.

Since the late 1970s important changes occurred on these two planes. The significance of the Arab-Israeli conflict as a cause for regional instability declined progressively since the 1979 signing of the Egyptian-Israeli peace treaty: no large-scale Arab-Israeli war broke out after 1973, although limited military operations continued to a great extent; Jordan too signed a peace treaty with Israel, joining Egypt in abandoning the cycle of war; a number of interim agreements were signed between Israel and the Palestinians; and various Arab states developed informal relations with Israel. In contrast, the Gulf area loomed as the focus of regional instability, as the last three major wars in the Middle East – the Iran-Iraq War, the Gulf War, and the 2003 Iraq War – occurred in this region. The undermining of the Gulf area's stability stemmed to a great degree from the groundbreaking change that took place in 1979: the rise of radical regimes in the two strongest countries in the region – the revolutionary Islamic regime in Iran and Saddam Hussein's dictatorial regime in Iraq. The struggle of these two regimes for regional hegemony and the rivalry between them have led to the buildup of massive armies and efforts at acquiring weapons of mass destruction. This arms race fostered regional instability, at a time when other countries in the arena, such as Saudi Arabia, were too weak to deal assertively with their radical neighbors and relied on the United States to guarantee their security.

Despite these developments, the stability that generally characterized the Middle East, especially since the beginning of the 1990s and until the 2003 war in Iraq, remained intact. First, although low-key military activity persisted for twelve years since the Gulf War, most notably between the Israelis and Palestinians, no major conflict broke out in the region. The lapse of a decade without a large-scale war was the first such interlude in the Middle East since World War II. This relative calm stemmed from a combination of inhibiting factors in the two main theaters of violence. In the Arab-Israeli circle, all-out war did not occur in the past generation for a number of reasons: the Arab states recognized Israel's overall strategic-military advantage over themselves; Arab countries incurred extensive damage in previous wars, and hence their assessment that launching another war in the foreseeable future would result in a similar defeat; the Arab states were unable to unite in a military alliance that could allow them to face Israel with their combined strength; Israel has enjoyed America's strategic backing and close friendly ties with American administrations, especially in the last decade, at a period when the radical Arab countries lost powerful outside support given the breakup of the former Soviet Union; and last but not least, major Arab countries, primarily Egypt, saw a vital interest in channeling national resources away from war preparations to the domestic sphere in order to stabilize the economy, social conditions, and their own regimes. Israel too, for its part, had no interest in initiating a war against Arab countries; quite the contrary, it preferred to exploit its strategic advantage to cement the peace process with the Arab states, even in exchange for most of the territories captured in 1967.

In the Persian Gulf, no major shocks occurred from the end of the Gulf War in 1991 until 2002. The region's relative quiet was preserved mostly due to the deterrent influence of American military presence in the region, and Washington's commitment to blocking the strategic arms buildup and aggressive intentions of the two radical states, Iraq and Iran. American pressure, despite limitations and problems in applying it in full force, rendered Iraq militarily and economically weak and appreciably isolated politically for over a decade, even though Baghdad continued to strive to restore its strategic non-conventional strength. To a lesser degree, American pressure also made it difficult for Iran to develop its military and economic capabilities. In the final analysis, the Clinton administration's policy of dual containment towards Iraq and Iran accomplished many if not all of its objectives.

Second, the end of the Cold War and the dissolution of the Soviet Union had an important stabilizing impact on the Middle East. The superpower competition that fueled the arms race and perpetuated instability in the region for nearly two generations, although not erased entirely, was greatly diminished. Russia ended its special relationship with the radical Arab states, and since the beginning of the 1990s the pro-Soviet bloc of Arab countries has ceased to exist. Russian arms supplies to the Middle East were sharply reduced and what remained was brokered on a commercial basis, not as a strategic-political arrangement. Russia developed normal political relations with Israel, and the two countries engaged in regular dialogue, a change that also led many countries in the former Soviet bloc and the Third World to reestablish diplomatic relations with Israel. Perhaps most importantly, radical Arab countries, especially Syria, no longer presumed Russian strategic-military support would be forthcoming in case of a war with Israel, as in the past. The inability to rely on superpower backing, at a time when the United States was explicitly and publicly committed to Israel's security, curbed Syria's strategic capability vis-à-vis Israel, and contributed to reducing the danger of an Arab-Israeli war.

With the end of the Cold War, a growing dialogue developed between the United States and Russia, especially under the presidency of Vladimir Putin. Putin was interested in expanding this dialogue in order to integrate his country into the Western system, revitalize the Russian economy, and enable Moscow to improve its international standing and deal with its host of socio-economic ills. The terror attack of September 11 introduced additional momentum into the superpower relationship and afforded fresh opportunities for cooperation, despite the ingrained suspicion among conservative circles in Russia as to America's intentions. Putin regarded the American decision to fight terror and topple the Taliban regime in Afghanistan as an important step in blocking both the radical Islamic and Chechneyan threats to Russia. The willingness to engage in greater cooperation was reflected in the May 2002 agreement by Presidents Bush and Putin designed to reduce the stockpile of nuclear warheads from 6,000 to 1,700-2,200, and to open a new era in relations between Russia and NATO.

In the congenial atmosphere of this dialogue, and against the backdrop of Russia's strategic decline, the United States became the only active superpower in the Middle East, and therefore abandoned its past fears of superpower confrontation, particularly within the context of a large Arab-Israeli war. At the same time, sharp differences still arose between the United States and Russia on central issues in the Middle East, for example, the war in Iraq, Russia's furnishing Iran with missile and nuclear technology, and Russian weapons supplies to other Arab countries.

Third, although the Middle East remained the world's leading region in defense expenditures, the arms race and the arms procurement trend have slackened. According to US State Department figures of 2000, Middle East states in the late 1990s imported 37 to 38% of the world's weapons. The Middle East led the world in defense spending statistics, with arms imports claiming the largest percentage (12%) of overall imports, defense expenditures accounting for the largest slice (7.5%) of the gross national product, and defense spending holding the biggest portion (approximately 22.5%) of the overall government budget. The Middle East was also the world's leading region in the size of its armies relative to the population (eleven military personnel for every 1000 people). Nevertheless, despite the region's foremost position in security investment, purchases dropped from approximately $30 billion annually (as of 1987) to $20 billion at the end of the 1990s, and security expenditures, relative to the gross national product, plummeted from 18% to 7.5% in the same period.

While the decline in the Middle East's conventional arms race was part of the general global decline in security spending since the beginning of the 1990s, several other important factors were involved. The economic crisis in the Arab world since the mid-1980s affected the regional arms market. Iraq, the Middle East's leading weapons importer in the 1980s, was banned from importing weapons since the Gulf War. Iran, also a major arms procurer in the 1980s, was forced to reduce significantly its import of conventional weapons for several reasons: the Western arms embargo; America's partially successful pressure on Iran's main suppliers, Russia, China, and North Korea, to reduce arms sales to Tehran; and domestic economic distress. The reduced import of weapons by Iran and Iraq also influenced other countries, including the Gulf States and Israel, to reduce their weapons purchasing. In the Arab-Israeli circle a number of developments slowed down the arms race and contributed to the reallocation of funds from weapons to domestic needs: peaceful relations between Israel and Egypt and Jordan, and their reduced perception of threat. Less money was spent on conventional arms because a number of countries in the region, especially the radical ones, decided to invest more resources in non-conventional weaponry. The sharp decline in the export of Russian weapons after the collapse of the Soviet Union also lowered the import of arms in the Middle East.

Fourth, in recent years, relations improved among Arab countries and between the Arab world and Iran. In effect, there remained no outstanding conflict dividing the Arab world, even if rivalries, disputes, and clashes of interest still abounded. Iraq, partially ostracized for years following the Gulf War, slowly made a comeback to the Arab arena and improved its political and economic relations with several countries, including its main rivals, Syria and Iran. Syria's relations with the two Arab states that have signed peace treaties with Israel, Egypt and Jordan, were correct, even though some suspicion lingered. Following Khatami's election to the Iranian presidency in 1997, Iran's relations with many Arab countries, including the Gulf States, Egypt, Jordan, and Iraq, also changed for the better. Particularly conspicuous within this atmosphere of goodwill was the Iran-Saudi Arabia rapprochement, which served as a beacon for other states in the Arab world and Gulf region. Their improved relationship lessened the risk of conflict between Iran or Iraq and neighboring states. Yet despite the improved atmosphere in the arena, Arab states were still marked by sharp differences of opinion and found it difficult to attend collectively to the main issues on the agenda, such as the Israeli-Palestinian crisis or the war in Iraq. Indeed, conflicting national interests and doubts of the ability to resolve the Arab-Israeli dispute through military means have helped forestall the creation of a military coalition against Israel since the 1973 Yom Kippur War. Thus, improved inter-Arab relations have not translated into any form of collective military alliance against Israel.

Fifth, despite the ongoing Israeli-Palestinian crisis, most of the Arab world continued to advocate a political solution to the Arab-Israeli conflict. The most outstanding expression of this support, Israeli-Palestinian violence notwithstanding, was the Saudi initiative of February 2002, endorsed at the Arab summit the following month, proposing a comprehensive political settlement between Israel and the Arab world, including the normalization of relations. Even with the damage caused to Arab-Israeli relations by the Palestinian uprising, and the consequent delay in the return of Egyptian and Jordanian ambassadors to Israel, the peace treaties with these two counties remained intact. Egypt and Jordan managed to thwart some serious pan-Arab attempts to impair their ties with Israel. Furthermore, while many voices in the Arab world were calling for a freeze in relations with Israel, almost no mention was made of reverting to the warpath, excluding among the radical fringes.

Finally, since the 1990s the influence of the region's radical bloc has steadily declined. Some radical regimes – Iraq, Iran, Syria, and to a lesser extent Libya – were still key regional players whose policy was characterized to a large degree by anti-Americanism and anti-Zionism, and the attempt to alter the regional status quo. Certain radical organizations, such as extremist Islamic and Palestinian groups, also flourished in many countries. Overall, however, radical forces generally operated independently because of interstate strife, for example Iraqi-Iranian contention and Iraqi-Syrian rivalry. Furthermore, the weakness of these regimes was rooted in the decline of conventional weaponry and economic distress: Iraq - because of the Gulf War and the threat of an American attack; Iran - because of the war with Iraq and American pressure; Syria - because of the economic crisis; and Libya - because of American pressure and Arab coolness towards its policy.

The American administration's declaration of war on terror and its preparations for an Iraqi operation increased the pressure on these radical regimes and organizations. Close ties to the Soviet Union, severed when the Soviet bloc disintegrated, had been the connecting thread between some of these countries. A number of states that had been considered as aligned with the radical group – Algeria, South Yemen (now part of Yemen), and even Sudan – were now more occupied with their domestic affairs. In the final analysis, the dominant tone in the Arab world in the past decade has been the moderate voice, despite continued attempts of radical regimes and organizations to wield their influence in the region.

Against these trends of stability and continuity, other factors risked undermining regional stability. Iran and Iraq were perceived by the US administration and by moderate regimes in the Middle East as posing strategic threats. Saddam Hussein's regime was considered a threat not only because of its continuing efforts to acquire weapons of mass destruction, but also for the ruthlessness Saddam had demonstrated in his use of chemical weapons and ballistic missiles against his own citizens and other Middle Eastern countries. Iran was regarded as a potential threat for several reasons: its successful buildup of an arsenal that included long-range ballistic missiles, chemical weapons, and possibly biological weapons; its continuing efforts to acquire a nuclear bomb; its deep involvement in terrorism; and the radical nature of its regime. Many moderate governments felt that the acquisition of weapons of mass destruction, especially nuclear weaponry, by either of these two radical regimes might threaten regional stability. A similar belief significantly contributed to the Bush administration's decision to disarm Iraq from its non-conventional potential by deposing Saddam's regime.

The Iraqi and Iranian efforts to acquire weapons of mass destruction should be seen in a wider regional context. In contrast to but concomitant with the de-escalation of the conventional arms race, the regional trend showed the continued development of weapons of mass destruction. A less restricted flow of materials, equipment, and nuclear technology between countries, applicable for weapons of mass destruction, enabled more small nations or relatively poor ones to obtain military strategic capabilities that were once the possession of the superpowers only. This trend has grown since the 1980s because of the eagerness of Russia, China, and North Korea to supply Middle Eastern states with weapon systems, components, equipment, raw materials, technologies, and overall assistance in the development and production of weapons of mass destruction. In the face of American pressure to halt the export of non-conventional weapon systems and technologies, the three aforementioned suppliers on more than one occasion pledged to cease or limit overseas shipments. However, they repeatedly violated their guarantees, since none proved capable of resisting the financial temptation, or because governmental control and the inspection of weapons-producing companies were ineffective.

This was the backdrop for the twenty-five countries throughout the world, one-third of them in the Middle East, that in 2003 were developing weapons of mass destruction or ballistic missiles. Most of them aspired to obtain independent production capability, although the integration of all the weapon systems components proved more demanding than production alone because of the complexity involved. The prominent feature of this phenomenon was the important role played by radical states, and therefore portended an extremely worrisome fusion of radical regimes and weapons of mass destruction. Terror organizations too, first and foremost al-Qaeda, displayed an increased interest in acquiring weapons of mass destruction, even of the relatively primitive variety. Among Muslim/Arab countries, Iran claimed a central position in the endeavor to develop non-conventional weaponry. Iran was on the threshold of producing its own Shehab-3 missile with a 1,300 kilometer range, and had plans of building missiles with even greater ranges. Furthermore, Iran was progressing quickly in its nuclear military program, and most Western estimates predicted that the Iranians would achieve tactical nuclear capability within the decade. Iran was also actively engaged in chemical and biological warfare programs, among the most extensive in the Third World. Alongside Iran, Iraq strove to obtain weapons of mass destruction, and according to the majority of Western estimates it too could acquire nuclear capability if it was not stopped.

Another source of instability was the severe blow that the Arab-Israeli peace process suffered. The Oslo arrangements dissolved, and in the summer of 2002 Israel reoccupied large chunks of Area A in the West Bank for an extended period of time because of Palestinian terror. The peace process vanished from the political horizon, and the perpetuation of violence precluded any return to the negotiating table. At the same time, the Bush administration chose to avoid investing energy in jumpstarting the peace process, in part because of the wider focus on the Iraqi crisis but also because it deemed conditions inauspicious for infusing the process with momentum. The unrelenting violence and the gaping void in the peace process gave rise, for the first time in years, to an overwhelming fear of deterioration in the general Arab-Israeli arena. The deterioration could occur primarily in the Israeli-Palestinian context, but might also extend to additional players – for example, Hizbollah, Syria, and Lebanon – even if the probability of a major escalation was deemed low. In addition, the peace talks between Israel and Syria were frozen in 2000, and conditions that could augur their renewal remained lacking.

The terror attack inside the United States did not shake essential Middle East stability. On the contrary, Washington's declaration of war on terror forced organizations and regimes affiliated with terror to curb their activity lest the United States take action against them. The ousting of the Taliban regime and the destruction of Osama Bin Laden's al-Qaeda strongholds in Afghanistan dealt a severe blow to the extremist terror infrastructure in the region. Yet the campaign in Afghanistan was not without negative results. Al-Qaeda activists and operatives connected with the organization scattered among many Arab and Muslim nations, from Southeast Asia through the Middle East and continuing to Africa. It became harder to track and locate these activists, who were still plotting mass casualty terror attacks against American, Western, and Israeli targets, and in the cases of the Bali attack in October 2002 and the bombing in Mombasa, Kenya two months later, succeeded in executing such attacks.

In addition, the economic and social destitution in many of the region's countries served as a breeding ground for fundamentalist organizations and other radical groups. Radical organizations were generally better coordinated than state bureaucracies, their members were highly motivated, and they were able both to provide the impoverished public with immediate material assistance and propound ideological-religious solutions that the regimes were incapable of giving. Radical organizations were skilled at exploiting the suspicions harbored by many people over globalization and the penetration of Western culture, and they adeptly channeled local frustration with the country's backwardness and fear of American hegemony to affiliation with their fundamentalist cause. For these reasons the radical organizations continued to pose a threat to the stability of moderate regimes, to Western interests in the region, especially American interests, and to Israel.

Finally, and above all, the regional ramifications of the war in Iraq will be extensive and far-reaching. In the short term, the consequent political instability in Iraq, the American military deployment there, and the reactions from the Arab world will combine to undermine regional stability. Yet in the long run, if the United States is able to install a new regime, moderate and with ties to the West, the results will significantly bolster regional stability.

The Middle East After September 11

The main background to the regional agenda was the September 11 terror attack and the twofold consequences on the Middle East: the war in Iraq and the war on terror declared by the Bush administration. Although the Bush administration did not accuse Iraq of explicit involvement in the September 11 attack or of direct assistance to al-Qaeda, it did present Iraq, and Saddam Hussein personally, as a factor endangering the stability of the Middle East and United States interests. Iraq figured as a pillar of what the US has coined the "axis of evil." The US government wished to take advantage of the anti-terror momentum in order to enforce firmly the prohibition on Iraq's development of weapons of mass destruction, for which the preferred solution lay in toppling Saddam Hussein's regime and its replacement with a moderate one.

The ramifications of the Iraqi crisis and the military campaign that ensued are considered extensively in the chapter on the Gulf. At this juncture, suffice it to say that the American efforts regarding Iraq encountered three major challenges. The first challenge concerned the marked withdrawal of international support for a military strike – in the Arab and Muslim world, in most Western countries, and within the United States itself. Anti-war sentiment, expressed through numerous anti-war protests throughout the world, gathered steam while the US delayed military action. Many countries refused to contribute to military efforts, and in addition, repeatedly created new diplomatic obstacles in the UN Security Council to the impending strike. The controversy regarding the war in Iraq sparked a severe crisis between European governments and the American administration and within NATO, and undermined the authority of the Security Council. At the same time, since the end of 2002 the United States managed to enlist support among several of Iraq's neighbors, which allowed the administration to prepare the logistical and military infrastructure necessary for the operation. By March 2003, the US and Britain had concentrated around Iraq and in the Mediterranean Sea about 300,000 fully-equipped troops, including task forces of eight aircraft carriers and approximately 1000 planes.

The second set of challenges concerned the execution of the military operation. The force assembled in the Gulf by the US and Britain was apparently sufficient for an attack, and there was no question regarding the balance of power in favor of the Western forces over the Iraqi military. However, the American administration did not define its objective as routing the Iraqi army or destroying its strategic infrastructure. Rather, the goal was to replace Saddam's regime with a new government prepared to destroy the country's non-conventional weapons capabilities. Therefore, the offensive would seek to undermine the Iraqi army's loyalty to Saddam Hussein, and if necessary, to penetrate and quash the regime's strongholds, especially in Baghdad and its environs. This would be a complicated process, liable to incur heavy casualties should the American force become entangled in urban warfare, and was heavily dependent on factors outside of US control, such as the cultivation and use of a viable opposition to Saddam.

The third set of difficulties concerned the aftermath of a defeat of Saddam. The American administration made it clear that even deposing Saddam and destroying its weapons of mass destructions would not fully achieve American objectives. Rather, the overt goal was to establish a more moderate regime, democratically-inclined and with ties to the US and the West. Merely ousting Saddam was liable to create an unstable political vacuum in Iraq marked by internal struggles as well as a humanitarian disaster, a situation that would invite the rise of a new radical regime to seize power. Therefore, the administration assumed that it would leave a sizable military presence in Iraq, perhaps even for an extended period, to stabilize the new regime. This force would help guarantee a government more suited to Western interests and to the cessation of plans to develop non-conventional weapons. At the same time, this force might become a prime target for terrorist attacks and encourage widespread anti-American protests in the Arab and Muslim world, both of which would make any extended presence difficult at best.

The second dimension to the September 11 aftermath was the American administration's war on terror, with implications first and foremost for the Middle East and its periphery, where the largest concentration of Muslim terror organizations operated. In many Arab and Muslim states, the struggle against terror, the approach to radical Islam, and the attitude to the United States and the West immediately became top priority issues. The trauma of September 11, America's determination to combat terrorism and its demand that countries declare their allegiances in this campaign, the US military action in Afghanistan, and the possibility of a massive American operation against a leading state in the Middle East such as Iraq all placed a great deal of sudden pressure on several countries in the Middle East and the surrounding region. These states again collided bluntly with the danger that radical Islam posed to their own regimes' survival, and understood that the future target of violent fundamentalist Islam was not only the United States and the Western world, but also moderate Muslim and Arab regimes. The United States government called on them to take practical steps against extremist Islamic organizations, despite their apprehension that these steps could ignite domestic unrest and jeopardize their stability. Some of the Arab and Muslim states worried about possible American military moves against countries actively developing weapons of mass destruction, first and foremost Iraq, or Middle East countries linked to terror whose aim was to create an anti-American front of regional instability.

After September 11, the war on terror became the central pillar of the United States foreign and security policy and the main test of the Bush administration. It promised to be a long-term campaign, complicated and arduous, spread out across dozens of countries, with a level of success that was not assured and might not always be recognized. It involved sensitive, controversial issues, for example, the feasibility of military operations against countries or organizations linked to terror, and intervention in their internal affairs. Although the first stage of this war, the military action in Afghanistan, seemed to have been waged quickly and successfully, in effect, it was still continuing long after it had begun and many of the top al-Qaeda leaders, including Osama Bin Laden, were not captured and their deaths not verified. Administration officials admitted that the military action did not achieve all of its goals, and that many terrorists were still at large, continued to operate from other countries, and posed a strategic threat to American objectives.

In preparation for the close of the Afghan stage of the campaign, the American administration examined a long list of military, security, political, legal, and economic options. Some of them were implemented, and others were in the planning and preparatory stages, including those still under debate within the administration. These options translated into three directions of activity. The first was the destruction of the al-Qaeda infrastructure and its affiliated organizations that succeeded in setting up cells and networks in scores of Muslim, Arab, and Western countries. This unremitting move would entail various diplomatic, legal, law enforcement, and financial measures and perhaps additional military ones to root out the al-Qaeda havens, and it required close cooperation with those countries where the strongholds were located. The US government was determined to proceed in this direction but stumbled across some formidable pitfalls – for example, blocking the flow of the terrorist organizations' funding was regarded in some countries as American interference in their domestic affairs.

The second form of activity was designed to destroy terrorism's infrastructure throughout the world. The background to this objective was an underlying assessment of terror organizations as an integrated system that threatened world peace and that could be eliminated through a full-fledged campaign. The decision to wage a wide offensive against terror has been made, and the administration has even decided on the various organizations to target, but as of early 2003 the full scope of its operations had not yet been determined. It can be assumed that the administration would assign priority to crushing terror organizations that endanger the United States and American interests directly or indirectly, but it is unclear to what extent it would invest its resources in destroying other terror organizations. It may well take aim first at Hizbollah because of its responsibility for deadly terror strikes against American targets, its links with Iran, its widespread terrorist activity directed from many countries, and its threat to Israel. Generally, great difficulties surrounded America's planned assault on these organizations: some were seen by their host countries and other states as legitimate liberation organizations that should be left alone, and these states were reluctant to yield to American pressure. The American administration has not yet indicated how it will deal with these organizations and their host countries, and apparently has decided to postpone any decision until after the campaign in Iraq.

Furthermore, the United States expected that states harboring terror cells would take firmer steps to "drain the swamp" that encouraged their proliferation. Long-range social, educational, religious, and cultural programs were required especially in Muslim and Arab countries, including changes in the school curricula and greater supervision of activity in the mosques, in order to transform the basic conditions that fostered the development of terror organizations. This expectation also lay behind the administration's aspiration to strengthen democratic proclivities in the Middle East. A strategy to effect cultural changes was under review by the administration but it has not yet been translated into a consolidated plan of action. We may assume, though, that American attempts to pressure countries to institute comprehensive changes will encounter severe opposition since they touch on the roots of the regimes' stability.

The third direction was the most problematic. The administration took pains to link the campaign against terror with other strategic threats against the United

States and world stability, especially those stemming from the development of weapons of mass destruction and their possible acquisition by radical regimes or terrorist organizations. In this Washington targeted Iraq as the main objective, while obscuring its intentions regarding other nations.

As with a military strike against Iraq, a central problem the American administration encountered in the war on terror was the absence of a supportive coalition, the international backing to which the administration assigned a crucial role in the war on terror. Furthermore, many of the steps planned in the war against terror could not be executed without the practical cooperation of additional countries. Therefore, the administration assigned a key role to the countries it wished to recruit: the destruction of terror networks, severance of their financial pipelines, legal action and law enforcement agencies to work against them, and intelligence cooperation. Yet the most challenging if not problematic element of the coalition that the Bush administration sought was the Muslim participation, especially the Arab component. This participation was of critical importance, since most of the states that provided safe haven for terror organizations were Muslim countries, and the United States had no desire to alienate the Muslim world.

Two main considerations influenced the Arab attitude towards the American campaign. One was the Arab countries' awareness of America's need to respond to the unprecedented attack on its soil, and of the threat that radical Islam posed, to whatever degree, to Arab and Muslim regimes as well, such that a common US-Arab-Muslim interest existed for fighting radical organizations. The degree to which Middle East countries were willing to cooperate with the American administration depended in part on the amount of pressure the administration exerted on them and their concern over Washington's reaction if they did not acquiesce. On the other hand, in practical terms their willingness to combat terror was greatly limited by the dilemma involved in extending support to an American operation aimed at Muslim/Arab regimes, or against organizations that enjoyed domestic favor. In several Muslim/Arab states support of this type had the potential of sparking severe domestic tensions because of hostility toward US designs.

The campaign in Afghanistan and the war against al-Qaeda seem to have been the limits of complicity. Arab and Muslim countries were inclined to accept the felling of the Taliban regime and destruction of Bin Laden's organization since both were ostracized and regarded as threats, and also because the link between them and the September 11 attacks was obvious. Otherwise, these countries related to the thought of additional American military ventures, especially against Iraq, with undisguised coolness. This was particularly true of Saudi Arabia, the home of the majority of the September 11 terrorists. Saudi Arabia claimed that it increased its monitoring of suspicious charity and welfare organizations and froze bank accounts with possible links to terror organizations. At the same time, the Saudis have specifically avoided detaining large numbers of Islamic activists, and it seemed that they would withhold significant tangible support to the planned American operation against Iraq.

Saudi Arabia's rationale influenced other Arab states that sensed the American pressure to join the war on terror. While publicly they expressed support for the need to extirpate terror, some of them applied a different definition to terror than that accepted by the United States, one that discounted the link between terror and Islam. If they did not hinder American activity in Afghanistan by their actions and declarations, neither did they supply it with practical assistance. A number of Arab states conveyed intelligence information to the United States regarding terrorist activity in their domains, and some of them, first and foremost Egypt and Jordan, arrested members of local terror organizations. Newly cooperative states even included Sudan, Yemen, Syria, and Libya. It was safe to assume that a number of Arab countries were prepared to take some degree of action against terrorist organizations operating on their soil as long as it served their domestic agendas, or at least left their interests intact, and on condition that the United States stayed out of their internal affairs.

Of these countries, Syria figured as a special challenge for the American administration. To date the Syrian regime appeared free from the threat of serious Islamic opposition. Damascus, however, offered safe haven to the headquarters of a number of Palestinian terror organizations, including the military arm of Hamas and Islamic Jihad, and retained a powerful influence over Hizbollah activity in Lebanon. Syria has always considered these groups not as terror organizations but as liberation movements, and it had no intention of expelling them in the wake of September 11. American pressure, however, was unrelenting, and when the Syrians realized they were liable to be a target in the American war against terror, they slightly modified their position. Intentional press leaks revealed that Syria was working with the American administration in investigating al-Qaeda activity, and Syria informed Washington that it was willing to explore ways of closing down al-Qaeda offices and terminating the activity of Syrian-based Palestinian organizations. Damascus' foreign minister also hinted that there was room for lowering the profile of the "opposition organizations." What this apparently added up to is that Syria was maneuvering to neutralize American pressure, though in fact no substantial change occurred and Syria remained a safe zone for Palestinian organizations and Hizbollah, affording them room for their activities.

Aside from Iraq, it appeared less likely today that military steps would be taken against other states. Since 1984 Iran has been officially labeled by successive American administrations as the state most involved in terrorism. Iran was also fully engaged in developing weapons of mass destruction and was further advanced than Iraq in this objective. This is why the administration assigned Iran membership to the "axis of evil" alongside Iraq and North Korea. Nevertheless, at this stage the administration preferred to make an intensive effort at maintaining a dialogue with the Iranians, and despite its disappointment at the pace of rapprochement and the weakness of moderate elements in the country, Washington made no threats of military action against Tehran. For similar reasons the administration did not threaten Syria with a military move despite Damascus' support of terror. The United States seemed to believe that political and economic pressures were the most expedient means of initiating changes in the policies of Iran and Syria. At the same time, the administration did not rule out military action against countries that continued to support terror groups, an option it hoped would exert pressure on these countries to cooperate in the campaign against terror.

The Americans' declaration of war on terror also had an impact on the Israeli-Palestinian crisis. Since September 11 the administration has displayed a greater understanding of Israel's situation as a state besieged by terrorism and of its policy for combating terror. The United States explicitly defined the Palestinian Authority (PA) and Yassir Arafat personally as parties required to exert a far greater effort at curbing terror, since their attempts to date, if any, were too few and their links with terror organizations remained intact. The Bush administration's classification of a number of Palestinian groups as terrorist or terror-affiliated organizations, including the PA-linked Tanzim, Fatah, and al-Aqsa Brigades, had two practical meanings. One, the PA was told in unequivocal terms to implement an immediate and absolute cessation of violence against Israel if it wanted to achieve an independent Palestinian state. Two, Israel gained unprecedented freedom to act against the PA and Palestinian terror cells, and above all, to operate inside PA territory, including for extended periods of time. When the Israel Defense Forces (IDF) first entered Area A during the intifada, the US administration limited the time span to a matter of hours. During Operation Defensive Shield of April 2002, Israel was allotted greater freedom of action, measured in terms of days, and in fact the administration showed even more flexibility by granting additional time. Once Israel launched Operation Determined Path two months later, Washington had no qualms at unlimited time stretches because of its unqualified recognition of Israel's right to self-defense. The Bush administration's unmistakable position on Israel's lengthy incursion into PA territory also convinced other governments to accept Israeli moves against the Palestinians' terror infrastructure.

In general, since September 11, 2001, many countries have offered greater cooperation with the United States in the campaign against terror than in the past, a change that made activity for terror organizations more difficult. Bin Laden was considered a pursued renegade but not a hero, even if he was still alive. The Muslim street may have realized that the pulverizing his organization suffered was also a blow to the greater radical Islamic movement and a sign of its failure. If this became the prevailing mood, then the American military action in fact contributed to the reinforcement of moderate Arab regimes vis-à-vis fundamentalist Islam. But this is still hypothetical, and achieving a decisive victory will require a long-term effort because organizations like al-Qaeda have the patience to lie in wait until the right moment presents itself, and have perhaps even received inspiration from September 11 to radicalize their activity.

Furthermore, the September 11 attack added tension to the United States relations with Arab countries, ironically with the regimes closest to it. Considerable anger was felt in the United States towards Saudi Arabia for not doing enough to clamp down on the terrorist cells it harbored and for what appeared as its unwillingness to offer meaningful assistance to the American military campaign against Iraq. Washington's plans to move against Iraq sparked tension in American-Egyptian and American-Jordanian relations. Egypt in particular grew increasingly critical of the administration's support of Israel, of Washington's reluctance to act more decisively in advancing the peace process, and of the alleged United States decision to withhold further economic assistance from Egypt because of the arrest of the Egyptian human rights activist Sa'ad al-Din Ibrahim following his denunciation of Mubarak's regime.

A year and a half after September 11, the American administration's war on terror was still in its early stages. United States military action in Afghanistan continued, and had not yet attained all of its objectives. The al-Qaeda organization was badly hurt and lost its territorial base, but its operational capability was not destroyed and continued to pose a threat to the United States, other countries, and Jewish and Israeli targets. Furthermore, preparations for the military move against Iraq eclipsed other elements in the war on terror, even as the administration continued to pursue al-Qaeda leaders.

Nonetheless, the American declaration of war on terror already produced a number of major ramifications for the Middle East. Most of the countries in the region, including radical regimes that showed no cooperation toward the United States in the past, were now willing to aid in crushing al-Qaeda cells. Some of these regimes were prepared to move against other terrorist groups, particularly those endangering their own stability. The war on terror granted Israel greater political and military freedom to operate against the PA, and encouraged heavy international pressure on the Authority, which was now presented as the problem rather than the solution to the Israeli-Palestinian crisis. The swift demise of the Taliban regime and al-Qaeda network in Afghanistan, even if initial American objectives there were not yet completed, added to the image of American power and deterrent capability in the Middle East, and contributed to the increased pressure on Arab and Muslim countries to cooperate with the United States. The next dominant factor concerned Iraq: if the administration succeeds in supplanting Saddam Hussein's regime with a moderate, Western-oriented one, then this will have enormous significance on the region.

Implications of the Israeli-Palestinian Crisis

The violent clash between Israel and the Palestinians impacted, first and foremost, on the two central parties in the conflict, but the fallout had regional implications as well. The seriousness of the crisis was reflected in its long duration, the high level of violence, the rising number of victims on both sides, and the destruction of the Israeli-Palestinian political process. The fragile trust that had been crystallizing gradually between Israel and the Palestinians during the Oslo process, based on intense negotiations and a series of agreements, broke apart completely once the violence of the second intifada erupted. Israel lost all trust in the Palestinian leadership and in Arafat personally after he violated the most basic commitment attained in the framework of the negotiations: the rejection of violence and terror for the advancement of political goals. Significantly, the intifada did not break out against the background of a deadlock or protracted crisis in the negotiations. Rather, the Palestinians' blatant reneging of their commitment against violence was particularly provocative as it began in the midst of serious discussions in which Israel offered the Palestinians unprecedented concessions. As a result, in Israel there was near-unanimous agreement that Arafat cannot be a partner to peace talks and conflict resolution. For their part, the Palestinians, who failed to afford the Barak government and its proposals sufficient value, had no confidence whatsoever in the Sharon government and its potential for brokering an agreement.

In addition to mutual distrust, other severe difficulties were involved. From the start of the crisis, no formula acceptable to both sides was found for renewing negotiations. The Oslo process was considered a failure by the majority of Israeli and Palestinian decisionmakers, rendering it – or any peace process - very problematic to reinstate. The approach that advocates immediately addressing issues of a permanent settlement, as the Barak government tried to do, was also deflated. Positions to emerge from the Arab and Palestinian circuit likewise provided little to advance a political horizon. The Saudi initiative won wide-scale Arab support and may eventually contribute to a permanent resolution, but it offered nothing of substance for ending the present crisis, and at this stage its practicality was limited. Thus, in the absence of a framework for dialogue and agreement, various ideas were broached in Israel, in the American administration, in Arab countries, and among the Palestinians that offered outlines for conflict resolution or, conversely, proposed unilateral steps independent of any formal settlement.

These ideas, however, lacked sufficient common ground, and it proved a challenge to consolidate any degree of consensus that would permit genuine progress. In the meantime, the Israeli government did not come forward with a coherent political plan for resolving the crisis and returning to the political track. The Palestinians rejected the idea of a long-term interim settlement, and the Arab states and the international community likewise failed to support it. An alternative suggestion, establishing a Palestinian state in part of the area and then quickly proceeding towards a final settlement, was unacceptable to the right wing of the Israeli government. The unilateral separation alternative won wide public backing in Israel, but without any consensus as to the location of the demarcation line, and in the absence of an agreement on so cardinal an issue, it was difficult to realize this type of disengagement.

Some members of the Palestinian leadership, including Arafat, appeared willing to return to the point at which the talks broke off in early 2001 and agree to President Clinton's proposals as a basis for renewing negotiations – perhaps out of an awareness of the horrific and misguided decision to destroy the political process. However, few in Israel, even on the Israeli Left, believed that it was possible to move directly forward to a permanent settlement, and most were not prepared to pick up the shattered pieces of the Clinton proposals, due to their distrust of Arafat and their dismissal of the present Palestinian leadership as a suitable partner for negotiations. Moreover, the existing gap between the Israeli and Palestinian positions when negotiations ruptured at the end of the Barak administration widened further, particularly in the wake of the ongoing crisis and violence.

The divergent positions also reflected the prevalent moods. The Israeli public curtailed its support for the Oslo process and the principle of "land for peace," and more people were of the opinion that a peace settlement with the Palestinians was unattainable. On the Palestinian side, too, belief in the peace process was shattered; the expectations of an imminent, peacefully-achieved permanent settlement and the establishment of a Palestinian state were replaced by strong approval of violent attacks against Israel, including suicide bombings, in the belief that violence would hasten the end of Israeli occupation. The Palestinian leadership thus far showed no willingness to curb the violence that was unleashed as a means of advancing its political objectives, despite the fact that voices were increasingly heard in the Palestinian public advocating policy reassessment, a halt to attacks inside Israel, and the transition to a non-violent struggle. Certainly as long as violence in the territories continued, it was exceedingly difficult to reengage in a dialogue, and even more challenging to achieve genuine progress.

The difficulty in finding a way out of the crisis and reigniting the political process encumbered both sides. Well into its third year, the intifada had not landed the Palestinian leadership a single gain, and instead, it displaced national objectives to the point that they appeared out of reach. Furthermore, it failed to crack Israeli determination to prevail in the struggle against violence. Worst of all, the Palestinian leadership forfeited one of its most valuable assets – the support and credibility of a large section of the Israeli Left regarding a tangible settlement between the two sides. The swing to the right in Israeli public opinion since the beginning of the crisis reflected the more liberal camp's weakness and the loss of ability to influence the political process.

Concurrently, the Palestinian leadership lost the backing of the American administration pending its fulfillment of several demands that would prove the Palestinians' meriting of statehood, including deposing Arafat or at least drastically curtailing his power. Thus the Bush government called for a change of Palestinian leadership and a volte-face in its conduct as a precondition to the establishment of a Palestinian state. Washington's priority in reforming the PA contributed, in effect, to deferring the renewal of the political process to sometime in the future. The Europeans too harbored reservations over the Palestinians' behavior. All of the PA's efforts to involve the international community in the Israeli-Palestinian confrontation failed thus far, and paradoxically, this failed attempt brought international pressure on the PA to modify itself. Moreover, the Palestinians won only minor practical support from the Arab world, despite the avowed identification with their suffering, and a number of the leading Arab countries called on the Palestinians to restrain their conduct in order to avoid regional upheavals; some even supported instituting basic reforms in the PA, including leadership change. Finally, the terrible suffering of the Palestinian people, their economic distress, the rampant unemployment, the absence of achievements, the surfeit of desperation, the external pressures, and the domestic rivalries all sparked major internal criticism of the PA's direction and domestic cries for serious reforms, including the transfer of part of Arafat's authority to the hands of others.

An important change took place in Israel's policy towards the PA in the middle of 2002, with the IDF's massive, long-term entry into Palestinian cities and Area A. This step translated into a significant reduction in the scope of terror strikes committed by Palestinians, mainly because of Israeli pressure on the Palestinian organizations and the severe blow to the upper echelon of guerilla activists. On the other hand, it damaged the daily life of the Palestinians, aggravating their misery and impairing the PA's administrative and security systems. The long-term stay in PA territory also thrust on Israel the problematic mandate of responsibility for the welfare of the Palestinian population.

The desperate reality prompted measures to create a window of opportunity for emerging from the crisis. The Quartet, an international body comprised of representatives of the United States, Russia, the European Union, and the United Nations, drafted a "roadmap" intended to steer a course from an end to the current violence to a permanent solution, including the establishment of a Palestinian state. The concept of the roadmap has now been accepted within international discourse and has become a subject for discussion between the Quartet and the Israeli government and the PA. At the same time, Arafat was under intense pressure from the Quartet and several Arab nations as well to appoint a prime minister, who would acquire most of the political authority and thereby improve the PA's international image. Succumbing to this pressure, Arafat was forced to nominate his deputy Mahmoud Abbas (Abu Mazen) as prime minister, a new position within the Palestinian hierarchy. Abbas was considered a moderate leader, not directly involved in terrorism, and had advocated putting an end to the violent confrontation.

In addition, several senior officials within the PA openly advocated a one-year abstention from terrorist activities, so that the IDF would withdraw from the PA-controlled areas. For its part, Egypt invested considerable effort in brokering an agreement between the PA and Hamas regarding a cease fire. Within Israel, there was hope that the creation of a new, more moderate Palestinian leadership would allow for an end to the violence and political progress, and Prime Minister Ariel Sharon openly expressed support for President Bush's vision of an Israeli-Palestinian agreement, which includes an eventual establishment of a Palestinian state.

Yet these developments, however encouraging, were not sufficient to sidestep many of the major obstacles to a resolution of the crisis. It was not certain that Arafat would transfer substantive authority to the new prime minister. Hamas rejected appeals to halt the violence. The American administration was occupied with the war in Iraq, and it was unclear when it would find the time and energy to restore the Israeli-Palestinian conflict to priority status on its foreign policy agenda. Nor was it clear how much political freedom Sharon would enjoy. More likely, the right wing coalition that formed his new government following the 2003 elections would, at the very least, limit the political overtures Israel extends to the Palestinians.

The lengthy duration of the crisis and the ongoing absence of a political exit placed Israel in a formidable situation, even though Israel earned freer activity in dealing with the PA and won considerable support from the American administration for its policy against terror. Israel's ability to act almost totally freely in PA territory and strike the terror infrastructure at will also reinforced its deterrent capability towards the Palestinian organizations. The Palestinians' deteriorating situation and the reduced scope of terrorist attacks, at least as long as the IDF remained in Palestinian territory, strengthened the perception of Israel leading in the confrontation. At the same time, however, the need for extensive troop deployment demonstrated to Israel the ordeal it faced in trying to overcome terror by military means alone, and conversely, the ability of Palestinian organizations to continue deadly terror attacks while under siege or renew terror attacks in a relatively short time after IDF withdrawal from Palestinian areas. The absence of a political solution underscored to Israel its own demographic vulnerability and the multi-tiered dilemma involved in simultaneously controlling the Palestinian population, dealing with the growing intricacy of the Israeli-Arab issue, and safeguarding both Jewish identity and democracy in the state. Israel also faced harsh criticism from many countries, especially in Europe, for its continued presence and military operations in Palestinian territories.

The basic assumption that the Israeli-Palestinian crisis was far from over demands an evaluation of the regional implications of the conflict. For several reasons the crisis elevated the Palestinian issue to a high position on the Arab world's agenda. Arab states were committed to the Palestinian cause but were aware that no political solution lay within sight. A number of Arab countries, especially Egypt, Jordan, and Lebanon, feared that popular expressions of support for the Palestinians in the Arab street might destabilize their regimes. Moreover, one of the concerns that emerged in Israel and other countries early in the violence was that the crisis could escalate into an all-out regional war. This form of deterioration was not expected as a result of a coordinated Arab decision to initiate a war against Israel. Israel's assessment of this probability was low, especially because of the estimate that Arab opinion itself favored Israel in the Arab-Israeli strategic balance.

Yet if the prospect of a major war seemed low, the danger still existed of a limited deterioration due to the miscalculation by one of the sides or from an attack or incident that produced an unacceptable number of casualties, either Israeli or Palestinian. A special case would be an outright strike at a holy site by either Palestinians or Israelis that could trigger an escalation with reverberations beyond the immediate Israeli-Palestinian arena. Or, for example, a significant worsening in the Israeli-Palestinian confrontation might lead to a massive attack by Hizbollah from inside Lebanon on Israel's northern settlements, thus exploiting Israel's military engagement with the Palestinians. In this case, Israel would have no choice but to respond with heavy force against Hizbollah and targets in Syria and Lebanon, a move that could trigger a Syrian military reaction against Israel and a wide-scale confrontation. The fear was that such a clash could potentially embroil other states in the region, such as Iraq (until the 2003 war) or Iran, and maybe even force Egypt and Jordan to take military steps against Israel.

But the likelihood of this type of domino effect was not high. It could only transpire when all of the braking systems against such a scenario, not just one or two of them, were malfunctioning, a configuration of factors that usually does not occur. It was particularly unlikely that that the Syrians would launch a major military move against Israel. They understood fully that they might be left alone to engage the IDF in battle because of the limited ability of Iraq and Iran to assist in the fighting, and Jordan and Egypt would vigorously avoid getting dragged into the fray. Overall, since the end of 2001, the fear of regional deterioration has diminished.

The main risk of local escalation lay on the Israeli-Lebanese border because of Hizbollah activity, especially – though not only – in the context of Israeli-Palestinian hostilities. In recent years Hizbollah has been faced with a strategic dilemma. With the conclusion of the civil war in Lebanon in the late 1980s and the process of Lebanonization in the country, Hizbollah had to concede an important element in its original ideology, namely, leading Lebanon to an Islamic republic. Consequently, it became merely another ethnic group competing for its own niche in the Lebanese struggle. To highlight its uniqueness vis-à-vis other organizations and retain its militant revolutionary image, Hizbollah sought to raise the banner of struggle against Israel. But the IDF's withdrawal from southern Lebanon in May 2000 significantly circumscribed the nexus of activity of Hizbollah's military struggle against Israel, and international pressure on Syria and Lebanon and fear of a massive Israeli retaliation forced Hizbollah to concentrate mainly on the Shab'a Farms sector. Moreover, after the September 11 terror attack, the American administration blacklisted Hizbollah, citing it as one of the leading terror organizations that must be immobilized, and applied pressure on Syria and Lebanon to restrain the organization's activities and its channels of funding. On the other hand, since mid-2000, with direct assistance from Iran, Hizbollah managed to build up a formidable strategic military system in southern Lebanon, equipped with thousands of rockets, some long-range, that placed a large section of Israel's northern region within striking distance. This military arsenal, adjacent to Israel's border, transformed Hizbollah into a dominant factor in South Lebanon and granted it the strategic capability of attacking Israel far more than in the past.

The Israeli-Palestinian crisis added a new dimension to the mainsprings of Hizbollah decisionmaking. With the outbreak of the al-Aqsa Intifada, the Palestinians became the leading player in the armed struggle against Israel, not only banishing Hizbollah to the sidelines but also effectively narrowing its field of activity. Within this constrained reality, the organization sought additional channels of operations against Israel – especially by stirring up the level of activity on the Lebanese border from time to time, and tightening its cooperation with the Palestinians by aiding them within Israel and the territories. Activities like these required Hizbollah to move cautiously, lest Israel respond and target Syria and Lebanon with great force; lest the United States pursue it actively; and lest the growing resentment on the part of the Lebanese towards its activities and their concern about escalation in the region unleash an irreversible backlash. For this multiplicity of reasons, the organization avoided taking military steps that could spark a strong Israeli retaliation that would in turn lead to severe deterioration in the region.

At the same time, apprehension increased in Israel over the possibility that Hizbollah might plan a "strategic ambush" in the near future. This fear was based on the assessment that with the bulk of Israeli forces engaged in the confrontation with the Palestinians, the organization was liable to presume Israel's preference not to open an additional front and refrain, as it had thus far, from a heavy-handed response to Hizbollah provocations. In this scenario, Hizbollah could escalate its operations so as to demonstrate its contribution to the Palestinian armed struggle and its assistance to Iranian and Syrian interests by applying intensive military pressure on Israel. Increased aggression on Shab'a Farms was liable to involve new tactics such as firing long-range rockets into the north of Israel. The initiative would probably receive the backing of Syria, whose young leader has not displayed sufficient wariness in his support of Hizbollah, and from Iran, which seeks greater involvement in the Israeli-Palestinian crisis and has already boosted its assistance to Palestinian organizations, including the PA. A major Hizbollah attack would perforce thrust on Israel the need to decide on a far-reaching response, despite the inconvenient conditions for opening a second front and the inherent risks in such an escalation. By late 2002, however, the fear of escalation had somewhat declined: Hizbollah seemed to restrain its aggressive activities out of the fear that Israel would take advantage of the war in Iraq to strike at the organization.

The danger of deterioration on the Lebanese border due to Hizbollah activity was aggravated in the summer of 2002 by the Lebanese government's unilateral initiative to increase pumping water from the Hazbani River that flows into Israel. Jerusalem was concerned that the diversion of water would upset Israel's water balance and prompt the Lebanese to greater control of the Hazbani's water. Thus, Israel announced it would react to Lebanon's attempt at pumping unless a mutual agreement was signed. Cognizant of the perils of deterioration, international parties, led by the American government, endeavored to pressure Syria and Hizbollah to avoid worsening the situation, and began mediating between Israel and Lebanon on the water issue. As a result, since the end of 2002 the issue lost, at least temporarily, some of its immediate significance.

Besides the danger of a limited confrontation, the regional implications of the Israeli-Palestinian crisis had political repercussions as well. The crisis roused a wave of identification with the Palestinians in the Arab and Muslim world, as well as hatred and incitement against Israel. Naturally, the anti-Israel sentiment played into the hands of Iran and Iraq, the region's leading radical countries, which consider the peace process a threat to their interests and have sworn to derail it. The peace talks between Israel and Syria, frozen since the spring of 2000, were unlikely to resume soon, in part because of the changes of government in both states, and in part due to the continuation of the Israeli-Palestinian crisis. The intensification of violence between Israel and the Palestinians was also liable to wreak further damage in Israel's relations with Egypt and Jordan, which witnessed an outpouring of enmity towards Israel, at the level of diplomatic representation as well as in economic and commercial connections. At the same time, there seemed to be a limit to the steps that Egypt and Jordan would take against Israel since neither state was interested in flagrantly violating the peace treaties or embarking upon large military moves that could lead to a regional flare-up and the possibility of a harsh United States response. On the contrary, both Egypt and Jordan had an interest in maintaining open channels of communication with Jerusalem in order to influence the return of the Israelis and Palestinians to the political track.

In addition, events in the PA territories and their coverage in the media caused unrest in several Arab countries, especially Egypt and Jordan, where they were exploited by opposition elements to incite against the governments. Until now, this incitement was a limited phenomenon that in no way jeopardized the regimes' stability, but Egypt and Jordan worried that domestic unrest would increase as long as Israel continued to act against the Palestinians. The economies of these two Arab countries were also hurt because of the crisis, especially due to the decline in tourism. This concern was another reason for their interest in resolving the crisis and renewing the political process, including via an intensive dialogue with the American administration. So extensive was the concern that it even led to overt Arab criticism of the Palestinian leadership alongside the criticism of Israel, and resulted in a readiness to transfer management of the crisis from Arafat to Arab governments and endorse the rise of an alternative Palestinian leadership.

The Stability of Middle East Regimes

The last generation has witnessed impressive, unprecedented stability in the Middle East Arab regimes, with some leaders remaining in power two or three decades, or even more. The only major regime changes in this period occurred with the deposition of the Shah of Iran in 1979 and the 1989 military coup that overturned the Sudanese government. Regime stability continued even since 1999 when novice leaders rose to the helm in Jordan, Syria, and Morocco, heirs to their fathers' positions. In these cases, the transfer of government was carried out in an orderly, smooth fashion. Arab regime stability was particularly impressive when one recalls the instability that characterized most governments in the 1950s and 1960s, and the massive problems that some of them still confront. A number of factors contributed to this stability: the strengthening of the regimes' internal legitimacy over the years; the weakness of opposition groups in most Arab states and the unattractive alternatives they represented; the creation and stabilization of the link between regimes and the state's military system, often the leading power in the country; the increasing difficulty to plot and execute military revolutions because of the magnitude of the armies; and the efficiency of the regimes' internal security agencies and the large military units whose main role is to protect the regime from enemies from within and without.

Current signs pointed to continued stability in most of the regimes in the Middle East. As far as an assessment permits, none of the key players appeared in danger of being overthrown in the near future by domestic elements, because opposition elements are neither strong nor organized enough to pose a threat. In most Middle East countries the army remained loyal to the regime, and the leaderships have demonstrated their ability to neutralize domestic pressures, keeping them from becoming a lever for regime change. Nevertheless, in early 2003 there were three regimes and leaderships in the Middle East where changes were likely to occur in the near future:

- Saddam Hussein's regime in Iraq was not in imminent danger of a domestic challenge but indeed seemed likely to collapse under the pressure of the coalition attack.

- The Iranian regime was under no serious external threat, but it was experiencing a gradual process of basic domestic pressures that were aimed at modifying its radical fundamentalist nature.
- The Palestinian Authority was under heavy international and domestic pressure to alter its composition, structure, and policies, as well as divest the chairman of most of his authority. The IDF's penetration into PA territory, the collapse of the PA's administrative mechanisms, the economic misery, the calls for a major restructuring as a way out of the economic crisis, the appointment of Abu Mazen as prime minister, the internal rivalries, and the de-legitimatization of Arafat and his entourage by the Bush administration all led to the pervasive feeling that Arafat may be in the twilight of his career. Given these circumstances, various parties were preparing for an inheritance struggle likely to emerge in the coming period.

A number of factors already prevalent in the Middle East may threaten regional stability in the more distant future. First, many Middle East states confronted a host of economic and social problems: a soaring birth rate that exceeded the rate of an increase in resources (although the birth rate in some of the region's countries has declined in recent years); runaway urbanization; growing unemployment, especially among young people; a freeze – in some cases even a drop – in the standard of living; outmoded infrastructures; inefficient, often corrupt governmental mechanisms that failed to address economic and social problems; distrust of political institutions by sections of the public, and the rising chorus of complaints against them; fear of the penetration of Western culture and its deleterious effect on tradition and religious values; difficulty in facing the challenges of modernization and globalization; and opposition to American hegemony in the region.

These problems have been exacerbated by the economic crisis that has plagued the Arab world since the mid-1980s, heightened especially by the relative slump in oil prices that lasted until the late 1990s. Economic conditions in a number of Arab countries have improved somewhat due to the renewed rise in oil prices that began in 1999, but for most states the effect has been insignificant. Fluctuating oil prices have had an influence primarily on the states whose economies are oil dependent and a secondary influence on surrounding countries. The gap between population size and available resources will likely widen further when the population in the Arab world exceeds 400 million, which is expected around 2015. The pressure on economic resources, infrastructure, and employment sources could then reach a breaking point.

In addition, fundamentalist Islam continued to threaten regional stability, although the radical Islamic movement has not managed to score many achievements in recent years, other than in Morocco. The strengthening of Islamic organizations in the region from the late 1980s to the early 1990s endangered the stability of Arab regimes and led to serious outbreaks of violence in the moves to counter them, especially in Algeria and Egypt. But since the mid-1990s the radical movement's upsurge has stopped, and in some states, notably Jordan and Egypt, its strength has waned. Even in the Islamic Republic of Iran, where Islamic fundamentalism won its most spectacular victory, moderate elements, backed by popular support, were striving to modify the nature of the regime. Nevertheless, fundamentalism posed an ongoing threat, even if limited, to a number of Arab regimes, to American and Western interests, and to Israel. This was because the social problems that brought about the rise and empowerment of radical Islamic elements in the 1980s still festered in many countries.

Finally, several states in the region were expected to witness a change of leaders because of their age and the accession to power of a younger generation. This process has already started, and in effect has begun in Israel too, though with Sharon's government it is on temporary hold. To date the transfer of government in these countries has transpired without political upheavals, but there is no guarantee that this smooth transfer will continue in the future, especially where the succession process has not been properly prepared.

Against this background, a brief survey of the domestic situation in the major countries in the region will be presented, with the discussion of Iran and Iraq reserved for the chapter on the Gulf.

The regime in **Egypt** has proven to be one of the most stable regimes in the Arab world since the 1952 Free Officers revolution. In the 1990s the regime triumphed in a bitter struggle against fundamentalist Islamic organizations after taking a series of steps to counter their operations. It unleashed its security forces against fundamentalist strongholds in Upper Egypt and in various quarters of Cairo. It took legal action against them, arrested thousands of activists, and barred or limited the activity of fundamentalist charity organizations and autonomous mosques that provided shelter and aid to the Islamic organizations. In general, the regime pursued its political rivals and successfully quashed opposition. In 2001-2002 the government arrested hundreds of extremist Islamic activists, some of them in the wake of the September 11 attack, and brought scores of them to trial. At the same time, however, the regime has displayed a willingness to cooperate with moderate Islamic elements and appease their demands, release detainees, and improve social services in impoverished areas that had become the breeding grounds for fundamentalist groups. Overall, since the massacre of fifty-eight tourists in Luxor in November 1997, terrorist activity by Islamic fanatics has declined due to suppression by state security forces in most of their strongholds; indeed, evidence of their distress has been their repeated calls to the regime for a ceasefire.

While the urgency of the Islamic fundamentalism challenge declined, economic affliction topped the regime's agenda. Egypt suffered from a fundamental economic crisis mainly because of the excessive demographic pressure on the state's meager economic resources, which has led to the rising frustration of the population. This crisis was reflected in the gaping deficit in its balance of payments, the decline in foreign currency reserves, the devaluation of the Egyptian pound, the huge budget deficit, the steep climb in prices, the growing rate of unemployment, and the diminished standard of living. Nevertheless, over the years there have been indications of partial, slow improvement in the financial agenda, and in the foreseeable future the regime's survival is not at risk.

Most significant is that the regime emerged strengthened from having withstood and overcome the challenge of Islamic fanaticism, and having rendered the opposition weak and disorganized. As of early 2003, the government rested securely on a trilateral pact between the political elite, the security organizations, and the business elite. The prevailing arrangement, if at times difficult, was under control, especially without the presence of any strong political parties or the vocal criticism of political forces in the public debate. Mubarak's government remained strongly anchored in power and the president had no rival in the highest echelons of power. Unlike his predecessor, Mubarak has preferred not to appoint a deputy so as not to create an additional power center within the regime, though he may be quietly preparing his son Gamal as his heir. Nonetheless, the government must continue to tackle a host of challenges likely to influence its stability in the future: basic economic deterioration, pressure for political freedom, aspirations of additional sectors to have their voices heard and to participate in government, and the prospect of another wave of violent Islamic fundamentalism.

The regime in **Syria** has been headed by Bashar Assad since June 2000, when his assumption of power took place smoothly immediately following his father's death. Even before his father's death and his own appointment as president, Bashar, with the help of his father, began to consolidate a support base in the military and in the security system, as well as in the dominant Ba'ath Party. Bashar engaged in military management, replacing a number of high-ranking officers with younger men now obligated to him for their promotion. He also disposed of potential rivals in the upper echelons of the regime, first and foremost his uncle Rifaat Assad. This groundwork proved of great value, for since coming to power the regime has not weathered any serious threats to its authority. Also contributing to the government's stability has been the rapprochement that began in the 1990s between the Ba'ath regime and Islamic circles, following the regime's rift with the Muslim Brotherhood in the early 1980s. Bashar Assad's regime exhibited more tolerance towards religious activity, releasing from custody the majority of activists in the Islamic movement and allowing moderate religious candidates to be elected to parliament as independents. For their part, the Islamic circles acknowledged the regime's authority and were aware of their inability to challenge it as its alternative.

Over the past years, Syria, like Egypt, has had to deal with a severe economic crisis, especially due to the fluctuations in oil prices, since oil accounted for two-thirds of exports. Syria also had one of the highest birthrates in the world, and this imposed heavily on the state's infrastructure and resources. The freeze in the GNP has led to a decline in the standard of living and a rise in unemployment. The regime tried to tackle the situation by improving economic planning, modernizing the financial and banking systems, increasing wages in the public sector, and redressing its trade relations abroad, especially with Iraq. These steps alone, however, were insufficient to generate a comprehensive improvement in the economy. The way to liberate the Syrian economy and make it accessible to desperately needed foreign investments will be by increasing the strength of the private sector and expanding cooperation with the business sector. As a step in this direction, Bashar set up a new government in December 2001, leaving some of the top posts in the hands of veterans from his father's regime, but also introducing eighteen new ministers, some of whom received key portfolios in economic projects. The government saw its main task in boosting the pace of economic growth and reducing unemployment and poverty through the rapid implementation of economic reforms.

Bashar Assad seemed more willing than his father to initiate changes in Syria's domestic and foreign policies. He has freed hundreds of political prisoners and, for the first time in decades, has permitted the publication of a newspaper not under government control and has allowed criticism of the state's economic policy to appear in the government press. The president promised to expand Syria's openness to new technologies and to link the country to the global economy, although his ability to influence the older elite to support this modernization remained to be seen. Indeed, his willingness to expand public debate has been limited because of the antagonism of the old guard, and Assad has been forced to reduce the pace of political change and even retract on certain programs. At the same time, he has redeployed some of the Syrian troops in Lebanon, withdrawing a number of units from Beirut in order to alleviate friction with the local population, especially because of demands in Lebanese circles – Maronites and Druze – to remove Syrian forces from Lebanon and reevaluate the relationship between the two countries. The most significant development in 2002 and early 2003 was the marked improvement in Syria's relations with Iraq, particularly in the economic and military spheres. Syria has obtained weapons for Iraq, thus violating Security Council resolutions and provoking the American administration at a time when Washington was planning to attack Iraq.

In its first three years the regime of the younger Assad has shown signs of stability, without any threat from domestic opposition. However, it faced a series of imposing challenges that could affect its future: the implications of the 2003 war in Iraq; the need to maintain long-term unity among the president's senior associates in a way that will offset any threat to the regime on the basis of its Alawite minority; the unrelenting economic challenge and its social implications; Hizbollah activities against Israel that could embroil the regime in a confrontation with Israel and the American administration; and if conditions permit, the attempt to reach a political settlement with Israel. Facing these challenges and lacking the experience and caution of his father, Bashar Assad has raised doubts in Western and Arab circles whether he is capable of leading his country wisely.

The regime in **Saudi Arabia** faced challenges of a different nature. While the country has been spared a financial crisis, fluctuations in the oil prices have taken their toll on the economy. Declining oil prices since the mid-1980s have lowered the Saudi GNP, although there has been a marked upswing in oil revenues since the late 1990s. Moreover, Saudi Arabia has been investing a sizable share of its oil income into the security sector. The desert oil kingdom was the world's leading weapons importer, purchasing nearly 60% of the arms in the Middle East and in recent years investing almost 35% of its budget and nearly 14% of its GNP in security. Demography also played a major role in the kingdom's development. The Saudi population increased by 300% between 1973 and 2000, from 6.8 million people to over 20 million, with 60% of the population twenty-five years old and younger. This skyrocketing growth rate has created pressures on the job market and diminished per capita income, while foreign workers, who made up over one-quarter of the population, posed a separate problem.

The Saudi regime thus far was reluctant to challenge the Islamic extremism operating in the country. The regime restricted the clergy's activity, paid its wages, and oversaw the construction and maintenance of almost all of the country's mosques. Even prior to the September 11 attack the Saudi government supported limiting the activity of Islamic extremism, tracking the activity of radical groups, and on occasion suppressing them. After September 11, the regime made it clear to the clerics that it would not tolerate their support of any kind of terrorist and radical activity. However, for the most part it avoided heavy-handed, large-scale crackdowns on Islamic groups, and preferred dialogue in the attempt to restrain the extremism. The Saudis' surveillance of terror groups and fanatical incitement in the education system and religious institutions has not been tight enough, and the government has even provided funds for Muslim organizations engaged in terror in order to win their good will, overlooking the true nature of their activities. The extent of change in Saudi policy in light of the September 11 lessons thus remained an open question, although the Saudi leadership was under pressure to amend its relationship with its closest ally, the United States, which deteriorated following the September 11 attack. More congenial relations depended on the regime taking firmer action against terror-linked organizations.

The present generation of Saudi leadership was likely to exit the political scene within the next few years. The three top figures – the ailing King Fahd, who has served only intermittently in recent years, and the princes Abdullah and Sultan – were all approaching eighty years of age. Their successors will emerge from a team of younger leaders twenty years their junior. Assuming that the transition proceeds without shockwaves, the new leaders will still have to attain some balance between traditional culture, religious values, the education system, and the political structure, on the one hand, and the challenges of modernity on the other. Until now the Saudi regime has displayed impressive skill in adapting to the needs of the present, without inducing major jolts to society. Prince Abdullah, the acting ruler, has shown willingness to institute some minor political amendments, and has allowed the Saudi media to carry on a limited discussion about economic and educational reform. However, the current pace of political-social-economic improvement will probably be too slow for the future. Saudi Arabia lacked institutions that allow broad, meaningful political participation in shaping the country. In addition, there were inadequate channels for moderates in both Islamic and liberal circles to criticize corruption in the uppermost levels of the state, and address the lack of representation in the political system, the heavy press restrictions, and the economic policy. The coming leadership will have to guarantee that the leading institutions in these areas will develop gradually into more representative bodies that offer greater public involvement in building the kingdom's future. The future leadership will also be required to diversify the Saudi economy, reduce its dependency on oil, replace some of the millions of foreign workers with a new generation of Saudis, and entrust the private sector with a larger role in the financial management of the state.

The Hashemite regime in **Jordan** will also be forced to deal with a host of imposing challenges. King Abdullah's ascent to the throne in February 1999 occurred smoothly following the crisis in the royal house on the eve of King Hussein's death, when the dying monarch, in a surprise maneuver, decided to divest his brother, Crown Prince Hassan, of the inheritance to the throne. Abdullah's style of rule was different from his father's. He appeared in public infrequently, and still lacked the special personal status his father enjoyed at home, in the Arab world, and in the international arena. At the same time, his popularity seemed to be strong among many layers of Jordan society, including the military. In general, the young king kept the domestic and foreign policy of Jordan intact, although the Israeli-Palestinian crisis impelled him to downgrade relations with Israel, and Jordan was disappointed with the limited economic benefit accrued so far from the peace treaty with Israel. Relations between Jordan and the Arab world were stable and congenial: Abdullah invested time and energy in inter-Arab diplomacy, restoring his country's relations with the Gulf States in the aftermath of the Gulf War. Jordan also worked at improving relations with Syria, and tried to manage its policy towards Baghdad with prudence given its economic dependence on Iraq.

Abdullah inherited the economic crisis that beset the country during his father's rule. Jordan has been in a deep recession since 1996, a downturn that retarded economic growth, decreased the per capita income, and resulted in high levels of unemployment (over 20%). The Gulf War crippled Jordan's main market for exports – Iraq – and of the 300,000 Jordanian workers, mainly Palestinians, who were expelled from Kuwait and Saudi Arabia, the majority returned to Jordan and joined the circle of the unemployed. The loss of the Iraqi market – which, to be sure, was partially restored over the years – also increased Jordan's foreign debt. King Abdullah attempted to focus on improving Jordan's economic plight and accelerate the pace of modernization. But the Jordanian economy was overly dependent on foreign capital, and the regime, unable to extricate itself from the financial crisis, has been only partially successful in its attempts at procuring American aid and amortizing its payment of debts. Against this background and facing the looming war in Iraq, King Abdullah – unlike his father in the 1991 Gulf War – chose to support quietly the American offensive in Iraq. In the coming years, the Jordanian regime will have to cope with the implications of the war, both positive and negative, on the kingdom.

Since the 1980s, Islamic political parties and organizations have been the main opposition movement in Jordan, and in recent years a number of their members were detained and those linked to al-Qaeda brought to trial. In general, the Islamic opposition, excluding fringe groups and some factions outside the country, did not plot to topple the regime but endeavored to alter Jordan's policy, especially its relations with Israel and the United States. The fear of the Islamic organizations' growing power has driven Abdullah to slow down the democratization process that his father, King Hussein, tried to initiate. In June 2001 the king dissolved the parliament, and announced new elections for November 2001, but these have not yet been held. Following the attack of September 11 the regime tightened its surveillance of the opposition and enacted laws restricting the media's criticism of state policy and the United States.

Despite the difficulties facing Abdullah, the regime in Amman continued to display remarkable stability. The Islamic opposition was not strong enough to endanger the regime, and the economic crisis, with all its exigencies, did not threaten the regime's survival. The main problem was likely to emerge from the Palestinian quarter. The Israeli-Palestinian confrontation has already had a negative impact, albeit limited, on the mood of the Jordanian public, the economy, and Jordanian-Israeli relations. An escalation of the crisis may well aggravate matters, although it seemed that the Jordanian regime would prevent a major deterioration in peace relations with Israel. The problem lay in the trends that could develop in the long run: the longer the Palestinian issue remains on the Arab and Jordanian agenda, even if an independent Palestinian state comes into existence, the more likely the Palestinian population in Jordan will understand its national identification in context of the Palestinian question. If such identification translates into political organization, it is liable to upset the Hashemite regime's stability.

Against the backdrop of stability in the Arab regimes, ironically, the government of **Israel** exhibited relative instability. The regime has not changed in essence and it is unlikely that a significant change will occur in the foreseeable future. Nevertheless, since the early 1990s six different prime ministers have ascended and stepped down from office, the government has shifted four times between the two main parties, and most governments were swept out of power before the end of their terms. There was no precedent in the history of Israel for this rate of government shuffling. The instability stemmed primarily from the divisions in the Israeli electorate that withheld power from the two major blocs, giving smaller parties a decisive role in coalition governments. The country's electoral split compromised the survivability of Israeli governments for a generation, paralyzing their ability to function, which in turn injured the political process and economic policy.

Israel's political structure, based on two main blocs of similar strength, has exhibited recent, if perhaps temporary, signs of change. The failure of the political process and the ongoing intifada have seriously weakened the Israeli Left, first and foremost the Labor Party, which led the peace negotiations with the Palestinians. The Labor Party's weakness was expressed in the sharp division between its different camps, a leadership crisis, a lack of consensus on a political platform for resolving the Palestinian crisis, the refusal of some senior party members to join the Likud-led unity government, and the possibility that Labor's left wing would break away and establish a new party. Added to this was the sway to the right by large sections of the public as a result of the violent, continuing crisis with the Palestinians.

Against this background, the elections of February 2003 changed the composition of the government. The right wing Likud party doubled its representation, and Ariel Sharon, the head of the party, continued as prime minister in the new government. The two left wing parties lost nearly one third of their seats, an electoral failure that testified to the growing right wing sentiment among Israeli voters since the current violence erupted in 2000. The election results, along with the marked differences between the two largest parties on a political option in the Israeli-Palestinian crisis, resulted in the inability to reestablish a national unity government. The Labor Party's decision to lead the opposition prompted the creation of a right wing extremist government, even if Sharon himself appeared more inclined to display pragmatic flexibility than rightist ideology.

The Israeli-Palestinian crisis has had a powerful impact on the fabric of Israeli society and the growing abyss between the country's Jewish majority and Arab minority. The gap stemmed from the feelings of discrimination held by Israeli Arabs regarding the allotment of resources, the standard of living, employment opportunities, and personal rights, and from the opinion of many Israeli Jews that the Israeli Arabs' loyalty to the state cannot be trusted because their primary loyalty is to the Palestinians in the West Bank and Gaza Strip and to the greater Arab world. The intifada has exacerbated the polarization between the sides, especially in the wake of Israeli Arab affinity with the Palestinians in the territories, an identification that was heightened by the militant Arab members of the Israeli parliament and the leaders of the Islamic Movement in Israel. In October 2000 this identification brought on a direct clash between masses of young Arabs and the Israeli police, which resulted in thirteen Arabs killed. Since then no further confrontation of this size occurred, mainly because Israeli Arabs were leery of taking steps that could impair the fragile status quo. However, a large part of the Jewish public continued to harbor doubts over the loyalty of Israeli Arabs, a feeling dramatically reinforced in light of the increasing number of Israeli Arabs involved in terror attacks inside Israel, even if the number was miniscule in proportion to the population.

Against this backdrop loomed Israel's economic decline, partially attributed to the intifada, and a bleak economic prognosis. The financial deterioration was expressed chiefly in negative economic growth, a general slowdown in economic activity, heavy damage to several branches, especially tourism, a rise in unemployment, and a sharp drop in foreign investments.

The government system of **Turkey** likewise suffered from an inherent instability. For years, Turkey has been ruled by a succession of unstable coalition governments, many of them incapable of resolving major issues or implementing decisions. The roots of the fragility lay in the divided party system, unstable parties, and an oscillating electorate. The tendency towards a divided political system, which began in the late 1960s and intensified since, was due to the adoption of a proportional voting system, economic-social-demographic changes that encouraged the emergence of new movements and parties, and the dissolution of the big parties. The division in the party system resulted in a series of unstable coalition governments whose participants competed not only with the opposition, but also among themselves in order to demonstrate quick achievements to their supporters. As a result, Turkey's governments preferred to deal with short-range problems, and shunned issues whose solutions would be realized only in the long term.

Such instability was also characteristic of the previous coalition government, headed by Bulent Ecevit. The three coalition partners lay on different ends of the political spectrum, while the wrangling among them intensified from early 2001 with the deepening of the economic crisis and the pressure on Turkey regarding its request to join the European Union (EU). The economic crisis forced the International Money Fund and World Bank to dictate harsh terms to be met before Ankara could receive a sizable loan of $16 billion . The EU continued to present Turkey with strict preconditions for membership, such as the revocation of the death penalty, increased rights for the Kurdish minority, and a resolution of the Cyprus problem. Despite the differences of opinion among the three coalition partners, the government passed a set of laws in the summer of 2002 revoking the death penalty and expanding citizens' rights for the Kurds. Yet notwithstanding these incipient changes in Turkish policies and heavy American pressure on the EU for Turkey's membership, in October 2002 the Union decided not to vote Turkey onto its roster of candidate states.

With this background, the Ecevit government was plunged into a deep crisis during 2002, following its loss of support from a large number of delegates in Ecevit's own party and the resignation of several senior ministers. Together with the declining health and functional incapacity of the 77-year old Ecevit, the government was obliged to advance the elections to parliament from April 2004 to November 2002.

The elections caused a major change in Turkey's political map. None of the traditional parties reached the 10% minimum for representation in the parliament. Instead, AKP, the Islamic Justice and Development Party, founded in 2001, scored a resounding victory, winning 363 of the 550 parliament seats, although earning only 34% of the popular vote. For the first time since 1991, the election results enabled the winning party to establish a government without coalition partners. Party Head Recep Tayyip Erdogan initially could not be appointed prime minister, since a previous sedition conviction prevented him from serving as a member of parliament. Party Vice President Abdullah Gul was appointed prime minister, until legislative changes allowed Erdogan to join parliament and then rise to prime minister. The sole opposition party in parliament was the socialist-democratic People's Republican Party.

It is too early to envision where this political revolution will lead. The sweeping victory of the Islamic party reflected less of a popular movement to fashion an Islamic society than a desire for change in the traditional political system. The financial crisis, and the failure of the previous government to address it sufficiently, spawned much anger and impatience towards the traditional parties, while the Islamic party projected confidence in its ability to rectify the situation. The new leaders that assumed power attempted to alleviate fears that they would intervene in civil affairs and impose an Islamic lifestyle on the population. However, the support of the American offensive in Iraq became a major issue, due to its implications on the American-Turkish relationship as well as on Turkey's economic situation and its Kurdish problem. Hence, the real test of the Turkish government was to amend its relations with the US, to cope with the repercussions of the war in Iraq, to improve the economic situation, to advance the process of joining the EU, and to prevent viable opposition from within the army.

A Look to the Future

Since the start of the present decade, powerful developments have impacted on the two circles of potential instability in the Middle East:

- The Iraqi crisis, and especially the outcome of the war, are likely to change the balance of power in the Gulf, and perhaps throughout the Middle East. The shockwaves that emanated from the massive military operation in Iraq will necessarily affect many of the players in the region.

- The al-Aqsa Intifada has undermined the framework for peace in the Israeli-Arab arena. Interim agreements and the belief in a negotiated settlement between the Israelis and Palestinians collapsed. The Israeli-Syrian peace process, already frozen prior to the outbreak of violence, has hardened further, and formal and informal peace arrangements between Israel and a list of Arab countries have been severely disrupted because of the Israeli-Palestinian crisis.

In the coming years the Middle East may well be less stable than in the 1990s and more likely to witness force being wielded in the region. This would be the result of a number of factors:

- The war in Iraq would create a locus of regional instability, in the near future at least, that could impact negatively on Iraq's neighbors and United States relations with the Arab world.
- The Israeli-Palestinian crisis did not appear close to an end, even if truces were signed, since no basis existed for renewing the political negotiations towards settlement. The prolonged violence will have a negative effect on the relations between both sides, on the political, economic, and social developments within each side, on Israel's relations with the Arab world, and perhaps on the domestic situation of Israel's neighbors.
- A possible attempt by Hizbollah to open a second front with Israel in the north could encourage further deterioration and entangle Syria in a fray, although the probability of this leading to an all-out confrontation remained low.
- It is still not clear how the Middle East will react in the long run to the American administration's declaration of war on terror. This will take years to find out. On the one hand, international cooperation against terror temporarily weakened the infrastructure of various terror organizations and imposed some restraint on their activity. On the other hand, these organizations were able to demonstrate their survival skills and operational ability – either against the United States and Western countries, including Israel, or against moderate Muslim-Arab regimes. The war on terror is liable to sharpen the polarity between fundamentalist Islam and the West.
- In the coming decade Iran might acquire more weapons of mass destruction. Iran has assumed the lead in this endeavor and may even obtain nuclear capability within the decade, a development that would significantly alter the region's balance of forces.

Against the signs that augured regional instability, other factors balanced the picture and pointed to the stabilization of conditions in the next few years. If the American offensive against Iraq is crowned with success and the United States replaces Saddam Hussein's regime with a more moderate and stable government, this will have a long-term stabilizing effect on the region. It would also contribute to halting Iraq's rush to attain weapons of mass destruction and might even have a positive influence on Iranian policy. Seen from another angle, despite the threats that motivated Iran to build up a non-conventional arsenal, there was a good chance that deep-rooted domestic processes now underway in the country would eventually lead to a more moderate regime in Tehran. Such a development could produce a more profound dialogue between Iran and the United States, and perhaps even with Israel, thus significantly reducing the Iranian threat.

Moreover, the possibility could not be ruled out that a formula will eventually be found to reach an Israeli-Palestinian political accord, simply because recent violence, distrust, and hatred notwithstanding, both sides desire such a settlement. If and when the Iraq affair is concluded, the American administration is likely to invest much greater effort in advancing an Israeli-Palestinian agreement. There is also a positive element in the fact that various considerations, including the Arab-Israeli strategic balance of power, act as braking systems against an escalation of the crisis into a full-scale confrontation.

CHAPTER 2

Developments in Iraq and Iran

Ephraim Kam

For over a decade since the Gulf War and until the new crisis in Iraq, the security situation in the Persian Gulf remained relatively stable. There were no serious military crises, and the changes that occurred were gradual and limited, certainly in comparison with the previous decade. The state of affairs in the region may be summarized as follows:

- Since the Gulf War until March 2003 no major conflicts erupted, although the region saw limited military action – especially American and British air attacks against targets in Iraq, usually when Baghdad deviated from the Security Council restrictions.
- The region's relative quiet was due to a number of factors. The United States served as a major deterrent towards Iraq and Iran by virtue of its extended military presence in the Gulf; its explicit commitment to guarantee the security of the moderate Gulf States; its policy – crystallized during the Clinton administration and known as "dual containment" – to weaken the strategic-military strength of Iraq and Iran; and its continual posture as a threat towards both states, a threat that increased since 2002.
- Militarily, Iraq and Iran were still relatively weak, especially in conventional weapons, primarily because of the losses sustained during two wars in the Gulf and the strict limitations placed on the export of weapon systems to them. The damage from the two wars was still fresh and deterred both radical states from military initiatives. Iran suffered a devastating blow in the fighting with Iraq, and has not yet recovered fully from its military and economic losses. Iraq was defeated soundly in the 1991 Gulf War, and has remained weak and partially isolated since then; it is hard to imagine it embarking on another military venture in the near future. Their weaknesses made it very difficult for either

country to contemplate a military move against the moderate Gulf States, let alone against American forces.

- On the other hand, some of the southern Gulf States, led by Saudi Arabia, forged ahead with their buildup of new weapon systems, especially naval and air systems, that may not be equal to the strength of Iraq's and Iran's arms but would bolster their security. As of 2003, Saudi Arabia's air and naval power was impressive on the regional level, consisting of weapon systems superior in quality to Iraq's and Iran's, and constituted a factor that would have to be dealt with seriously should either of the two northern states decide upon military action in the Gulf.

- Added to this was the political situation. In recent years Iran and Iraq, each separately, took political and economic steps to forge new relations of trust with other Gulf States, as well as with each other. As a result, the political atmosphere in the Gulf was friendlier, with the fear of aggressive moves by Iraq or Iran greatly diminished.

Nonetheless, seeds of change appeared that were likely to influence the region's stability in the coming years:

- A wide-scale American military move against Iraq, with the goal of toppling Saddam Hussein's regime, could generate instability in the region, at least in the immediate future, and the fallout could spread to some of Iraq's neighbors. If the US-led venture is crowned with success and Saddam Hussein is replaced with a more moderate regime, this would have a stabilizing impact on the whole region in the more distant future.

- A military move against Iraq, especially a successful one, was likely to lead to additional American steps, not necessary military ones, to block Iran's non-conventional armament.

- Both Iran and Iraq strove to develop weapons of mass destruction in order to compensate for their weakness in conventional arms. Iran was actively engaged in a program to produce nuclear, biological, and chemical weapons, and was poised to manufacture a long-range ballistic missile. Iraq was suspected of trying to recover its non-conventional capability that was crippled as a result of the Gulf War.

- Iran was undergoing a major process of domestic transformation, with large segments of the population calling for greater individual and political freedom, and less corruption in government. Recently the process has suffered a setback, but if it regains momentum in the coming years, perhaps after a more vigorous internal struggle, then the nature of the Iranian regime could change in a way that would have ramifications on its foreign affairs and security policy.

This chapter will concentrate on developments relating to the Iraqi crisis, the transformations that Iran experienced, and the US policy towards the two regimes. Other issues connected with the Gulf States, especially concerning Saudi Arabia, are included in the opening chapter on the strategic survey of the Middle East.

The Crisis in Iraq

Saddam Hussein's regime displayed impressive survival skills. Iraq was badly bruised in two Gulf wars, both launched at the explicit initiative of Saddam Hussein. If the Iraqi victory partially compensated for damage sustained in the war with Iran, any long-term gains were offset by the comprehensive defeat in the Gulf War. Iraq's military, economic, and political losses were sweeping, impacting on the entire Iraqi population then and to a great extent ever since. Despite Saddam's personal responsibility for defeat, the collateral losses, the economic suffering of his country, and the ongoing misery of the Iraqi people - all of which gained him many enemies - his regime remained secure and no significant organized opposition was active in the country. The destitution of the Iraqi people did not compel them to organize against Saddam; on the contrary, it heightened their dependence on the regime. Saddam succeeded in channeling popular anger over domestic conditions towards the United States, and he exploited American support of the opposition in exile to depict these foreign-based Iraqis as traitors who have teamed up with the country's archenemies.

The opposition to his regime was made up of Shiite groups, Kurds, and fundamentalists, but they were divided and militarily weak, with many of them residing outside Iraq. Saddam succeeded in building efficient domestic security agencies and a network of internal loyalties that gave him firm control of the country's main centers of power – the army, the security branches, and the Ba'ath Party – all of which were dependent on him and fearful of him. His dictatorial control enabled him to quash a number of attempted coups, and for years no further attempts were heard of. Although Saddam was forced to come to terms with Western-imposed Kurdish autonomy in northern Iraq, protected by the United States and European countries, this region did not become an independent state detached from Iraq, nor did it serve as a springboard for undermining his regime. The Shiite rebellions in the south in the early 1990s were brutally suppressed, and since then did not resurface on any significant scale. Saddam's regime managed to survive severe challenges because of its brutal ruthlessness, the opposition's weakness, and the fear it engendered by its control of the in the country's centers of power.

Anchored by its relative domestic stability, the main goals of Saddam's foreign policy were to reduce if not eliminate the stringent international restrictions on

Iraq's capabilities and freedom of action following the Gulf War so as to restore its strategic might. These restrictions can be categorized according to four groups:

- The Security Council's unconditional demand that Iraq destroy all the programs, facilities, equipment, and fighting material it built in the field of nuclear-biological-chemical weapons, including ballistic missiles with ranges exceeding 150 kilometers. The establishment of a UN inspection mechanism was designed to verify that Iraq complied with these demands and refrained from restoring any such facilities and materials.
- Total prohibition on the sale of weapons and military equipment to Iraq.
- Economic sanctions, mainly in the form of limitations on the export of Iraqi oil and the use of oil revenues. In 1996 Saddam was forced to acquiesce to the Security Council decision on the "oil for food" program, which allowed Iraq oil revenues of no more than 1.8 billion dollars every six months to be used for food and humanitarian goods only.
- Restrictions on Iraq's sovereignty and its freedom of action; restrictions on Iraqi flights in northern and southern Iraq; and a requirement to grant the Kurdish people the opportunity to set up an autonomous protectorate.

At the end of the 1990s Saddam scored two successes in limiting UN restrictions. The most important was in late 1998, when he ousted the UN inspectors who were monitoring the sites for development of mass destruction weapons. Despite enormous pressure, the inspectors did not return until November 2002. The second triumph was Saddam's success in convincing portions of the Arab and international public that the Iraqi people's suffering was due to economic sanctions. To this end he exploited differences of opinion among the permanent members of the Security Council and the Arab delegates regarding the continuation of sanctions and Arab business dealings with Iraq. His success was evidenced by the weakening of the international consensus on the sanctions. Convinced that easing his isolation and restoring Iraq to the international community would provide a positive incentive to Saddam, some countries, including Russia, China, and France, urged for a lightening if not outright lifting of the economic measures. Thus, in 1999 the amount of oil that Iraq was allowed to sell within the framework of "oil for food" was raised to $5.2 billion every six months, and in reality few actual limitations on oil exports remained. However, Iraq was unable to increase its oil production by significant amounts because the infrastructure was severely damaged during the Gulf War and recovery has been only fragmentary. Iraq still needed huge foreign investments in order to restore its production to full capacity.

Iraq's military capability was drastically reduced, and Iraq lacked the power to attack its neighbors, though it still possessed a large army that was apparently capable of defending the country against regional foes, even if only with antiquated weapons. Yet there was no doubt that Saddam Hussein still aspired to rebuild

Iraq as the leading superpower in the Gulf and the Arab world, and to accomplish this he would continue striving to regain his military strength and develop and manufacture weapons of mass destruction. His dedication to this goal motivated him to defy Security Council demands, which in turn resulted in a prolongation of the sanctions and the increased probability of an American military operation.

As far as was known, international inspections following the Gulf War uncovered most of Iraq's weapons facilities, and the majority of weapons of mass destruction and ballistic missiles were destroyed. Nevertheless, it was assumed that during those years Iraq managed to retain a small, undetected stockpile. Following the expulsion of the inspection teams in late 1998, Iraq was free to attempt to produce chemical and biological weapons to the best of its ability. The consensus among Western observers was that Iraq also succeeded in concealing a small number of launchers and ballistic missiles, and that in the last decade it progressed in the permitted development of short-range missiles, while possessing a forbidden infrastructure for producing longer range missiles. The status of its nuclear weapons program was less clear. Iraq was not close to achieving nuclear weapons capability, but it may be assumed that Iraq was putting to use its nuclear science knowledge and experience gained until the Gulf War, when it was within a few years of producing a nuclear device. The main concern was that foreign sources would provide Iraq with fissile material that would enable it to proceed quickly to achieving nuclear capability. Western sources estimated that if the limitations were removed, Iraq would race to build up its strategic power.

Thus, the loosening of restrictions on oil exports, and especially the ousting of UN inspection teams in 1998, created a large breach that made it easier for Iraq to continue developing weapons of mass destruction. The restrictions that remained in force – the prohibition on the import of military supplies and arms, limitations on Iraqi sovereignty, the American presence in the Gulf, and the rest of the economic proscriptions – were important in themselves for curbing Iraq's strategic rearmament. But the slackening of international sanctions placed a question mark over their effectiveness in the future. Despite the international community's weakened resolve, the American administration was able in May 2002 to push through the Security Council what was termed "smart sanctions." The idea was to increase the volume of civilian goods Iraq was allowed to import, but to tighten UN supervision over the use of the money that Iraq received from its oil exports and to enforce strictly the prohibition on the import of sensitive weapons and materials.

The September 11 terror attack changed the previous parameters of the Iraqi issue. Although the US government refrained from linking Iraq directly to the attack or Bin Laden's organization, it claimed that Saddam's regime posed a threat to stability in the Middle East. Furthermore, if weapons of mass destruction wound up in Saddam's hands, they might be channeled to purposes of terror, with catastrophic results for the United States and other countries. The administration

emphasized that its basic objective was to replace Saddam's regime as the only
sure way to obstruct Iraq's attempt to obtain weapons of mass destruction. Clearly,
though, ousting Saddam served as a goal in itself – to rid the arena of a ruler who
harbored aggressive intentions towards his neighbors and had already used
weapons of mass destruction against them. The administration believed that the
post-September 11 reality created an opportune time to oust Saddam, before he
obtained nuclear weapons and it would be too late to disarm him, thereby
constituting a serious threat to United States interests in the region. The
administration, therefore, sought to make full use of the conditions created after
September 11 and the willingness of numerous governments to join the campaign
against terrorism in order to conclude its "unfinished business" with Iraq.

The American administration examined at least two limited alternatives to bring
down Saddam: subversive activity and covert operations inside Iraq, or a relatively
limited military operation, Afghanistan-style, based on a massive air strike, the
deployment of limited American troops, the use of opposition forces to the Saddam
regime, and possibly targeted killings of figures in the Iraqi government. Yet
Washington was not enthusiastic over these alternatives. Although simpler and
less risky than a large-scale operation, their chances of overthrowing Saddam
Hussein were much lower. Both alternatives depended on an Iraqi opposition
that was weak, divided, disorganized, and militarily feeble. No element in Iraq
was comparable to the Afghani Northern Alliance that could be tapped to fell
Saddam's regime. The only organized force were the Kurds in northern Iraq, but
their military strength was limited and they hesitated to act in any way that might
threaten the autonomy they had achieved. Indeed, since their interests were focused
in the northern part of the country, they made it known that they would avoid
any form of military action against the regime. Moreover, the American
administration itself was committed to a unified Iraq, in part to prevent regional
shockwaves and primarily to avert any threat to Turkey's stability, and therefore
was loath to rely on Kurdish participation, which might ignite an attempt at
secession.

A US air attack would probably cripple Iraq's strategic infrastructure and
military power, and in theory it could drive elements hostile to Saddam, perhaps
even in the Iraqi army, to rise against him. But this meant that throughout the
whole operation the United States would be dependent on Iraqi elements it had
no control over. Furthermore, there was no guarantee that they would overcome
their fear of Saddam's revenge and organize effectively against him, or display
the determination and capability needed to overturn his regime. The US secretary
of state also made it clear that without a ground attack it would be impossible to
destroy Iraq's non-conventional capability.

With other options relegated to the background, the Bush administration
reached a decision at the end of 2002 to launch a large military offensive to depose
Saddam Hussein. Already by the summer, the US had begun an assembly of forces

in the Gulf and elsewhere around Iraq, eventually numbering about 250,000 troops. The force also included six task forces of aircraft carriers, including two in the Mediterranean Sea, more than 1000 planes – fighters, bombers, early warning, transport, and refueling aircraft – as well as helicopters and a large assembly of precision guided munitions. Added to this force were 40,000 troops and two aircraft carriers from Britain, and a small Australian force. The forces were heavily dependent on a broad logistics infrastructure that was built in the Gulf States and other Middle Eastern countries primarily after the Gulf War. By March 2003, the American and British forces were prepared for a large scale strike against Iraq, following the massive buildup and extensive preparatory drilling in Kuwait.

Preparations for the campaign, however, encountered serious difficulties. Within the United States itself a dispute arose regarding the legitimacy of a military offensive. Beginning as a dispute within the administration that centered on the dangers entailed in a military strike, the controversy grew and extended to the Congress and the media. Yet despite the strong public disapproval expressed by prominent figures of previous administrations, and despite large anti-war demonstrations across the country, the Bush administration succeeded in winning strong support from Congress for a military campaign and in persuading most of the American public as to the legitimacy of the war.

Joining American domestic opposition to a military strike was the strong disapproval voiced by many governments abroad. Great Britain and a small number of states favored the strike, notwithstanding their own significant domestic opposition. Against them, however, was a bloc of countries led by France, Germany, Russia, and China that objected strongly to military action and tried to avert it. The result was a sharp polarization between the US and Britain on the one side, and other European states on the opposing side, a division that threatened to create a serious rift within NATO and the European Union and to impinge on the authority of the UN Security Council. This diplomatic resistance severely complicated the US attempt to achieve international backing for a military campaign and to anchor the offensive in UN legitimacy. Once France announced its intention to veto any Security Council resolution favoring military action, and in light of its inability to muster a majority, the United States was forced to abandon its hope of a new UN resolution that would authorize a military offensive in Iraq.

Perhaps predictably, most of the Arab and Muslim states opposed a strike on Iraq. Rather than any inherent support for Saddam Hussein, their objection stemmed primarily from the fear that the strike would appear to be a US attack on the Arab and Muslim world, and would arouse strong anti-American sentiment that might threaten their stability. Arab and Muslim support was important to the US in part for international legitimacy for the attack, but no less for the logistical support that one or two of Iraq's neighbors could provide, for without a land base in at least one country bordering Iraq, a ground attack into Iraq was not feasible.

While most Arab countries remained steadfast in their opposition, the administration managed to attain a minimum degree of cooperation. Kuwait, Qatar, and Bahrain agreed to let the US launch ground attacks from their countries. Saudi Arabia, which had initially refused support for the offensive, announced in September 2002 that it would allow US forces to operate in its territory if the Security Council sanctioned military action, and in practice, Saudi Arabia permitted American forces to operate to a limited degree within its borders. The Turkish government too allowed the US to assemble ground forces and launch a northern offensive from its border. Turkish consent was obtained with a pledge of extensive American aid and the promise to allow Turkey limited activity in northern Iraq, in order to protect Turkish interests in Iraqi Kurdistan and prevent an uprising on the part of the Kurdish minority in Turkey. However, the Turkish parliament refused to support the agreement between its government and the US administration, and eventually agreed only to allow the Americans the use of Turkey's airspace for operations. As a result, the Americans had to cancel the planned ground invasion into Iraq and the launch of aerial attacks from Turkey, and were obliged to move the forces already assembled on ships near Turkey to Kuwait. Jordan likewise voiced its objection to a strike against Iraq and announced its refusal to serve as a base for US military activity, yet in practice it appeared that the US had reached an agreement regarding limited assistance for a military offensive in western Iraq.

The final difficulty was the set of complex military challenges entailed by the offensive. The main problem was not achieving a victory over the Iraqi army: there was no question that the balance of power would allow the US to defeat the Iraqi army soundly. Yet because the objective was deposing Saddam's regime, the offensive assumed greater complexity. Should the military strike fail to encourage Iraqi commanders to join forces with the US to depose Saddam, the Americans would be forced to fell the regime on their own. This would mean entering Baghdad and possibly fighting in a densely populated urban area, a move that would likely incur heavy casualties, among American soldiers and Iraqi civilians alike. It was feared that significant losses might be sustained through terror attacks or guerilla warfare, or perhaps Iraqi use of chemical or biological weapons. The overall financial cost of the war would unquestionably be steep, and this time, unlike in the Gulf War, there would be no one to assist the United States in financing the operation.

In an attempt to thwart United States military preparations, Saddam Hussein maneuvered to assemble international political opposition, especially among the Arab states. Thus, as international pressure mounted against him, and apparently from his assessment that the American administration was determined to attack, Saddam agreed in mid-2002 to readmit unconditionally the international inspectors to Iraq. Through this ploy he hoped to channel international preoccupation towards the attempt to ascertain whether Iraq was manufacturing weapons of mass destruction. Capitalizing on the difficulty in obtaining proof of this nature, which in any case would require an extended period of time, Saddam hoped to strip a military offensive of international support and legitimacy, or at the very least postpone it.

The lack of sufficient international support for a military campaign prompted the US and Britain to attempt to win approval through a Security Council resolution. Following much bargaining and compromise with other powers, in November 2002 the UN passed Resolution 1441. The resolution accused Iraq of violating previous Security Council resolutions ordering disarmament of weapons of mass destruction, and mandated the return of the UN inspection regime, although this time under more stringent conditions. It also determined that Iraq "will face serious consequences as a result of its continued violations of its obligations."

Following the resolution, UN inspection teams returned to Iraq, and their inspections indeed made it difficult for Iraq to continue to develop non-conventional weapons. At the same time, the inspectors' regular reports to the Security Council denied the US of the formal basis to construct a framework for a forthcoming attack. The inspectors complained of insufficient cooperation on Iraq's part, yet they did not determine that Iraq possessed weapons of mass destruction. The lack of such decisive proof bolstered the efforts of those objecting to the use of military force, led by France, Russia, and Germany, who refused to allow the administration to pass a new resolution that would grant legitimacy for a military strike. Yet the American administration decided that it would no longer settle for a continuation of the verification regime in Iraq, which Saddam had successfully deceived in the past and which proved unable to uncover Iraq's non-conventional capabilities. Against the failed attempts to pass a new resolution, or even to obtain a Security Council majority, the Bush administration decided in mid–March 2003 to end its futile diplomatic efforts and launch a military strike, even without UN backing and while embroiled in unprecedented disagreement with other major states.

On March 20, 2003, a military campaign against Iraq was launched with the explicit goal of deposing Saddam Hussein's regime and replacing it with a more moderate government willing to abandon Iraq's development of weapons of mass destruction. It was assumed that several factors would determine the success of the campaign: the rate at which it progressed and the extent to which ground forces would be involved, possibly in urban warfare; the response of Iraqi military commanders and their potential willingness to assist in deposing Saddam and in building a new Iraq; the extent of international opposition to the American offensive; the degree to which the Bush administration is determined to attain its goals, even in the face of complications and heavy losses; and the ability of the US and moderate Arab states to stifle strong anti-American sentiment that the war may arouse.

The offensive also promised to actualize the question the United States had long grappled with, namely, the Iraq that would emerge following a military operation. Even if the United States succeeded in toppling Saddam's regime, overall results would probably be mixed. On the one hand, the administration expected the regime change to bring about a major transformation in the region. Establishing a moderate, US-allied government in Baghdad willing to cease its pursuit of weapons of mass destruction would undermine the region's radical camp, add to the stability in the Gulf, strengthen United States influence in the area, reduce the risks to American allies, including Israel, and contribute to the political process in the Arab-Israeli conflict.

But all of these results were mere speculation since stability in post-Saddam Iraq remained far from certain. The Iraqi regime was built around Saddam and his entourage over more than two decades, during which any potential alternative government was forcibly crushed. The establishment of a stable, new order based on representatives from central groups in the Iraqi system, including the army and security services, and the assurance of their joint cooperation would be a formidable task. It would undoubtedly demand the investment of enormous resources and an ongoing American military presence until the regime stabilized. Also, there was no guarantee against the dangerous features of Saddam's regime – the quest for regional hegemony, the ambition to enhance Iraq's status as a strategic military power based on weapons of mass destruction, the offensive security concept, and the hostility to Israel and the peace process – reemerging among his successors, in the near or distant future. The American administration was concerned, therefore, that instability might prevail in Iraq, requiring a long-term American military presence in the country, with the risk of US forces getting dragged into internecine fighting.

A major cause of concern was the Kurdish north, a worrisome prospect to the US and to regional states, especially Turkey. The Kurds could exploit the American action in order to expand the autonomy they won after the Gulf War. In this scenario, unrest could awaken a demand for liberation among the large Kurdish populations in Turkey, Iran, and Syria, and this in turn might bring about Turkish military intervention in northern Iraq. The Shiites in the south of Iraq might also rise up and as a majority sector insist on their share in the new government. Unless the future Iraqi regime would be strong and stable, then the fragile balance in the Kurdish north and Shiite south could thrust the country into civil war and anarchy, with the possibility of Iran and/or Turkey entering the fray. Such a development could turn Iraq into the center of regional instability.

Iran and the Winds of Change

The Iran of 2003 was undergoing a process of gradual changes that were expected to continue in the coming years. They included:

- Significant domestic changes, although they were somewhat erratic and occurred at a pace that did not satisfy their proponents.
- Post-September 11 changes in the strategic environment, with the United States invasion of Iran's eastern neighbor, Afghanistan, and the military intervention in its western neighbor, Iraq.
- Gradual amassing of strategic military power, in contrast to its limited conventional strength. In 2002-2003 it became clear that Iran has progressed significantly towards developing nuclear weaponry.

Since the 1990s, a discernible process of reform has occurred in Iran: its significance lay in its rise as a groundswell and not as policy dictated from above. Focused on domestic issues, the drive for reform emanated from many sectors of society, especially the younger generation, who called for expanded personal and political freedoms, greater rights to organize politically and voice criticism of the state, a stronger economy, and a reduction in the corruption rampant in the system. Supporters of reform have won four prominent victories at the polls over the past six years: the election of Mohammed Khatami twice as president of Iran, and winning parliamentary as well as municipal elections. Hope ran high among the moderates that the chain of victories, Khatami's status, and the electoral gains in parliament would enable the president to push ahead with reforms. This did not happen. It soon became clear that the moderates' parliamentary majority was not strong enough to overcome the radicals' control of the key centers of power in the country: the army, the Revolutionary Guards, and the legal and economic systems. In addition, the radicals have turned to the "Council of Guardians," a conservative body with the authority to block legislative proposals, chaired by the past president Hashemi Rafsangani, to stymie reforms that threatened their interests. In this way they succeeded in neutralizing the moderates' majority in parliament.

After the moderates' parliamentary victory in February 2000, the radicals counterattacked by taking advantage of their hold on powerful positions. Nearly all of the newspapers that supported domestic reform were shut down. Some moderates were ousted from office and arrested; others were put on trial or threatened with indictment because of criticisms they voiced in parliament. The radicals impeded the moderates' efforts to reform the election process, ease the press restrictions, and initiate a dialogue with the United States.

Beset by this opposition, President Khatami displayed his weakness as a leader. In general, he drifted with the popular sentiment rather than direct it. He abandoned his supporters who had been arrested and arraigned, and he did not even try to interfere in the closure of newspapers. Aware of the subsequent criticism aimed at his leadership, Khatami felt it sufficient to distribute occasional verbal barbs at the radicals about their obstruction of change and to threaten to resign if he failed at advancing reforms. Yet overall he made no use of his popularity to confront the radicals, nor did he exercise his power in dealing with their provocations.

Consequently, the reform movement lost momentum over the last few years and even regressed. One prominent indication was the radicals' victory in the February 2003 municipal elections – the first victory since 1997 following four previous electoral failures. The stagnated progress created bitter disappointment in large sections of the Iranian public as well as among Iranian exiles who had pinned their hopes on the reform movement. The focus of their frustration was the inability of the president and parliament to shake off the radicals' hold on government, and the impotence characterizing Khatami's leadership. The disappointment has brought many observers, especially in Western countries, to realize that Khatami is probably incapable of introducing major changes in the Iranian system, and that a breakthrough in reform will be delayed for at least a few years.

Yet despite the setback, the reform movement was still alive. Iran in 2003 was far different from what it had been a decade before. Greater political and personal freedom existed and there was more political openness than in previous years. Public debate occurred on issues that were closed to discussion in the past, such as relations with the United States. Occasionally, unrest broke out among students. In all, a large percentage of the Iranian people made it known in various ways they favored change, and it seemed that this would generate a continuation of the reform process even if it took years. Moreover, with the political venue for reform effectively blocked, indications pointed to the Iranian street as a potential alternative for advocating change through student and worker demonstrations that decried the stifling of individual and political freedom, and the ongoing economic affliction.

Although the reform process focused on domestic affairs, it also influenced Iran's foreign policy, especially in the direction of improving relations with the Gulf States, first of all Saudi Arabia, and even with Iraq and other Arab countries. Relations with the United States improved only slightly. The moderate camp, which included Khatami himself, expressed its willingness to enter a dialogue with the American people. However, they would be willing to open a dialogue with the American administration only if certain strict conditions were met, such as the removal of economic sanctions from Iran and the withdrawal of American forces from the Gulf. The radical camp, led by the spiritual head of Iran, Ayatollah Ali Khamenei, rejected dialogue with the Americans on principle, and persisted in its hard line on other foreign policy issues, such as events in Afghanistan. In practice, an informal dialogue with American individuals has grown over recent years, and from time to time secret contacts between the governments took place at the working level. On the other hand, consensus was strong in Iran regarding relations with Israel, with both the radical camp and the moderate establishment, excluding individual moderate academicians, rejecting a dialogue with Israel and clinging to a solution based on the creation of a Palestinian state in place of Israel, not adjacent to it. On matters of national security the two camps also saw eye to eye: the moderates fully supported the continued strategic arming of Iran, including the development of long-range missiles.

American policy in the aftermath of September 11, 2001 was likely to have a major impact on Iran. After the Islamic Revolution, the regime in Tehran perceived itself facing a series of threats in its strategic environment: the Iraqi menace from the west, the American threat from the south, the Soviet peril from the north, and Soviet intervention in Afghanistan from the east. During the 1990s the Iraqi threat abated and the Soviet Union collapsed; on the other hand, the American threat to Iran was exacerbated and loomed as the country's primary danger. After September 11, the American threat increased in the eyes of the Iran, especially as US troops began operating inside Iran's eastern neighbor. Although the Taliban regime, which had been a source of concern to the Iranians, was quashed, in its place was a regime linked to the United States. Furthermore, the American presence in Afghanistan and in some of the new, ex-Soviet republics in the north intensified, and Iraq was targeted next.

The US declaration of war on terror had further significance for Iran. Since 1984 the Islamic Republic of Iran has been officially defined by Washington as a state heavily involved in terror. Iran was also actively engaged in the development of weapons of mass destruction, and in fact has overtaken Iraq in this regard. Indeed, the American administration invested a great deal of energy in obstructing Iran's weapons programs. For this reason, it seemed likely that the administration would treat the Iranian regime as it did Baghdad, yet interestingly, the administration adopted different attitudes to each regime. This divergence stemmed mainly from two reasons: hopes regarding Iran's moderating trend and the opening of a more substantive dialogue that would lead to a reduction of the Iranian threat; and awareness that it was much more difficult to launch a military offensive against Iran.

After September 11, there were glimmers of a positive turn in relations between the two countries. Iran strongly condemned the attack. President Khatami publicly expressed sympathy for the American people and victims of the attack, and dissociated himself from Bin Laden and al-Qaeda activity. Commiseration with the United States after the terror strike was also heard in the Iranian street. Talks were held between the two governments at the working level, and information and ideas were exchanged pertaining to the war on terror. In advance of the American action in Afghanistan, Iran pledged to assist in rescue operations of American military personnel downed inside Iran, and declared it would close its borders with Afghanistan and Pakistan to prevent al-Qaeda and Taliban militants from fleeing to Iranian territory. Tehran also cooperated in the establishment of a transitional government in Afghanistan after the fall of the Taliban.

Meantime, the Bush administration toned down its anti-Iranian rhetoric, despite its basic opposition to the regime, and in the first months after September 11 it refrained from assigning Iran to the next stage in the war on terror. This restraint apparently reflected an exercise in quiet diplomacy to reach a serious dialogue with the Iranians. The administration believed that its powerful position in the wake of the terror attack, and the common ground with the Iranian regime regarding the future of Afghanistan and Iraq, both countries of great concern to Iran, could jumpstart a dialogue. A rapprochement like this, the administration hoped, would induce basic changes in Iran's conduct, at least regarding anti-terror measures, and later perhaps in the area of non-conventional arms development.

These expectations, however, never materialized, and it soon became apparent that the radical wing of the Iranian government rejected any expansion of the dialogue with the administration. In late October 2001, Khamenei fulminated publicly against any impulse to improve relations with the United States, particularly after a group of Iranian delegates in parliament called for the renewal of relations with Washington. Two additional developments convinced the administration that Iran continued to act against American interests, and that nothing had altered in its anti-US policy. The first was Iran's endeavor to regain influence in Afghanistan after the Taliban collapsed by distributing arms to Iranian-linked parties in a way that sabotaged the embryonic stability the United States sought to anchor. The American secretary of defense and head of the CIA also confirmed that a considerable number of Taliban and al-Qaeda activists had entered Iran during American operations in Afghanistan, through an arrangement with senior figures in the Iranian government. The second development was the exposé of an arms shipment from Iran to the Palestinian Authority on the vessel *Karine-A*, which proved that Iran had developed a new channel for disseminating terror and was working to derail any peace process. This incident was another indication of the marked increase in Iran's assistance to Palestinian Islamic organizations, joining its attempts to infiltrate the ranks of Israeli Arabs and to encourage intensification of military pressure on Israel by Hizbollah.

Recognizing Iran's resistance to reorienting its policy, President Bush was prompted in January 2002 to proclaim that Iran represented one of the three pillars of the "axis of evil," in company with Iraq and North Korea. This declaration, coupled with the American intention to strike at Iraq, created a new level of tension and mutual suspicion between the United States and Iran. Radical and moderate leaders virulently attacked the Bush administration for its posture towards Iran, and rejected American allegations of evil. Furthermore, the prospect of a US military operation against Iraq was very worrisome to the Iranians even if its objective was the removal of Saddam Hussein's regime. While Iran had an interest in the ousting of Saddam and in Iraq remaining weak, the thought of another military move – coming on the heels of US operations in Afghanistan – against a neighboring Muslim state, with the goal of regime toppling and the obstruction of mass destruction weapons programs as the basis for American aggression, served as a clear warning for Iran. Moreover, if the American offensive in Iraq resulted in the establishment of a US-backed government there, it would leave Iran almost completely surrounded by pro-American regimes, with US troops deployed directly across the Iranian border.

While Iran, unlike Iraq, did not for the time being figure on the list of potential American targets, since September 11 the Iranians nonetheless grew increasingly wary of an American military move that could be initiated against them too. Disclosures in the American media in March 2002 of a secret Defense Department memo concerning the administration's intentions to prepare for the possibility of using nuclear weapons against seven states threatening the United States, including Iran, undoubtedly added to the anxiety. This spurred Iranian leaders, led by Khamenei, to issue several sharp warnings to the United States against an attack on Iran. The most caustic comment came from the deputy commander of the Revolutionary Guards, who declared that if the United States attacked Iran, Iran would respond by striking at American interests wherever they were, including oil facilities in the Gulf. After April 2002 the rhetoric on both sides toned down, and there was reason to believe that secret, low-level contacts resumed, including in context of the impending war in Iraq, although the atmosphere remained charged with suspicion.

From the American point of the view, the most problematic issue was Iran's pursuit of weapons of mass destruction, led by its nuclear program underway since the 1980s. The program has been plagued by serious technological, organizational, and financial difficulties, in part because of US efforts to obstruct its progress. The power plant under construction by Russia in Bushehr, for example, will not be completed before 2005, following a delay of at least five years. Given these complications, it seemed that Iran had yet to reach the point at which there would be no stopping its nuclear program by blocking external technological assistance, although it may be rapidly approaching this watershed. On the other hand, there were increasing indications that Iran may have succeeded in progressing towards a capability to produce fissile material. In 2002 and early 2003 several important components of the Iranian program came to light, particularly the construction of two nuclear facilities in Iran: a facility for uranium enrichment using gas centrifuges, which could advance Iran's capability to develop nuclear weaponry through uranium enrichment; and a facility for heavy water production, which would advance the declared Iranian plan to build a heavy water research plant, which in turn might provide Iran with fissile material capability through the separation of plutonium. Furthermore, the likelihood also existed that Iran could acquire fissile material from outside sources, notably former Soviet Union states. If this happened, the timetable for Iran to become a nuclear power would be shortened. At the present stage, therefore, it seemed that Iran was at least a few years away from producing significant amounts of fissile material, yet at this rate, Iran would be able to produce a nuclear warhead for a ballistic missile in the latter half of the decade.

Since the mid-1980s, Iran also has also been actively engaged in developing chemical and biological weapons. It has amassed a formidable stock of chemical weapons – one of the largest in the developing countries – built with material and equipment from Western and Eastern companies, but mainly with Chinese technological assistance. Despite its signature to the limitation treaty on the spread of chemical weapons, Iran's arsenal expanded steadily both in size and variety of weapons. It was not known if Iran progressed to the next generation of chemical agents, chiefly nerve gases. Most experts agreed that Iran was capable of delivering chemical payloads by means of artillery shells, short-range air bombs, and rockets, but it was still unclear whether it managed to fit chemical warheads onto ballistic missiles. Iran was also working intensively on biological weapons programs, and it seemed to have attained limited delivery capability for biological weaponry, via artillery, air bombs, or rockets. Apparently, though, a full-scale biological program based on ballistic or guided missile delivering systems lies well in the future.

Iran had one of the largest missile stockpiles in the Middle East, containing Scud class ballistic missiles, mainly from North Korea, with ranges of 500 kilometers; similar missiles that were licensed to be manufactured and assembled in Iran; and artillery rockets produced in Iran, with ranges of 200 kilometers. Iran also possessed naval cruise missiles imported from China, with ranges of 120 kilometers (some have also been produced in Iran). However, the most significant and disturbing feature of the Iranian missile program was the effort being invested in developing long-range ballistic missiles. The most conspicuous of these weapons was the Shehab-3, powered by liquid fuel and with a range of 1,300 kilometers, and built on the basis of the North Korean Nodong-1 missile and Russian technology. It was believed to be already operational in emergency conditions; that is, Iran could deploy a limited number of Shehab-3 missiles if necessary, and it was expected to begin serial production in the near future.

Moreover, the Iranian defense minister announced that Iran would develop missiles of an even more advanced class, the Shehab-4 and Shehab-5. Later he proceeded to dissemble, claiming that Iran had no need of long-range missiles and was merely improving the operational capabilities of the Shehab-3, with the Shehab-4 designed for satellite launching rather than military purposes. At the same time, it is estimated that Iran had at least three additional missile programs underway. One, the Shehab-4 program was being built for ranges of 2000 kilometers, and there may have been plans for missiles of longer ranges, based on the North Korean Taepo-Dong and Russian technology. It is assumed that the program was still in its early stage, and that even if the missile was intended officially for satellite launching and thus presented as designed for civilian needs in order to counter pressure to halt its development, it provided the basis for a long-range military missile. The second program was the solid fuel program for producing a ballistic missile with a range similar to that of the Shehab-3. The solid fuel would upgrade the operational capability of the missile. In 2002 Iran announced it had succeeded in developing a 200 km range solid fuel missile, which may well lend it capability to develop such missiles with longer ranges. The third program was designed to extend the ranges of Iran's naval cruise missiles made in China.

In all, Iran was constructing a formidable capability in mass destruction weapons. American measures have impeded progress, forcing Iran to rely heavily on foreign sources for acquiring equipment, technology, and raw materials. However, if the development programs are not stopped, their results will be forthcoming in the near future even if the weapon systems are not very sophisticated and accurate. If and when Iran's weapons programs are completed, especially the nuclear devices and long-range missiles, then the balance of power in the Gulf and Middle East will be altered, and the threat will have an impact on the various states in the region, including Israel, as well as on American interests in the area. The threat does not necessarily come from the possibility that Iran would unleash weapons of mass destruction against other countries, as it would probably prefer to retain them as a deterrent factor and use them only under exceptional circumstances of national survival. However, even assuming this estimate holds true – and there is no absolute certainty of that – the very existence of these weapons in Iran's hands has disturbing implications: Iran possesses a safety net for committing aggressive acts against other countries, including the United States and Israel. In turn this would provide motivation to other countries to develop their own nuclear weapons programs, thus accelerating the strategic arms race in the Middle East. Radical elements in the region would be strengthened and allied more with Iran, while moderate countries would be forced to readjust their strategic policy to the Iranian line.

Iran's military buildup in conventional weapons was less impressive. Excluding Turkey, it had the largest army in terms of manpower and number of divisions in the Middle East, but its main drawback was its weapon systems. Most of the arms in the regular Iranian army and the Revolutionary Guards were outdated; some were purchased from the United States and Britain in the 1970s during the period of the Shah, and other weapons were bought in the East, mainly from China. After the revolution, the United States and other Western countries ceased supplying arms, spare parts, and ammunition to Iran except in limited quantity, an embargo that significantly contributed to the obsolescence of Iran's equipment. Since the 1990s Russia has become Iran's leading weapons supplier. Between 1989 and 1991, four arms deals were concluded between Russia and Iran, for the sum of $5.1 billion. Until the mid-1990s, Iran received the weapon systems and military equipment – primarily tanks, aircraft, air defense systems, and submarines – at the value of $3.6 billion. The remaining weapons in the agreement were not supplied to Iran, primarily because it was unable to find the money to pay for them.

The arms supply from Russia enabled Iran to obtain quality weapon systems for the first time since the revolution, but this source quickly dried up. Since the mid-1990s Iran procured only a limited number of weapon systems from Russia due to its lack of funds and because of American pressure on the Russian government to cease its arms sales to Iran. In the middle of 1995 Moscow yielded to American demands to halt further arms deals with Iran, and agreed to complete only transactions it had already signed. In November 2000, the Russian government informed the Americans it was canceling this agreement. The following year, in October 2001, Russia and Iran signed a framework agreement outlining the sale of weapons to Iran, worth $1.5 billion – and according to other sources, $7 billion – to be spread out over a five year period. This agreement too suffered from the previous constraints: Iran's incapacity to pay for the merchandise and American pressure on Russia to limit arms supplies to Iran. As a result of these strictures, as of early 2003 only one deal was realized within the framework of the Russian-Iranian agreement: the sale of military helicopters.

Despite these obstacles, one area of Iran's military capability has witnessed remarkable advancement – naval power. Iran accorded high priority to maritime power because of the importance of the Gulf. Iran's vast oil resources were concentrated there; it served as a route for Iranian oil exports; the American presence in the region posed a threat to the Gulf; and finally, Iran's control of the eastern coast of the Gulf and of the Straits of Hormuz acted as a deterrent to Iran's enemies. For these reasons Iran invested large sums to upgrade its naval capability, specifically in fast missile boats, cruise missiles, submarines, and various mining devices purchased mainly from Russia and China. Thus, in contrast to the forced neglect of its air and ground forces, Iran has significantly upgraded its naval forces.

The issue of arms supply to Iran created a challenge for American relations with other governments. Western countries did not present special obstacles over this issue. All of them have agreed to honor the American-initiated embargo on weapon systems and sensitive technologies to Iran in effect since the 1980s, although some Western companies, including American ones, continued to supply Iran with dual use equipment and materials, managing to sidestep the restrictions and inspection checks. These materials were used by the Iranians primarily for developing weapon systems, especially weapons of mass destruction. At the official level the problem centered on the Russian, Chinese, and in certain cases, North Korean governments. Russia was Iran's key supplier of nuclear know-how, ballistic missile technology, and conventional weapons; China was the main supplier of chemical warfare capabilities and naval military equipment, as well as nuclear and missile technologies; North Korea furnished vital assistance in missile development and perhaps in nuclear technology. All three states reached agreements and understandings with the Americans, mostly during the latter half of the 1990s, regarding the cessation or limitation of military assistance to Iran, but all three found ways to maneuver around these commitments. Financial profit motivated them to continue supplying Iran, as did the awareness of Iran's importance as a key state in the region, and perhaps the desire to receive larger benefits from the United States in exchange for disengagement from Iran.

The issue tied in with the question of the success of the Clinton administration's "dual containment" policy, announced in 1993-1994, which was designed to block the threat emanating from the efforts of Iran and Iraq at obtaining weapons of mass destruction. The policy vis-à-vis Iraq was remarkably successful. Most of Iraq's non-conventional weapons were destroyed during the 1990s. Washington's attempt to thwart Iran's strategic growth also indicated some measure of success. The United States did not alter Iran's policy that still supported terror and sought to sabotage the peace process, nor did it manage to stymie Iran's pursuit of weapons of mass destruction However, US efforts greatly hindered Iran's strategic armament programs, both conventional and non-conventional, and there was no absolute certainty that Iran would eventually succeed in developing nuclear weapons. Without the American containment policy, Iran would be much stronger militarily today and would undoubtedly have gotten hold of an arsenal of long-range missiles, and probably possess nuclear weapons too. The setback in Iran's nuclear capability was important in itself, but the timing may be of greater importance if the moderate forces in the country are strengthened, and a meaningful dialogue develops with the American administration prior to Iran's acquisition of nuclear weapons. A scenario of this nature would create the opportunity for halting Iran's nuclear program through an agreement, and would transform the significance of the Iranian threat.

The partial success of the containment policy can be looked at from another angle: until now no better practical alternative has been proposed for reducing the Iranian threat. The only other option, suggested by Europeans, was the "critical dialogue" approach. This proposal called for removing economic sanctions from Iran, developing economic and political ties, and launching a dialogue in the hope that these stimulants would have a palliating effect and incline Iran towards moderation. While this approach allowed the European countries to cultivate economic ties with Iran, it had no practical influence on Tehran's continued efforts to procure weapons of mass destruction, its involvement with terror, or its attempts to derail the peace process. It was even questionable if the European approach contributed in any way to strengthening the moderate forces in Iran. While the Americans' containment policy achieved a partial success, the European option of "critical dialogue" was a failure.

In all, the Iranian threat towards a slate of countries is liable to assume graver meaning in the coming years, the more its nuclear and missile programs progressed. In the future, it will be possible to narrow the Iranian threat by means of two political measures. One is by influencing Iranian capability, that is, by cutting off the foreign supply of technologies and equipment necessary to its nuclear program. If the American move against Iraq proves successful, it may be easier to slow down the rate of Iran's weapons development since American ability to pressure Iran and its arms suppliers would increase. The second way is an Iranian change of priorities. If Iran's domestic path towards moderation gathered renewed momentum and transformed the character of the regime, then the Iranian threat would likely be reduced. The differences between the moderates and the radicals on issues of strategic buildup and relations with Israel were currently imperceptible, but a gap in these issues could widen if the moderate trend in Iranian leadership strengthened, and an enhanced dialogue with the United States ensued in order to improve the economy. Moreover, if a genuine peace process emerged between the Palestinians, Syria, and Israel, it might diminish Iran's ability and motivation to continue as the region's radical element as well as one that stands to harm Israel.

CHAPTER 3

Military Balances in the Region

Shlomo Brom

When violence erupted between Israel and the Palestinians in late September 2000, concern grew that the conflict would spill over to Arab states or other neighboring adversaries. This fear, however, did not materialize. The majority of Arab states, first and foremost Egypt, declared unequivocally that they had no intention of being dragged into a military confrontation with Israel. Even Syria, which supported Hizbollah provocations against Israel, acted to restrain the organization's operations when it was made clear to President Bashar Assad that such support could embroil Syria in an all-out war. The moderate Arab states harbored valid political reasons for avoiding a clash with Israel, but from their leaders' statements it was clear that their assessment of the military balance between Israel and its neighbors is what played a major role in avoiding such a confrontation. Arab leaders estimated that entanglement in a military conflict under the circumstances they faced in 2002, which resembled those on the eve of the 1967 war, would end with similar results. This appraisal reflected the growing perception in the Middle East regarding Israel's military superiority over its neighbors in a potential clash between regular armies.

It was the military balance in the Persian Gulf region that dominated the agenda in late 2002, in light of the American decision to change the Iraqi regime in stage two of its global war against terrorism. Debates in the United States about how to change the regime focused on the estimated strength of the Iraqi army. Assessments on the balance of forces in the Gulf once the Baghdad regime is replaced also influenced considerations on the way the region's strategic balance can be preserved.

The following analysis considers the balance of military power with regard to two key dimensions of Middle East issues, the Arab-Israeli conflict and the Gulf region, and will also examine the balance in the region's weapons of mass destruction. The analysis is based on the data that appears below in the second section of the book.

The Arab-Israeli Balance

In 2002, the factors that discouraged a military buildup in the majority of Arab countries surrounding Israel or in those that were candidates for a future anti-Israel coalition remained principally unchanged. Syria, Jordan, and Lebanon continued to suffer from serious shortages of funds that almost completely froze their arms buildup. Although indications were that Syria was to be re-supplied with fighter planes by Russia and that Jordan received a number of new tanks, the first deal did not materialize and the pace of the second was slow and the numbers insignificant. Iraq and Libya remained stymied by sanctions that prevented a refurbishment of their armed forces even when financial means were available. Even Saudi Arabia, the world's number one oil magnate, found itself financially struggling when it came to weapons procurement projects that were planned when oil prices were at their peak, and in 2002 was forced to cancel or postpone a number of deals for basic military hardware, such as Leclerc tanks. Only the Gulf States and Egypt, which receive annual American financial aid, continued their military buildup alongside a parallel buildup by Israel, which also enjoys massive American assistance on a yearly basis.

The implication of these developments was that no change transpired over the past year in the quantitative balance between Israel and the Arab countries that could form a coalition against it. Although the proportions have always been to Israel's disadvantage, they remained at a degree that allowed Israel to grapple with them successfully because of its own qualitative advantages. In addition, the scant likelihood in 2003 of an anti-Israel military coalition being formed renders at present the analysis of the balance of forces between Israel and an Arab coalition of this sort a theoretical exercise.

A rough quantitative balance in main weapon systems existed between Israel and Syria, and Israel and Egypt. Israel had 3400 tanks to Syria's 3700 and Egypt's 3000. Israel possessed 470 warplanes to Syria's 490 and Egypt's 480, and had 105 combat helicopters to Syria's 90 and Egypt's 100. In field artillery Israel was at a distinct numerical disadvantage: its 1300 artillery pieces did not stand up to Syria's 2600 and Egypt's 3500. If Egypt and Syria were to combine forces against Israel, the power ratio would be approximately 2 to 1, and if other Arab countries joined the coalition then the imbalance would reach approximately 3 to 1.

However, the picture alters when factoring in the dimension of quality in the main weapon systems. For example, Israel had 350 top-of-the-line warplanes compared to Syria's 24 and Egypt's 210. As for first class tanks, the relative difference dropped to 1.5 (Egypt and Syria) to 1 (Israel), from the previous 2 to 1, and even this was not an accurate picture since most of Israel's tanks not categorized as qualitative have nevertheless undergone a thorough upgrading. In naval matters Syria lost its submarine fleet and now operates only a surface navy comprising outdated missile boats incapable of competing with Israeli vessels.

The Egyptian fleet has undergone full-scale modernization and was comparable to Israel's surface navy, if Israeli air superiority was overlooked. Under the water Israel retained certain advantages. It possessed modern Dolphin-class submarines, whereas Egypt could only muster antiquated subs made in China.

However, more critical than the qualitative difference in the traditional arsenal was the edge fostered by information-age technologies, otherwise known as the Revolution in Military Affairs (RMA). Indeed, the most dynamic factor in the Middle East balance continued to be the widening qualitative gap between Israel and its neighbors in areas of strength not considered main weapon systems by traditional armies: command and control systems, drones, precision guided weapons, night-fighting and all-weather systems, and intelligence collecting technologies.

The American success against the Taliban regime in Afghanistan, on the heels of the military achievements in the Balkans and in the Gulf War, underscored to observers in the Middle East and elsewhere that armies equipped with advanced RMA technologies can subdue traditional forces while suffering few human casualties among themselves. Central to this advantage is the ability to project accurate, long-range fire to targets detected in real time. Although the Taliban had relatively limited weapons compared to the Iraqi army at the time of the Gulf War, its militia-like nature and the experience in guerilla warfare gained in its struggle against the Soviets turned it into a tough, complex, asymmetric foe for armies equipped with the most advanced military capabilities. In fact, the "low signature" nature characteristic of lightly-armed guerillas made them particularly difficult to locate in real time. Nonetheless, the US forces were able to demolish the Taliban with pinpoint aerial and naval fire, thus allowing the opposition forces to defeat the weakened Taliban with relative ease.

The American victory in Afghanistan also greatly influenced the perception of Middle East countries regarding the balance of power between Middle Eastern countries and the Western superpowers, first and foremost the United States. Specifically, there were no illusions regarding the Middle East armies' ability to meet the challenge of superpower intervention.

It was understood in the Middle East of 2002-2003 that only Israel possessed the military capability derived from advanced technologies, the ability to form a real time image of battlefield targets, fire precision weapons at great distances, and direct the fighting from command and control centers that enable the optimal use of force. In the past Israel's capabilities were limited to relatively short ranges, but in recent years it vastly improved its ability to project its power, and could now reach targets in Iraq and Iran. These distances required the construction of long-range intelligence gathering systems such as Ofeq photo reconnaissance satellites, the last of which was launched in 2002, and accurate, long-range fighter aircraft such as F-15s and F-16s.

Even in the limited fighting against Palestinian terrorism that restricted the full implementation of the IDF's firepower, a number of RMA capabilities emerged that were expected to have a decisive impact on confrontations with regular armies. Combat operations in the Palestinian territories have revealed the IDF's enhanced ability to pick out low-signature targets (individuals, lone vehicles, and so on) based on verified intelligence data and technological know-how, and to track and destroy the objective with pinpoint accuracy at a minimal cost in collateral damage. In effect, the IDF has been hunting targets of lower signature than the Taliban targets in Afghanistan and destroying them with less collateral damage than the US army in Afghanistan. Military observers in other Middle Eastern armies were undoubtedly taking note of these developments and drawing conclusions about the IDF's fighting potential in future wars where the current restrictions would not be applied.

Israel's new capabilities were such that they could quickly erode the enemies' current main weapon systems inventory. Not only was this advantage recognized, but other Middle East armies themselves seemed increasingly skeptical as to their chances of acquiring capabilities similar to Israel's. The costs entailed in weapons upgrading are prohibitive, and advanced nations such as the United States still refused to make available certain basic RMA technologies in order to maintain their own military superiority. Israel was the only country in the Middle East with the development and production means for these technologies. The Arab countries still lacked the human, technological, and industrial infrastructures demanded for the successful assimilation of such advanced military capabilities. Sweeping changes in force structure, organization, and manpower infrastructure, essential prerequisites for the adoption of advanced capabilities, can occur only when the proper social and economic infrastructures are in place.

Even the Egyptian army, which has upgraded its fighting ability with advanced American weaponry (so that it possessed over 200 F-16s and 550 M-1 tanks), seemed to understand it would be at a severe disadvantage in an all-out armor clash with Israel as in 1973, since the IDF has already leaped ahead by a generation in war management technology. The Egyptian army was very limited in its ability to deal with new generation warfare where the battlefield is managed from great distances. Similarly, the armies of the other Middle East countries had to take into account that in the new political reality, superpower assistance would not be forthcoming with vast amounts of hardware, chiefly planes and tanks, as were supplied in the past by the former Soviet Union. For example, if Syria were to lose the majority of its armor and airpower, no source today would replenish it with new equipment.

The inability of Arab armies to absorb advanced weapons technologies forced them to concentrate on the development of asymmetrical solutions at the operational level. For example, greater emphasis was placed in the Syrian and

Iraqi armed forces on low signature elements such as various branches of special forces and on camouflage and deception.

Furthermore, the inability that confronted the rivals of Israel and the United States to match the capabilities of the regular forces propelled them to avoid regular forces warfare and seek asymmetrical responses at the strategic level. Options of this nature ranged from a low end – types of low intensity warfare, such as terrorism and guerilla operations – to a high end, specifically, the development of weapons of mass destruction and their delivery systems. It came as no surprise, then, that both the United States and Israel were facing similar challenges from these kinds of asymmetrical responses whose source is the Middle East. The United States was dealing with al-Qaeda terrorism and its branches worldwide, and with the threat of weapons of mass destruction in countries such as Iraq and Iran. Israel was engaged in a struggle against Palestinian terror and Hizbollah provocations on the Lebanese border, and in countering weapons of mass destruction in countries such as Syria, Iraq, and Iran.

Israel's campaign against Palestinian terror and the Hizbollah organization has underscored its own weaknesses, especially its lack of strategic depth, its relatively open borders, and the proximity of its population centers to enemy forces. The cumulative effect of these weaknesses resulted in a growing rate of deadly incursions. Palestinian suicide attackers could reach major cities quickly and with relative ease, causing heavy loss of life. The primitive, short-range mortars and rockets that the Palestinians manufactured were lobbed into Israeli neighborhoods only a few kilometers from Palestinian areas. Although highly ineffective, their psychological effect forced Israel to address this threat seriously and work vigorously at neutralizing it. In similar fashion, Hizbollah created a tangible threat to a large section of Israel's northern border by deploying a great number of rockets in South Lebanon, thus establishing a balance of mutual deterrence between itself and the strongest conventional military power in the Middle East.

Fighting the Palestinians included combating terrorism and guerilla tactics. The most taxing aspect to rooting out terrorism was the suicide terrorist or what may be termed the "precision weapon of the weak." Suicide terrorism allows an accurate delivery of explosives or other firepower directly to the enemy's sensitive areas – generally high density population concentrations. It was extremely difficult to prevent potential bombers from penetrating these areas. Therefore, in 2002 Israel embarked upon an ambitious plan for setting up a physical barrier along its border with the Palestinian-populated West Bank. Based on the local obstacles in each sub-area, the barrier would consist of electronic fences or walls with sensory ocular devices and patrols on high alert to block infiltration.

Moreover, suicide terrorism has brought the issue of effective border control to the top of the daily security agenda in other trouble spots in the Middle East as well as in Israel. Jordan, for example, regarded frontier surveillance with Iraq and other neighbors as a major security issue.

In counterinsurgency in the occupied territories the IDF has devised a wide range of operational and technological solutions to the present crisis. Since the Palestinians have been proven incapable of withstanding a full-scale confrontation with Israel or operating guerilla cells in IDF controlled areas, their struggle with the IDF in these areas has turned to launching mostly low level, usually low damage, hit-and-run guerilla attacks from areas under Palestinian control. It seemed that the IDF's lessons in the prolonged guerilla war with Hizbollah in South Lebanon were implemented with increasing skillfulness in the West Bank and Gaza Strip. Consequently, Hizbollah also found it difficult to score operational successes in the narrow fighting arena it has chosen at the Shab'a Farms (originally a Syrian area that has acquired the status of a "contested zone" because of official Lebanese demands for its control).

The struggle against terrorism and Palestinian guerilla warfare tied down a large part of Israel's regular army, especially infantry units, and required an excessive amount of reserve duty. This interfered with the training schedule of both the regular army and the reservists, but experience from the first intifada of the late 1980s indicated that the damage could be amended in a relatively short time. Another related question is whether the army's involvement in the low-intensity struggle with the Palestinians has affected its ability to operate on other fronts if the necessity arises. Here too, no serious dents seemed to have penetrated the IDF's capacity to engage in high-intensity, short-term wars with regular Arab armies. The structure of the IDF was based on the work of fully-equipped reserve brigades who are called up to handle the regular army's daily security assignments. The present, drawn out, low-intensity conflict with the Palestinians could create difficulties for the IDF, but the widening qualitative gap between Israel and its potential enemies reduced the likelihood of protracted, high-intensity wars.

The Israeli-Palestinian confrontation has exposed a fallacy regarding Israel's weakness: its sensitivity to casualties. When the Israeli public is convinced of a struggle's justifiability, it has the stamina to incur heavy losses. Israel's military strength has also provided it with the capability for "escalation dominance"; that is, at each stage in the conflict the Palestinians have been shown that their escalation will result in a heavier Israeli escalation. This was demonstrated in Operations Defensive Shield and Determined Path, which followed the waves of suicide bombings.

An intriguing question to emerge from the present struggle with the Palestinians is whether Israel's deterrent image has been eroded in areas other than low-intensity conflicts. Such was the claim that Israel's withdrawal from South Lebanon weakened the IDF's deterrent image vis-à-vis Arab countries. However, more than two years of violent confrontation with the Palestinians and the mild reaction on the part of Arab countries have clearly demonstrated that although many in the Arab world correctly understood from Israel's extended confrontation in Lebanon that even an army unmistakably superior in classic military terms can also have difficulty coping with low-intensity warfare against terrorists and guerillas, they did not assume that Israel's conventional strength, and certainly not its non-conventional capability, was at all diminished. What has weakened markedly is the image of Arab strength – as the Arab world observed helplessly while Israel wielded its military might against the Palestinians.

Thus, the Arab lesson has been to avoid a head-on clash with Israel's strength by endeavoring to circumvent it strategically and operationally.

The Military Balance in the Gulf

The military balance in the Gulf remained steady in 2002, with the three principal Gulf countries unable to improve their military capability substantively. Although Iran and Russia signed a long-term arms deal for billions of dollars, this deal has yet to materialize. Financial constraints stemming from the instability of oil prices and the increased demands of its population have impeded Iran from completing large-scale weapons transactions.

Similarly, no significant arms buildup took place in Saudi Arabia over the year either. Indeed, the noteworthy development was the cancellation or postponement of signed arms deals due to the lack of available funds. As with Iran, this cutback stems from an exceptionally steep reduction in oil earnings (because of OPEC's measures to safeguard prices through reduced production, and Saudi Arabia in particular shoulders the brunt of the curtailed oil production), and from an increase in the needs of the burgeoning population.

Since the Gulf War, the international community has forbidden Iraq to purchase any kind of weapons. This ban was monitored through the "oil for food" program whereby Iraq could sell large amounts of its oil production but the income was kept under United Nations control and every outlay was subject to UN approval. However, the inspection of goods brought into Iraq was less effective. In the aftermath of the Gulf War, Saddam Hussein developed an elaborate system of smuggling and illegal acquisitions that allowed Iraq to export certain amounts of oil apart from UN supervision and use the cash flow to import prohibited goods. These infractions enabled the entry of conventional weapon systems parts and some components for the production of weapons of mass destruction, but they were not sufficient to enable Iraq to acquire major weapon systems such as planes, helicopters, tanks, APCs, artillery, and missiles. The upshot was that the Iraqi army retained its limited capability based on the illegal import of spare parts and some production in the indigenous military industries, while its conventional equipment grew increasingly antiquated.

In the overall military balance and with the exception of the Turkish army, Iran continued to have the largest standing army in the Middle East, consisting of thirty-two divisions, mostly low-level infantry. Its armored corps was about equal in size to post-Gulf War Iraq's, approximately 1700 tanks to Iraq's 2000. The size of the air force in both countries was also roughly equivalent – around 200 aircraft, most of which were obsolete. The small Iraqi fleet was almost totally wiped out in the Gulf War, but the Iranian navy has built itself an armada of surface vessels and submarines. Iraq's air defense was antiquated; in contrast, Iran's was based on the steady procurement of air defense systems from Russia, although the rate of their supply was slow and Iranian air defense systems were thinly spread out because of the country's vastness and the number of sites to be defended. To sum up, neither country has succeeded in recuperating from the blows their armies suffered – Iraq in the Gulf War, Iran as a result of the Khomeini Revolution and the cutoff of Western arms sources, and both countries from the losses incurred in the Iraq-Iran War. The two states were militarily weak in comparison to other armed forces that have upgraded their equipment in the last decade. Both countries maintained a rough balance of military strength, although the war in Iraq will of course drastically weaken the Iraqi armed forces and alter the balance of power in the Gulf.

Saudi Arabia's ground forces, comprising only 750 tanks, were much smaller than Iraq's and Iran's, but its air force was stronger and more sophisticated than those of either of its northern neighbors. The Saudis had 360 planes, mostly advanced aircraft, and a modernized command and control center and air defense system. Saudi Arabia had a superior surface fleet, although it lagged behind Iran in submarines. Saudi Arabia's main problem was enlisting enough quality manpower to operate all of its weapons, a shortcoming, for example, that has rendered its ground forces operational only at the brigade level.

To sum up the military balance in the Gulf: Iraq and Iran lacked the capability of threatening their neighbors with conventional military forces. Saudi Arabia and the other Gulf States could defend themselves successfully, given the number of US forces permanently stationed in the Gulf region - about 12,000 American military personnel in various countries and an additional 14,000 on ships cruising the Persian Gulf and Arabian Sea, apart from the forces assembled for the war in Iraq - and the advance stationing of American military equipment on land in the Gulf States and in the area fleets, which can reinforce the American forces in the area on short notice. The Saudis' sense of growing discomfort with American troops on their soil indicated that they no longer perceived Iraq as a serious, imminent threat. Indeed, there were early signs of a process whereby Saudi Arabia devoted increasing attention to issues of internal security while viewing the American military presence as more of a threat to internal stability than a guardian against an external menace.

On the eve of the war in Iraq, neither Iraq nor Iran could vie with a military power such as the US armed forces and their RMA capabilities. Even prior to the war it was clear that the United States had the potential to destroy or neutralize the Iraqi army and replace its regime. The delaying factors in the American decision to intervene in Iraq revolved mainly around two questions: whether the current political conditions allowed an operation of this nature; and if so, then how to ensure that the situation created after the American military victory guarantees the realization of the war's prime aim – the destruction of Iraqi projects for the development and production of weapons of mass destruction and the replacement of Saddam's regime with a more moderate one.

Non-Conventional Weapons

Geographical subdivision is unnecessary when discussing the balance of non-conventional weapons in the Middle East, since countries possessing mass destruction capability are also armed with long-distance delivery systems, usually ballistic missiles, that place many potential enemies, in the region and beyond, within striking range.

The discussion of RMA capabilities above indicated that one of the primary reasons the Arab states and Iran aspired to gain weapons of mass destruction was the awareness of their inability to emerge victorious from a conventional war with Israel. Other salient motives that contributed to their ambition included: past military conflicts in the region that have witnessed a limited use of these weapons, such as the war between Iraq and Iran; Israel's image as a nuclear power; the prestige factor; and the desire to deter foreign superpowers from military intervention in the Middle East. The last reason was probably the most pressing, particularly once the United States adopted a preemptive policy of fighting terrorism and halting the proliferation of mass destruction weapons by means of forcing regime changes in the Middle East.

Iran has recently made important strides in nuclear research and the production of long-range, ground-to-ground missiles. Sources indicated that it has masked its development of weapons of mass destruction in the guise of civilian projects such as the nuclear power plant under construction in Bushehr in southwestern Iran. According to Western intelligence estimates, Iran was still five to seven years away from nuclear military capability. The international media's focus on the countdown to the completion of Iran's first nuclear reactor has diverted attention from the slow but real progress being made on the classified military project. The publication by Iranian opposition sources, later verified by the US administration, that Iran was building a site for enrichment of uranium and a second site for production of heavy water revealed significant achievement by Iran in acquiring essential technologies needed for a military nuclear program. The early uncovering of the construction of these sites embarrassed Iran and forced it to invite the IAEA to monitor these sites. IAEA monitoring will make it more difficult for Iran to utilize these sites for a covert military nuclear program.

Quite possibly the first stage in Iran's long-term goal was to gain control of all the basic technologies for producing a nuclear weapon in order to free it from dependence on foreign assistance programs. Afterwards, the amount of time needed to become a nuclear power would depend mainly on Tehran's resolve and political conditions. It is difficult to state definitively whether this decision has already been made, and if so, how Iran intends to overcome its signature to the NPT (Non-Proliferation Treaty) – whether it will withdraw from the NPT or continue to conceal its program. Moreover, Iran was being carefully monitored by the United States, which has assigned it to the "axis of evil" and could move against it if convinced that Iran were near to nuclear capability. As of early 2003, Iran's nuclear program was progressing more discreetly and gradually than Saddam Hussein's was in the 1980s, which testified to the Iranians' acute awareness of the political hazards it faced. The unfolding conflict between the US and North Korea regarding the latter's nuclear program may also influence the Iranian decision. If North Korea withdraws from the NPT without being punished for its withdrawal, Iran might be encouraged to follow suit.

Although Iran ratified the Chemical Weapons Convention Treaty (CWC), there are signs that it intended to retain its chemical weapons production capability by using dual use technology. Similarly, research continued on the biological weapons program.

Iran has made far greater progress in developing long-range, surface-to-surface missiles. In June 2002 it conducted an additional test of the 1,300 kilometer range Shehab-3 missile, although the success of this test was unconfirmed. This followed the successful test of a solid-fuel engine missile with a range of 200 kilometers, whose development was assisted by China, which supplied the technology for the M-11 missile. At this rate, within a few years Iran would have the capability of launching missile strikes with conventional warheads against targets in Israel, and deep into Turkey and Saudi Arabia, and at a later date, if its nuclear project is successfully completed, it will be able to reach these ranges with nuclear warheads. There was as yet no information available on Iran's progress on even longer range missiles capable of hitting targets in Europe.

Despite the presence of United Nations monitoring teams following the Gulf War, it was suspected that Iraq managed to conceal from inspectors several dozen of missiles, as well as chemical and biological warheads. In 1998, UNSCOM and the IAEA Action Team suspended verification inspections in Iraq, and it was assumed that this hiatus was exploited by Baghdad to renew its development and production programs of weapons of mass destruction and ground-to-ground missiles, undoubtedly taking immense caution lest the United States find a pretext for an attack. In the meantime, there were no indications that they progressed in the production of fissile material – the key to their nuclear weapons project. To sum up, it appears that Iraq had retained the theoretical capability to launch missiles armed with conventional, chemical, or biological warheads deep into Israel and Saudi Arabia, albeit in a very diminished capacity since the Gulf War. Nevertheless, the war in Iraq will significantly reduce its capability to develop and produce weapons of mass destruction.

Syria has stockpiled a chemical weapons arsenal that includes evaporable and resistant materials along with various delivery platforms, such as Scud C and D missiles that can hit any target in Israel. Syria was also working on the development of biological weapons.

Egypt had a chemical and biological military capability and, with the assistance of North Korea, was also involved in developing long-range, surface-to-surface missiles. Similar projects were likewise underway in Libya.

Israel's image as a nuclear power has increased over the past year, and among other estimates, it was thought to be developing the capability of launching nuclear-tipped cruise missiles from its German-built submarines. The estimate of intelligence agencies in the Middle East and West regarding Israel's chemical and biological capabilities remained the same. It was also generally believed that Israel has a superior capability in launch systems for surface-to-surface missiles and in manned platforms.

Israel's civil defense program against an attack by weapons of mass destruction was still far ahead of its neighbors' programs. It has developed a storehouse of defense measures based on the eradication of weapons of mass destruction and their launch platforms before liftoff and the interception of airborne delivery systems.

Israel was the first country in the Middle East to establish a national missile defense system (NMD), which is built on the Israeli-developed Arrow missile. The first operational battery has already been deployed; the second battery was also already operational. It was estimated that three Arrow batteries will provide the necessary defense for most of the population centers. Israel's detection capability of surface-to-surface missiles was based on its own defense means and on cooperation with the United States. In addition, the entire civil population was equipped with personal protective gear in the case of chemical and biological warfare, and building codes required safety features against a chemical or biological attack. Concurrently, the air force was upgrading its long-range striking capability against the stockpiles of weapons of mass destruction and their long-distance delivery systems. This capability was based on sophisticated intelligence coverage whose effectiveness has been upgraded by the successful launching of an additional Ofeq-class photo satellite.

Clearly, Israel held a distinct advantage over its potential foes in the Middle East in the field of non-conventional weapons. However, given the unique nature of the region, it is not clear if equality is necessary in the various types of weapons of mass destruction in order to retain a balance of mutual deterrence. Israel is exceptionally vulnerable to an attack by weapons of this sort because of its circumscribed territory and small population. A large number of chemical or biological warheads do not have to be detonated over Israel's population centers in order to present it with an immediate existential threat. For this reason, despite Israel's ballistic and delivery superiority, it would hesitate before launching a strike against strategic targets, such as population centers in Syria, out of fear that Syria would respond with a toxic attack against Israel's population centers. This stalemate might change only if Israel assesses that its storehouses of defense means are capable of protecting it from a major enemy attack with weapons of mass destruction. As of early 2003, Israel did not appear to be sufficiently confident about the effectiveness of its own countermeasures.

CHAPTER 4

The International War on Terror post-September 11

Anat Kurz

"The war on terror will not be won on the defensive. We must take the battle to the enemy, disrupt his plans, and confront the worst threats before they emerge. In the world we have entered, the only path to safety is the path of action."
President George W. Bush, West Point, N.Y.
June 1, 2002

From the clouds of smoke at Ground Zero in Manhattan and the Pentagon in Washington on September 11, 2001, a blueprint emerged for a new, intense, determined struggle against international terrorism.

The targets, symbols of American economic and military power, were struck in tightly-planned, simultaneous attacks that took the lives of over 3000 people and were carried out by the Islamic fundamentalist organization al-Qaeda. The United States was violently confronted with relentless elements that felt themselves challenged by America's vast power and global influence and were resolved to undermine its peace and security. No less poignantly, the attacks laid bare the extent of death and devastation that militant elements could wreak even without the use of non-conventional weapons.

The events of September 11 had a clear link to the Middle East. They represented an unmistakable escalation in the methods of globally dispersed, radical Islamic groups whose roots are embedded in the region. The intensification of violence reflected an increasingly militant strategy, an operational infrastructure that extended beyond local borders, and the acquisition of extensive operational capabilities, primarily under the aegis of Middle Eastern governments. Sources of ongoing tension between Middle Eastern governments and Islamic opposition groups included the strategic ties between the governments and the United States, the presence of American military forces in several Arab states, and most certainly the close relationship between the United States and Israel. The combination of these factors, especially since the 1980s with the rise of a radical, vehemently anti-Western Islam in the Middle East and other areas around the globe, has made American objectives preferred targets for attack. During the 1990s the threat to American interests in different parts of the world was concretized following a series of sporadic but brazen attacks carried out by Islamic zealots. Notable among these incidents was the attack on the World Trade Center in Manhattan, which was carried out in February 1993 by Egyptian Islamic radicals linked to al-Qaeda.

The unprecedented attacks in September 2001 prompted a United States campaign that was also unparalleled in scope and determination to fight international terror in general and Islamic fundamentalist terror in particular. The battle was officially announced already on September 11, and took shape in the weeks that followed. Initially it concentrated on a punitive expedition against al-Qaeda, aimed at destroying the organization's logistics base and reducing the operational capability of its various offshoots. Since the prior assumption that the terrorists' fear of an American response would prevent them from carrying out a mega-strike on US soil was proven wrong, restraints were lifted from the use of military might overseas in general, and against terrorist groups specifically. Given the extent of the catastrophe, the offensive in Afghanistan was designed both to topple the Taliban regime and deter other governments from hosting or providing logistical assistance to radical Islamic and other terror organizations. As a long range answer to the threat of terror, the Bush administration began to draft and implement new rules of engagement for the war on terror by means of vigorous intelligence gathering, police work, and strict law enforcement. These steps intended to address the assessment that international Islamic terror would not only continue but would escalate unless action was taken to destroy its perpetrators and their supporters through aggressive punitive, preemptive, and deterrent measures.

Governments in the Middle East that harbored al-Qaeda training camps and bases for other militant Islamic groups were expected to become the front lines of the war to extirpate international Islamic terror. In addition, however, the American administration's global campaign confronted all Middle East regimes with an acute dilemma bearing domestic and international implications. On the one hand, refusal to assume an active role in the struggle carried the risk of a diplomatic entanglement with the United States. On the other hand, support of the United States, which endorsed Israel's strong-arm methods against Palestinian terror and was now seeking the elimination of an Islamic regime, risked aggravating domestic threats by Islamic extremists. This was why the Arab governments' support for the war on terror was highly reserved, at least on the official and public level.

The first stage of the war on terror focused on attaining international legitimacy for the attack on Afghanistan. As the administration sought to capitalize on the concerns of other governments that they not appear opposed to a campaign that was morally justified and motivated by security concerns, it strove to create a political and organizational basis for broad international cooperation in thwarting terror threats. It was clear that these threats would eventually have to be confronted even if the immediate objectives in Afghanistan were achieved. An awareness of the link between socio-political frustrations and global terror was reflected in the US government's declaration that it intended to work at alleviating the sources of misery around the world. However, no drastic steps were taken to address the complex origins of social and political tension worldwide, and from September 11, the war on terror centered primarily on military attacks in Afghanistan and intelligence gathering.

Enlistment in the campaign was presented by the American administration as a litmus test for moral and strategic identification with the United States. Nonetheless, the administration did not seek to build an international coalition based on equal contributions by all participating governments and international bodies. Instead, the administration worked to procure cooperation in various other ways – through moral support for the campaign, active participation in the military effort, or long-term involvement in countermeasures – depending on particular operational and political needs. At the same time, it took care to minimize requests for larger commitments, since those were likely to be rejected. Indeed, the administration's appeal for open support and assistance met with refusals on more than one occasion. In these cases, the broad international front that the Bush administration wished to present threatened to falter, jeopardizing the international legitimacy of the military option and the estimated effectiveness of force in the war on terror.

Middle East links were only one albeit central characteristic of a complex international anti-terror campaign that carried with it operational and global implications. The following chapter deals with the main motifs of the campaign, its stages, and avenues of development. Specifically, the discussion focuses on the roles played by governments and international agencies in three frequently overlapping areas of the struggle: political, military, and preemptive. The **political arena** will be discussed first, since it is the framework in which international legitimacy was accorded the struggle. Political support for the war on terror, which crystallized immediately after the attacks of September 11, was broader than in the other spheres of the struggle, although it translated into only a limited practical commitment. The **military arena** was both narrower and harder to organize because of the time span required for American forces to launch the offensive in Afghanistan, to coordinate the attack with Afghani opposition factions, and to acquire military and intelligence assistance, mainly in Central Asian countries. At the same time, the military arena remained active even after it lost prime media interest and the political-rhetorical support it had enjoyed in the first phase. The **preemptive arena,** constructed as the US government was preparing to attack

Afghanistan, was designed partially to provide solutions to operational needs but primarily to be the basis for a systematic, long-term campaign against terror.

The Political Realm

Expressions of sympathy by heads of states and leaders of political organizations throughout the world for the September 11 victims and for the American people in their hour of affliction were numerous and ran deep. They were complemented by bitter condemnation of the terrorists, their sponsors, and their supporters, and the underlying approval of a concerted military attack on the al-Qaeda infrastructure and Taliban regime in Afghanistan. Emotional understanding ran deep for countering the threat of terror by means of long-term, preemptive action. On the other hand, the actual support given to American preparations for the punitive military strike and tenacious war against terror was usually lukewarm and noncommittal.

The tendency to back the administration in a war depicted as a struggle between good and evil, whether it was from belief in the war's aims or from the strategic benefit likely to be gained from this allegiance, was balanced by other interests. The interests that restrained all-out identification with the war included economic and political ties with countries said to be supportive of terror – particularly Iran, Iraq, and Syria. Outright support of an activist approach to the war on terror was also offset by differences of opinion over the intensity and immediacy of the threat, the actual sources of the conflicts generating terror, and the steps to be taken to resolving them. In addition, skepticism regarding the effectiveness of military force in reducing international terror tempered support of this option, along with the serious concern that a relentless struggle might serve to exacerbate the threat of terror itself, inflame Islamic fundamentalist militancy, and perhaps even propel terrorist organizations to turn to the use of non-conventional weapons.

Among those most wary of a massive American response were Middle East governments that for years have endeavored to contain the influence of Islamic opposition organizations and their potential for political upheaval. For their part, West European governments were also guarded in their support of the American campaign, careful to minimize damage to their cordial relations with Middle East states, avoid confrontation with Islamic communities at home, and pacify local groups opposed in principle to American economic and political hegemony. An additional factor that inhibited many governments from offering sweeping support to American efforts was the fear that entanglement in a military conflict might escalate and expand into a wider international sphere.

Nonetheless, the administration counted on official public support from the Arab states and other countries with large Islamic populations. It believed that this support would lessen the danger of the campaign against al-Qaeda being interpreted as a battle of cultures and religions. The willingness of several Islamic countries – such as Turkey, Jordan, Indonesia, and Bangladesh – to join in the attempt to stabilize Afghanistan after the fall of the Taliban helped dispel claims that the invasion was a declaration of war on the entire Islamic world. Another international forum that backed the American determination to root out terror was the Conference of Islamic Nations, which published a general statement condemning terror and al-Qaeda-sponsored terrorism in particular, although it stopped short of denouncing the radical ideology that motivated Islamic militancy, and it also embraced measures employed by the Palestinians in their struggle against Israel. Out of fear that it would be accused of granting legitimacy to the war in Afghanistan, Egypt declared it would not participate in the effort to stabilize the country after the military campaign. Saudi Arabia, on the other hand, promised financial aid for stabilizing the country. Other Middle East states in varying degrees of conflict with the United States and ranking high on the State Department's list of states abetting terror rejected the attack on Afghanistan but at the same time stopped short of openly sanctioning al-Qaeda activity. Iraqi authorities repeatedly denied any connection with the September attacks or their perpetrators. Palestinian Authority Chairman Yassir Arafat was quick to condemn al-Qaeda in order to stave off international isolation of the Palestinian leadership, as had occurred in the early 1990s following the PLO's support of Saddam Hussein.

The difference between verbal backing for the struggle against terror, especially the American assault on Afghanistan, and actual involvement in the war effort, was highlighted in instances of what had seemed to be unqualified displays of support. On September 21, 2001, the foreign ministers of the Organization of American States reiterated their commitment to the clause in the Inter-American Treaty of Reciprocal Assistance dealing with the guarantee of collective defense. NATO members recalled their obligation to Article 5 in the organization's charter, whereby an attack on one member would be considered an attack on all. Support for the war on terror was also given by the Asian-Pacific Cooperation Forum. However, none of these rhetorical declarations translated into practical assistance within the context of the military engagement in Afghanistan. In fact, from the outset, they were intended to grant legitimacy to the attack, but not to serve as a basis for active involvement. Furthermore, the declaration of support, as widespread as it was, did not provide sweeping legitimacy to military operations against terror. Thus, the principle stressed by the administration's spokespersons, according to which "terror is terror," was not assimilated fully in the international sphere and failed to become the unifying platform for a counter-response.

In fact, from its inception, the "Coalition for the War on Terror" that the United States strove to create suffered from breaches. Major differences divided the various governments regarding the extent of their obligations to principles drafted in Washington. Despite the initial shock of the September 2001 attacks and the subsequent anxiety regarding the future, many countries stood confirmed in their belief that the threat of terrorism could be substantially reduced by the rectification of the social, economic, and political injustices that formed the roots of the conflicts in and between countries and societies, and that actualizing the military option should be avoided as much as possible.

At the same time, the extensive rhetorical support was a diplomatic accomplishment in itself and a salient indication of American political dominance. In preparation for the attack on al-Qaeda, support of the administration's principles was essential for advancing the main American objective: the consolidation of broad international approval for the war and the new, aggressive approach to combating terror. To achieve this, the Bush administration portrayed international terror as a global challenge. Governments that openly expressed support for the attack in Afghanistan were not pressured by the United States to translate their words into practical deeds. Verbal backing itself granted legitimacy. Intelligence assistance, at times covert, expedited the attack at the operational level. These displays of support and cooperation were no less crucial to Washington, and apparently even more so, than the participation of foreign units on the battlefield.

The Military Sphere

The attack in Afghanistan was the opening stage in the war against worldwide Islamic terror, but this was not the first time the United States exercised a military option in response to al-Qaeda aggression. After the bombings of the United States embassies in Kenya and Tanzania in August 1998, the American air force struck at al-Qaeda bases in Sudan and Afghanistan. However, the scope of the campaign following the September 2001 attacks was much wider, given the extent of the provocation. Beyond the complete destruction of al-Qaeda's infrastructure, the US government sought to overthrow the regime that sheltered it.

In addition to international political and moral support, the administration needed immediate intelligence assistance in order to identify and strike those directly responsible for the September attacks. To the Americans this was both more important and more realistic than direct contributions to the fighting, although symbolic military involvement was useful to buttress the moral backing – not because American forces required ground assistance. Indeed, the Bush administration had no plans to establish an international military alliance, for fear that it would complicate the job of toppling the Taliban regime and smashing al-Qaeda's infrastructure. Much energy was invested, however, in operational coordination with the Northern Alliance – a loose coalition of anti-Taliban groups that on the eve of the American campaign controlled approximately one-tenth of the country. In exchange for Northern Alliance assistance during the assault, which conveniently coincided with the Northern Alliance's own needs, the United States supplied it with arms and guaranteed its leaders the government in Kabul after the Taliban's ousting.

The US call for intelligence assistance stemmed from its own intelligence agencies' inability to meet single-handedly the complex, multi-faceted challenge of locating bases and networks used by al-Qaeda and other extremist Islamic elements. Intelligence agencies throughout Asia were deemed an important source for information on the al-Qaeda infrastructure, and the administration requested their cooperation in order to facilitate the war management. In addition to intelligence material, Pakistan, Uzbekistan, Russia, and India were asked to grant air space and land passage through their countries into Afghanistan.

International cooperation generated some interesting diplomatic consequences, particularly regarding India and Pakistan. Pakistani assistance was especially relevant to the United States for operational exigencies. India's assistance was less vital than Pakistan's, but Washington-New Delhi collaboration – including cooperation in the war on terror – was considered to harbor long term importance because of India's regional status and the role it could play in counterbalancing China's growing influence in Central Asia. Significantly, the enlistment of these two sub-continent superpowers forced the administration to deviate from its active opposition to their independent nuclear programs. Restrictions on arms sales to India and Pakistan, previously imposed on both countries because of nuclear testing, were lifted. Pakistan, the focus of regional instability, in part because of its drive to gain influence in the Islamic republics of the former Soviet Union, even won a pledge from the Americans for substantial financial aid.

Satisfaction with Indian and Pakistani participation was dampened by the concern that the removal of sanctions on nuclear testing would make it difficult to restrain their nuclear policies in the future. In May 2002, heightened tension between the two countries, the result of an escalation in India's struggle with Kashmiri separatists who were helped by intelligence agencies in Islamabad, threatened to ignite the sub-continent into a conflagration that would have forced the Bush administration to intervene and would have sidelined the war on terror. The administration grew increasingly vexed at the build-up of Pakistani forces along India's border, not least because Pakistani military deployment left the vast border with Afghanistan permeable to the massive penetration of fleeing al-Qaeda activists. After Indian-Pakistani border tensions subsided in June 2002, Karachi troops marched back to the Afghani border and tightened their control there. Nevertheless, Pakistan had become a main refuge for al-Qaeda guerillas escaping from American forces and Northern Alliance fighters, and according to State Department sources, many of the guerillas found safe haven in the northwest of the country. Indeed, while the war in Afghanistan was still actively underway, al-Qaeda carried out a series of strikes in major cities in Pakistan, proving the difficulty in extinguishing the organization's operational capability.

The threat of international terror also headed the agenda in American-Russian relations. Rapprochement was facilitated by operational needs: land and air passages into Afghanistan, and Russia's contact with the Northern Alliance. At the time the US was fighting in Afghanistan, the administration announced its unilateral withdrawal from the treaty prohibiting the deployment of anti-ballistic missile (ABM) defense systems. Moscow thus had to accept a move that otherwise might have been interpreted as a strategic threat, had the Americans not cushioned it with token compromises and assurances of cooperation. In May 2002 Presidents George Bush and Vladimir Putin signed a ten-year agreement for the joint reduction in nuclear weapons stockpiles. Furthermore, the thaw in Moscow-Washington relations that developed around the war on terror, which included training of Russian troops in anti-terror warfare by American forces, also expedited Russia's approach towards the NATO framework. The "NATO Russia Council Agreement," ratified in May 2002, granted Russia influence on a number of critical NATO issues – such as the war on terror, the monitoring of mass destruction weapons, missile defense, crisis management, and peace missions – although Moscow was not accorded the right to veto decisions, vote on the acceptance of new members, or participate in joint military defense pacts.

The development that could have put a freeze on the American-Russian thaw was the rapprochement between Washington and Beijing, which also took place against the background of Chinese support for the American campaign against international terror. China's backing, though, came with a stipulation: approval from the United Nations Security Council for a military move. Another thorn between Washington and Moscow was Russia's relations with Iran, Iraq, and North Korea – the leading triumvirate in what Bush termed the "axis of evil" – that involved extensive trade in military technologies. Unlike Washington, Moscow saw Iran as a potentially stabilizing element in the Gulf region and Central Asia; at any rate, Russia did not succumb to American pressure to cease delivering to Iran nuclear technologies that it claimed were intended for civilian purposes.

A number of states combined their moral support for the campaign in Afghanistan with the dispatch of a symbolic contingent of military personnel. Japan and Australia, for example, augmented the American naval task force in the Indian Ocean. Great Britain, Canada, Germany, and Australia sent troops, although only the British army took an active part in any fighting, including aerial bombings. (Britain's participation recalled 1986, when Britain was the only United States ally that permitted its air bases to be used for the American strike against Libya, in response to Libyan sponsorship of terror.) Meantime, other European allies, such as France, Germany, and Italy, promised assistance in stabilizing Afghanistan after the ousting of the Taliban, not an automatic or easy commitment for countries that had to deal with vocal if limited domestic opposition to both the American assault and to European participation in the stabilization and rehabilitation of Afghanistan.

In December 2001 the Taliban regime in Kabul collapsed. In the immediate aftermath the United States coordinated its efforts with the governments of China, Tajikistan, Pakistan, Uzbekistan, Turkmenistan, and Iran in bolstering the new Northern Alliance government. Meantime, the military campaign against terror continued, with its focus in Asia. The US reinforced the Philippine army in rooting out the al-Qaeda-linked Abu Sayyaf organization. US military assistance also helped the Indonesian army and the civilian security forces in their struggle against Islamic rebels likewise connected to al-Qaeda. Significantly, however, neither of these cases involved the deployment of American troops in preparation for a massive attack such as in Afghanistan. Therefore, they should not be seen as an expression of American readiness to apply force in every instance but as supplementary activity in the overall campaign.

Certain immediate political challenges confronted the administration in light of how the military option in Afghanistan was interpreted by a number of governments. Israel, for example, applied its own spin on the American intention to extirpate terror, coining the catchphrase "Arafat is Bin Laden" in the hope of gaining international legitimacy for its military operations against Palestinian organized forces involved in terror, including the Palestinian Authority (PA). Although some European governments, including France, Germany, and Italy, backed the American move despite loud domestic protest over the suffering caused to Afghani civilians, they rejected the Israeli interpretation and emphasized the context of the Israeli-Palestinian confrontation: Israeli occupation of the West Bank and Gaza Strip. The brunt of European criticism was targeted at Israel's recourse to military means for dealing with Palestinian terror and the absence of any political horizon from Jerusalem.

In the months following the attacks on the Twin Towers and the Pentagon, the Bush administration counted on the Israeli government to soften the military pressure on the Palestinian Authority. This reflected an American concern that support of Israel in a period of escalating Israeli-Palestinian violence would threaten the already precarious backing afforded the administration by countries in the Middle East and Western Europe for the Afghanistan attack, and that the loss of such support could subsequently hamper covert arrangements for the upcoming attack on Iraq. As the fear subsided that American military action in Afghanistan would undermine the strategic partnership between the United States and countries in the Middle East, led by Egypt, Jordan, and Saudi Arabia, and as it became clear that the level of Palestinian violence would not abate by either military means or political pressure, the administration, led by the Defense Department, began to display a greater understanding of Israel's tough stand on terror. The absolute cessation of terrorist activity by all Palestinian groups was presented as a precondition for a political settlement. In June 2002 President Bush challenged the Palestinian people to replace its leadership because of the PA's direct involvement with terrorist acts, as well as its systematic rejection of various plans proposed by the administration for a return to the negotiating table.

Elsewhere, the war on terror, however comprehensive it was declared to be, evoked similarly nebulous issues. The administration insisted that its resolve to eradicate terror not be interpreted as a green light by Russia to intensify its war against Chechnyan rebels or by India to escalate its struggle against Kashmiri separatists. While Beijing expressed support for the United States campaign in Afghanistan and even committed itself to the war on terror, it also announced that it expected the administration to recognize China's need to combat its own break-away Islamic extremists. Another example of the dilemma in implementing a policy based on the rubric "terror is terror" outside of its original circumscribed context was Washington's criticism of the Egyptian, Saudi, and other Middle Eastern governments' coolness towards the American campaign and the reluctant response of these countries to explicit requests for assistance. The Royal House of Saud was especially blunt in its refusal, and the Omani government replied negatively to the administration's appeals to allow the use of American bases on Omani soil for air strikes in Afghanistan. Subsequent American criticism implied marginalization of the internal struggles being waged by Islamic opposition groups in countries cooperating with the United States. Washington criticism also seemed to downplay the link between the stability of these governments and key American interests and strategic understandings in the Middle East.

Additional reservations over the military option reflected the rejection of the war on terror as tacit approval of the United States advancing its interests beyond the specific sphere of counterterrorism. In the months following the al-Qaeda strikes on US soil, voices were heard in Washington claiming that Baghdad's non-conventional armament de facto implicated it in terrorist activity, as these weapons of mass destruction would surely be made available to terror organizations. Indeed, this claim, which intended to link the threat of terrorism with the threat of unchecked proliferation of weapons of mass destruction around the globe, was employed by the administration in its concerted diplomatic campaign to recruit international backing for the war on Iraq. West European and Arab governments, however, rejected the concept promulgated by the American government, especially by the president and the Defense Department, that a military strike against Saddam Hussein's regime should be perceived as part of the all-out war against al-Qaeda and like-minded terrorist organizations. The considerations and political motivations underlying the efforts of Middle Eastern and European countries to divert the administration from realizing its war plans in Iraq are beyond the scope of this chapter. Suffice it to note, however, that one critical factor was the concern that the war would intensify anti-Western sentiments among Islamic zealots and thus serve as a pretext for retaliatory terrorist activities. Explicit threats to this effect by al-Qaeda in advance of the war greatly aggravated the concern.

Preemptive Activities

In the planning stage and during the attack on Afghanistan, many governments took steps to limit the activity of radical Islam, obliterate expressions of identification with al-Qaeda, and gather information on its extended activities. Concurrently, security and intelligence agencies in numerous countries were on alert to identify and thwart any intended terrorist strike at its earliest stages. Part of this intelligence work was coordinated by American security agencies and foreign governments, a joint effort that Washington perceived as an important phase in the long-term, systematic, international project to wipe out global terror.

Intelligence agencies in many countries joined in the aggressive effort to track al-Qaeda cells, largely based on information obtained through arrests of Islamic activists in Saudi Arabia, Egypt, Kuwait, Lebanon, Algeria, Yemen, and Sudan. The government of Somalia, eager to be divested of any responsibility in this effort, rushed to announce the country purged of Jihad activists. Security officials in Syria, Egypt, Algeria, and Saudi Arabia relayed information on al-Qaeda's infrastructure in the Middle East, even if they remained cautious lest they display too much identification with American agencies. In May 2002, referring to the ongoing American-Egyptian cooperative intelligence efforts, President Mubarak stated that prior to September 2001, Egypt had handed the US information regarding al-Qaeda plans to carry out a strike on American soil.

The intelligence gathering efforts notwithstanding, the detentions in the Arab countries were designed chiefly to stifle groundswells of popular protest against the declaration of war on Islamic terror and the preparations for an attack on Afghanistan. Concurrently, the arrests also served to counter accusations about direct or indirect aid being lent to international Islamic terror. The energy with which street demonstrations were suppressed and seizures carried out, while at the same time efforts were underway to veil the connection between these steps and the US global campaign against terror, testified to the Arab world's awareness of the inherent tension between pacification of internal Islamic opposition and avoidance of a confrontation with the American administration.

Intelligence sources in Bosnia and Kosovo came forth with information on al-Qaeda infrastructures in the Balkans. In Britain and West European countries, Islamic activists were held for questioning. In Greece, fear of public protest over possible concessions of Greek sovereignty through its cooperation with American intelligence agencies forced the government to deny the Sixth Fleet the right to carry out searches on suspicious vessels in Greek territorial waters. The Turkish government, however, free from having to deal with any serious internal opposition to its strategic pact with either Israel or the United States, allowed the measures. Arrests were carried out in Malaysia, the Philippines, Indonesia, India, Pakistan, and Singapore. In exchange for information on al-Qaeda cells in Asia, the administration lifted sanctions that had been imposed on certain regimes the previous decade, in some cases for the systematic violation of human rights, and in the case of India-Pakistan, to curb the potential for producing regional shockwaves.

Indeed, the administration's policy change towards India and Pakistan illustrated vividly the immediate effects the September 2001 attacks had on operational and political contingencies in the war on terror, and their primacy over previous policy guidelines. Hence also, in exchange for assistance in tracking down Jihad cells, the US canceled the weapon embargoes imposed on Armenia and Azerbaijan.

Dozens of countries responded to the American administration's call for the long-term dismantling of fanatical Islam's capability by confiscating their financial holdings. Within two weeks after the attack on American soil, Washington began withholding money and assets of organizations suspected of maintaining al-Qaeda links. In the same move, funds and holdings intended for the Palestinian Hamas were also frozen. Ultimately, however, the effectiveness of these steps will depend on the degree to which other countries conduct a systematic pursuit of the money. Saudi Arabia, for example, bluntly criticized the way the assets of individuals and organizations suspected of ties to international terror were expropriated. Saudi royalty also refused to cooperate with the administration in locating cash flows to al-Qaeda. Nevertheless, for reasons of its own domestic security, it allowed its security forces to trace the money of Islamic organizations, but here too the effectiveness of this move depends on the degree to which these financial resources are reached. According to one estimate, al-Qaeda's assets are worth $5 billion, with the accounts and transactions of this fortune spread across the globe to make detection extremely complicated.

Many offers of support for the war made in international forums in the immediate aftermath of September 11 remained mere declarations of intent in the long-term preemptive sphere as well as the in the political and military arenas. Such was the United Nations Security Council Resolution 1373 (September 28, 2001), which called on countries to curb money transfers to terror organizations, guard their borders more vigilantly, obstruct enlistment in terror organizations, withhold asylum from terror organizations, and strengthen joint intelligence cooperation in the war on terror. Nothing was innovative in this resolution: it simply joined a long list of resolutions from other international forums – many affiliated with the United Nations – with detailed programs for curtailing international terror.

For NATO the challenge of international terror reinforced the relevancy of collective security among Western countries. Preparation for a long-term struggle topped the agenda at the organization's convention held during President Bush's visit to Europe in May 2002. NATO defense ministers received a mandate to reform the organization's branches, first by making the military force more flexible and adaptable to the specific demands of an anti-terror campaign. Likewise, countries in the European Union (EU), together with American security agencies and NATO, began to consolidate a second line of defense. The EU's spokespersons emphasized the terrorists' mockery of political solutions to grievances large or small, as illustrated on September 11, 2001. Paradoxically, though, the mega-strike actually strengthened Western Europe's resolve for a peaceful solution to conflicts on the assumption that this approach would significantly reduce the motivation for violent struggle.

A practical attempt to bolster cooperation was made within the European Union where plans concentrated on improving intelligence partnerships that had commenced prior to the September 2001 attacks, and tightening intelligence and police connections with American security agencies. EU security agencies drew up regulations for improving their preemptive ability to obstruct terrorist acts, which reflected the Union's official announcement at the end of September 2001 to prepare for the war on terror. An operational definition of the terror threat was approved, which granted justice officials the right to apprehend terrorists and block illegal money transfers to terror organizations. The infrastructure of a European border police was authorized (to be completed by 2007) and directives for cooperation with American intelligence and security agencies were updated. Overall, the European Union viewed the steps to create a joint alignment to obstruct terror as an expression of unequivocal solidarity with the United States. To West European governments, enlistment in intelligence coordination with the United States allowed them to contribute to the war on terror in a way that seemed to them more effective than the military option, and far less risky.

In December 2001, the EU, in conjunction with the Bush administration, began compiling a list of terror organizations. The list was finalized in June 2002 at a Brussels meeting of the Union's foreign ministers. Included among the eighteen organizations were the Fatah's al-Aqsa Martyrs Brigades, the Popular Front for the Liberation of Palestine, the Palestine Liberation Front, the Hamas military wing Izz al-Din al-Qassam, the Palestinian Islamic Jihad, the PKK (Kurdistan Workers' Party), the Egyptian Islamic Jihad, and others. Most of the organizations on the list had no financial holdings in Europe, and since it was beyond the EU's jurisdiction to enforce regulations in various countries, they seemed destined to remain theoretical activities only. Furthermore, with the death penalty illegal in EU countries, any attempt at extraditing terrorists to the United States, where the death penalty is still in effect in some states, will be met with opposition. The crux of the division between the administration and the EU was the distinction, adhered to in West European countries, between military and political branches of subversive organizations. This distinction kept Lebanon's Hizbollah and the Palestinian Hamas off the list of terrorist organizations.

US coordination of preemptive measures with foreign governments, strategic allies, and other bodies was not intended to substitute for a reorganization of domestic security and intelligence agencies that would orchestrate the long-term confrontation with international terror. Rather, it was only one aspect, and not necessarily the primary one, of the administration's efforts. In May 2002 Congress approved a budget of billions of dollars for the war on terror, the bulk of which was designated for internal security, largely by means of investment in advanced technologies for information gathering. An emergency sum of an additional $31 billion was authorized by the Senate. A prohibition went into effect against contact with members of groups on the list of terrorist organizations. Entrance into United States territory was banned to members of these organizations, and the collection and transfer of money to associations linked to them was also outlawed. Plans were drawn up for trailing suspects, and numerous regulations were issued, including the requirement to report information on suspicious money. These procedures were implemented despite objections in liberal circles regarding the tension between preventing terror strikes in their early planning stages and upholding democratic principles of individual privacy and personal freedom.

The formulation of these security regulations was accompanied by comprehensive organizational reform. Changes were made in the operational procedures of the FBI, domestic security agencies, and other task forces, focusing on inter-agency coordination and improved, integrated preventative capability. The army's authority was broadened, allowing it to operate on United States soil. Undoubtedly these organizational reforms were prompted by the criticism leveled at the administration and security branches for their failure to prevent the September 2001 attacks. In an attempt to counter the impending political disaster from the disclosure of intelligence blunders, and before the conclusions of Congressional and Senate investigating committees became public knowledge, President Bush presented Congress with a comprehensive plan to preempt future terror threats. At the heart of the proposal was the establishment a new government department, created especially for the war on terror – the Department of Homeland Security. The announcement that the new department would coordinate the operations of other agencies actively engaged in fighting terror was a clear attempt by the White House to restore the image of the administration and presidency that was so charred after the intelligence fiasco. By the same token, it was a further indication that the war in Afghanistan, whose effectiveness was still unproven, was only the first step in a prolonged anti-terror campaign. An ongoing, concentrated effort was likewise demanded to mitigate the political implications of the war on terror on both the domestic and international spheres.

Conclusion

The attack in Afghanistan represented an impressive display of resolve to strip al-Qaeda of its military and political resources. Nevertheless, it would be a mistake to assume that another mega-attack against the United States will elicit the same response. Evidence that the military option against terror and the pursuit of governments harboring terror cells will no longer be an automatic counterstroke can already be seen in the many conflicting strands within American policy on terror. An outstanding example is the administration's reluctance to apply the military option against Iran and Syria. These states feature prominently on the list of terror-supporting countries published annually by the US State Department in "Patterns of Global Terrorism." In the May 2002 report, Iran was highlighted – as it has been since 1984 – as the country most active in providing assistance to terror organizations. Under present political and strategic circumstances, however, a major offensive against Iran with sponsorship of terrorism as the primary cause does not appear to be a realistic option for the administration. Similarly, Washington has continued to apply diplomatic and economic pressure on Syria to alter its policy of promoting Hizbollah and radical Palestinian groups instead of threatening it with an immediate military attack.

Certainly the war in Afghanistan was not – and was never intended as – a signal for the opening round of an all-out, step-by-step, roving military campaign against terror organizations and governments assisting them. The policy that the American administration and other governments adopted in the wake of September 11, 2001, and the response to the American request for enlistment in a joint campaign, have remained bound by the same limitations that in the past hindered the formulation of unified standards for anti-terror operations and the establishment of a broad, long-range, international front committed to the eradication of global terror.

International enlistment in a US-led campaign against al-Qaeda and other terror threats did not result in the "widest global coalition in history," as vaunted by administration spokespersons. It would be more accurate to describe the alignment – impressive in scope as it may be – as a series of ad hoc agreements between the American administration and governments or international forums that decided to participate in the campaign according to a multiplicity of stipulations and diverse levels of commitment. Several governments that proffered official backing to America's determined efforts in Afghanistan refrained from translating these declarations into practical commitments. Others avoided issuing any statement of support at all after weighing the possible loss of American aid against the dangers inherent in their high-profile condemnation of terror organizations and states sponsoring terror. Even governments and international forums that agreed wholeheartedly with the United States' tenacious campaign, for example, EU members, took care to retain their freedom in selecting areas of operation, and the methods and range of pursuing the struggle.

The same factors that explained the discrepancies in dealing with terror also shed light on the divergent ways governments addressed the manifold sources of the threat. The main factors included: the fear that involvement in the campaign against terror would escalate into an all-out inter-state war; the inevitable cost in human lives and human rights; and damage to economic and/or strategic relations with countries accused of links to terror organizations. Against these factors were balanced the immediacy of the threat and the estimated price of rebuffing the request of an ally such as the United States. The factors that weakened the resolve to eradicate terror were sharpened significantly when the challenge of domestic threats was acute.

In addition to the risk of embroilment in a drawn-out campaign, another inhibiting factor to the military option was the limited ability that force appeared to wield in significantly reducing the threat of terror. In June 2002 the commander of British forces in Afghanistan stated that completion of the mission to destroy the al-Qaeda infrastructure would last one year. The prolonged challenges in stabilizing Afghanistan and alleviating any consequent suffering among the local population could erode the international support, already tepid at best, that the campaign enjoyed in its first phase. Additional questions about the efficacy of the military option emanated in June 2002 from American military sources themselves, claiming that the battle in Afghanistan had not only failed to curb the long-term threat of terror but had also failed to achieve its immediate goals. Many al-Qaeda leaders and fighters found safe haven in Pakistan and other Asian countries where government stability is imperiled by local Islamic organizations. Al-Qaeda branches continue to operate in the Middle East and North Africa. Their infrastructure remains a tangible threat as long as manifestations of American hegemony – especially President Bush's zealous military campaign to root out terror – reinforce the motivation of radical Islamic groups to strike at American and Western targets.

Dealing with international terror will demand long-term, preemptive efforts. The international front that directs these preventative operations will be in a continuous state of realignment with fluctuating degrees of commitment on the part of allied governments. Despite these shortcomings, it seems that the preemptive sphere will constitute the main effort in thwarting the threat of international and radical Islamic terror. Middle East governments have the opportunity to play a key role in this international alignment. The regimes in Egypt, Jordan, Saudi Arabia, North African countries, Syria, and Yemen share the same fear with the United States and other Western states over the upsurge of radical Islam, which explains why various degrees of participation may be expected of them in the long run. In other words, fear of the rising influence of destabilizing, radical Islamic groups, which was a decisive factor in the unwillingness of these governments to support the American campaign in Afghanistan, is ultimately likely to rouse them to join the international struggle against Islamic terror. For obvious reasons these regimes will continue to conceal their contacts with American and Western intelligence officials. The eventual end of the war in Afghanistan and dwindling of public interest will serve to anchor this channel of cooperation. On the other hand, developments such as an attack on Iraq will force Middle East regimes into a pronounced anti-American stand and will work against the consolidation of an orderly network of intelligence cooperation with the United States.

It appears, therefore, that initiatives on the American administration's agenda other than the war against terror are likely to wear down the fragile coalition that crystallized following September 11, 2001. Participation in the campaign did not alleviate the potential for atrocities that could ensue from the stockpiling of non-conventional weapons by India, Pakistan, and Iran. Other issues throughout the world continue to threaten world peace, including the Israeli-Palestinian and Indian-Pakistani conflicts, the instability of Russia and the former Soviet Union republics in Central Asia, the massive arms buildup in China, and the instability in the Gulf following the toppling of Saddam Hussein's regime by the US-led coalition forces. Attempts at reducing the sources of tension may well lead the administration to challenge governments that lent their support to the counterterrorism campaign, even if any such confrontation would halt the rapprochement with Washington. The trauma of the events of September 11, 2001 will not be erased; however, neutralization of the terror threat might be compromised in order to preserve other strategic interests, as was demonstrated by the war in Iraq. Although the invasion of an Arab country and the deposition of its regime clearly presented Islamic zealots yet another pretext for anti-American terrorist attacks, it did not prevent the administration from proceeding with the offensive.

CHAPTER 5

The Arab-Israeli Arena

Mark A. Heller

Two and a half years after the outbreak of violence known as the "Al-Aqsa Intifada," whatever political content there may once have been in the Palestinian uprising had long since disappeared. The Palestinian movement was no closer to realizing any of its national objectives than it was when the violence erupted in late 2000, and in some important respects, it actually suffered severe regression. The Palestinian economy and society were seriously compromised, and the stature of the Palestinian Authority (PA), both domestically and internationally, was dramatically undermined. At the same time, Israel also paid a high human and material price, but after more than two years was nevertheless no more successful in finding a formula that would enable it to advance its own more limited objective: to end the violence on terms that would deny the Palestinians any political advantage. Thus, it found itself constantly improvising but failing to produce a conclusive policy. In these circumstances, the confrontation seemed destined to ebb and flow, and neither escalation nor de-escalation yielded any decisive change of course. Each new act of violence seemed divorced from any larger context and increasingly resembled nothing more than the result of what had happened the day before and the cause of what would happen the day after.

Palestinian and Israeli Strategies

The ostensible trigger for the violence was a highly publicized visit by then opposition leader Ariel Sharon to the Temple Mount on September 28, 2000. Prime Minister Ehud Barak's precarious hold on power, due to disagreements with some of his coalition partners and the consequent loss of his parliamentary majority, encouraged expectations of early elections. Capitalizing on this uncertainty, Sharon intended his tour as a political ploy, to strengthen his position within his own party in anticipation of a leadership challenge by former Prime Minister Binyamin Netanyahu. But in the charged atmosphere that prevailed at the time, Palestinians immediately interpreted it as confirmation of the threat, propagated for years by Islamic factions, that the "al-Aqsa Mosque is in danger." Palestinian media contributed to the atmosphere by describing Sharon's presence on the Temple Mount as a "defilement of the al-Aqsa Mosque." (Hence the immediate adoption of the term "Al-Aqsa Intifada" for the violence.) The next day, following Friday prayers, Israeli police used lethal force against demonstrators and seven Palestinians were killed.

That incident sparked an extended period of bloody confrontation, but it fails to explain either the duration or the intensity of the violence. After all, there had been several previous outbreaks of similar violence, most recently in May on the anniversary of Israeli independence, designated by the Palestinians as "Nakba (Disaster) Day." Yet on all prior occasions, the violence had subsided after a few days following a PA decision to intervene. This time, it spread throughout the West Bank and Gaza (and briefly into Israel), and the PA, rather than acting to bring it under control, encouraged, supported, and glorified it.

One possible explanation for the PA's approach was Yassir Arafat's unwillingness to confront his own public by trying to contain what was presented as a spontaneous popular expression of frustrated desires to achieve independence and end the occupation. Indeed, the early months of the violence were sometimes characterized by the alternative term "Independence Intifada." In principle, however, independence and an end to the occupation could have been achieved peacefully two months earlier at Camp David. This suggests two other possibilities: that Arafat, quickly recognizing the potential benefits of the violence, refrained from suppressing it in order to reap those benefits, or that he even provoked and instigated it.

The second interpretation is supported by both direct and indirect evidence, including a PA-directed campaign of mobilization for armed struggle carried out in youth camps by the political guidance department of the National Security Forces during the summer of 2000. Moreover, records later confiscated by the Israel Defense Forces document Arafat's approval of PA funding of salaries and equipment for members of the Tanzim – the Fatah-based militia responsible for a large part of the violence after September 2000. Finally, in March 2001, one Palestinian Cabinet member, Communications Minister Imad Faluji, told an audience in the Ein el-Hilwe refugee camp in Lebanon that the violence had been planned after the breakdown of the Camp David talks in July. However, Faluji, an independent with ties to Hamas, subsequently retracted this claim, and the thesis that Arafat had actively prepared the violence and simply unleashed it when Sharon provided him with the pretext was strenuously denied by official Palestinian spokesmen and contradicted by many independent observers.

Whatever the background, PA policy in the months that followed indicated a strategic or instrumental approach, namely, an expectation that the violence could serve political objectives. In particular, Arafat, on the defensive after Camp David, hoped or anticipated that the large-scale, highly-publicized violence would reverse the Israeli-Palestinian political balance and improve his bargaining position in subsequent negotiations. This could result from either one or both of two developments. The first was that the Israeli government and public, worn down by human casualties and other costs, would be more forthcoming and concede, or at least come closer to conceding, what the Palestinians defined as their minimal demands. Indeed, Palestinian perceptions of Israel's unilateral withdrawal from southern Lebanon in the spring of 2000 encouraged the hope that the scenario could be copied in the occupied territories. Although the withdrawal had been planned in advance and was carried out with no Israeli casualties or loss of equipment, televised scenes of Israeli forces pulling back in what looked like disarray from the "security zone" precipitated widespread rejoicing among Palestinians and led to public demands for Palestinians to abandon the "illusion" of negotiations and embrace the "Lebanon model."

The other projected development was that the drama of violent conflict, in which the Palestinians would inevitably be seen as the weaker side or the underdog, would internationalize the conflict. In fact, at one point, Arafat rejected the interpretation that Israel was prompted by Hizbollah violence to withdraw unilaterally from Lebanon, and argued instead that Israel had been forced to withdraw by the power of international legitimacy, that is, a United Nations Security Council resolution. Reasoning dictated that at worst, internationalization of the conflict could produce sympathy, material support, and perhaps an international presence on the ground; at best, it might lead to unrelenting political pressure on Israel to grant even more generous terms. To improve the chances of this outcome, Palestinian leaders, including Arafat himself, immediately made every effort to characterize Israeli countermeasures in the most extreme manner, claiming, among other charges, that Israel had used depleted uranium shells against Palestinian targets and distributed poisoned candy to Palestinian children.

Although Palestinian spokesmen frequently described the violence as a struggle for independence, they also occasionally described it as defensive or reactive, arguing that Israel had actually initiated it in the hope of imposing by force its version of a political settlement. In fact, Israel had no such political strategy. Its use of force, like the Palestinians', was instrumental, but the strategy was essentially one of crisis management, and the only political component was a denial of Palestinian political objectives. Otherwise, what guided Israeli policy was the desire to end the violence while limiting both Israeli casualties and political damage at the bilateral, regional, and international levels.

In practical terms, these goals were inconsistent and somewhat contradictory. The desire to limit Israeli casualties, and perhaps to restore some degree of deterrent power, indicated a recourse to large-scale firepower. But the desire to contain the political damage indicated the opposite. As long as Israel hoped to sustain the possibility of reviving the political process at some point in the future and felt that the PA, as the organizational extension of the PLO, was the most promising or, indeed, the only potential interlocutor, it had an interest in minimizing Palestinian casualties and avoiding any action that would inflict irretrievable damage on the PA. The desire to avoid a further deterioration in Israel's relations with its Arab neighbors, especially Jordan and Egypt, also dictated some measure of self-restraint, as did the need to ward off the kind of international criticism that might lead to massive pressure for Israeli political concessions. The result of these contradictory interests was an Israeli policy that fluctuated between escalation and de-escalation in the use of both military force and economic pressure (closure of territory, withholding of tax revenues collected by Israel on behalf of the PA, and so on). Escalation normally came in response to particularly destructive Palestinian attacks, especially those of suicide bombers and car bombs against civilian targets inside Israel. De-escalation normally took place when the collateral political damage from "excessive force" threatened to become unacceptable.

For the first four months of the violence, the Israeli government also tried to combine military and economic countermeasures with diplomatic engagement. With American support, negotiations resumed at Bolling Air Force Base near Washington toward the end of the year and resulted in a set of "bridging proposals" by President Clinton. These included the transfer to Palestinian control of 94-97% of the West Bank and the exchange of Israeli territory as partial compensation for the remaining 3-6%. On Jerusalem, the proposed principle of "what is Arab should be Palestinian and what is Jewish should be Israeli" would enlarge the proportion of the city that would pass to Palestinian sovereignty. These proposals served as the basis for yet more negotiations at Taba, which extended into January and moved the center of gravity even closer to Palestinian positions. Nevertheless, the talks ultimately foundered on the Palestinian refusal to recognize any Israeli authority over the Temple Mount and to compromise on the principle of the refugees' "right of return" to Israel, and they broke off about a week before the Israeli elections. Meanwhile, the violence continued.

Despite the Barak government's willingness to offer more conciliatory terms in the post-Camp David negotiations, it is not at all certain that those terms would have been ratified by the Israeli political system even if the Palestinian side had accepted them. In fact, Barak came under intense criticism, including from his own supporters, for continuing to negotiate at all after December, once new elections were already scheduled. The Attorney General questioned his legal authority, and some Palestinian analysts suggested that one of the reasons for rejecting the package was that Barak did not have any real mandate to offer it. Most importantly, however, the violence had hardened Israeli public opinion and further intensified suspicions about Palestinian intentions and good faith. The left was disillusioned if not outright embarrassed, and the "peace camp" went into hibernation.

All this was reflected in the special prime ministerial election in February 2001 that swept Ariel Sharon into office with a huge margin (almost 2:1). Sharon had no substantive political platform, but the Israeli public was so repulsed by the Palestinian reversion to violence in the face of what was seen as offers by Barak that went very far (for his critics, too far) toward meeting Palestinian aspirations and by his willingness to continue negotiating despite the violence. Consequently, voters rejected both Barak and Arafat and placed their faith in Sharon's explicit refusal to negotiate under fire and his implicit threat to crack down hard in order to restore personal security to Israelis. With this rather amorphous mandate, Sharon established a broad-based "unity government" that included Labor Party representation, and he committed himself to not resuming negotiations until the violence came to an end. Even if that happened, however, there was little chance that the new government, dominated by right wing and religious parties, would repeat the offer made at Camp David, much less the one made at Taba, and little chance that public opinion would press it to do so.

In fact, negotiations did not resume, violence did not end, and Palestinian terrorist attacks exacted a growing cost from Israelis. Indeed, the incidence and intensity of these attacks increased after Sharon took office, as Palestinians resorted more frequently to suicide bombers operating inside Israeli cities. By the spring of 2003, Israeli casualties since the outbreak of violence numbered more than 750 killed and over 5,000 wounded, approximately three-fourths of them civilians. The ongoing violence frightened away tourists and foreign investors, thereby magnifying the local consequences of the global economic downturn.

Chief among the government's responses to heightened Palestinian militancy was a steady escalation in the frequency and intensity of military actions. Under Barak, Israeli retaliation was largely confined to "demonstration" attacks against PA facilities, installations, and security forces, and were intended to signal Israel's insistence that the PA act more forcefully against perpetrators of violence, without subverting the viability of what it continued to see as the ultimate address for conflict resolution. Indeed, most Israeli attacks were actually preceded by warnings in order to allow those inside targeted buildings to evacuate. But under Sharon, Israel no longer had the same political investment in the PA's ability to function. It rejected the principle of persuading or attempting to compel the PA to ensure the security of Israelis, insisting that Israel itself should assume direct responsibility for its citizens. The government was thus increasingly prepared to translate into military idiom the conclusion that Barak had already drawn but not acted upon, namely, that Arafat, as head of the Palestinian government, was no longer a partner for peace. As a result, it was progressively less restrained in the measures it used, subject only to concern about diplomatic repercussions. These measures included greater reliance on firepower (especially airpower), targeted assassinations of terrorists as well as those who recruited, trained, equipped, and dispatched them, tighter restrictions on the civilian population, and increasingly frequent and prolonged incursions into areas officially under the control of the PA (Area A). By the end of 2001, Israel had even destroyed Arafat's headquarters in Gaza and had him under virtual house arrest in his Ramallah headquarters.

None of these measures had the desired effect. Indeed, the results were to some extent counterproductive, since they often prompted at least outward manifestations of greater Palestinian solidarity with a besieged leader and increased the motivation of young Palestinians to take part in the most radical kind of anti-Israel activity: suicide bombing. Public opinion polls at the end of 2001 revealed that almost 60% of Palestinians supported suicide bombings and over 90% opposed any action by the PA against them. The level of violence peaked in March 2002, when Palestinian bombers killed more than 130 Israelis – the highest single month casualty toll in Israel's history (except during full-scale wars). After a particularly gruesome bombing in Netanya on the first night of Passover, Israel launched Operation Defensive Shield.

Defensive Shield was qualitatively different from any measure Israel had taken since September 2000 because it involved a protracted presence in six of the seven main Palestinian cities on the West Bank and set for itself the highly ambitious goal of rooting out the "terrorist infrastructure." In practical terms, this meant arresting or killing terrorist suspects, acquiring information through interrogations or expropriation of databases (including those in Arafat's headquarters) to be used in future counterterror operations, confiscation of weapons and explosives, and dismantling of bomb factories. International pressure to terminate the operation mounted quickly, especially following allegations of a massacre in the Jenin refugee camp and after Palestinian gunmen took refuge in the Church of the Nativity in Bethlehem. Israel was able to resist these pressures for about three weeks, during which time it achieved some of the tactical objectives it had set for itself. In particular, it uncovered evidence in Ramallah documenting that Arafat had not only made no significant effort to combat terrorism, but had actually financed and equipped organizations, such as the Tanzim and the al-Aqsa Martyrs Brigades, that had flaunted their role in "military operations" or "resistance activities." However, Israel was not able to accomplish the broader goal of rooting out the terrorist infrastructure. This was made clear by a new rash of attacks almost immediately after Israel withdrew from the cities.

At the end of June, therefore, Israel launched a second major incursion, Operation Determined Path, vowing that this time the operation was open-ended and that the IDF would remain in Area A (except for Jericho, which had been relatively free of terrorist activity, and Gaza, which was effectively fenced off) until terrorism stopped. It was not clear, however, how long the vow to remain in the Palestinian cities could be sustained, particularly in face of the growing impoverishment and misery of the Palestinian civilian population. Israel's previous actions against the PA had undermined whatever capacity the Authority still had to deliver social and economic services to the local population. Moreover, the measures associated with counterterrorism included semi-permanent town closures or at least serious hindrances to movement between towns as well as prolonged curfews. These intensified the disruption to the daily lives of Palestinians and further exacerbated the economic distress of the previous two years, caused by the exclusion of Palestinian workers from the Israeli labor market, and by Israel's withholding of tax revenues collected on behalf of the PA on the grounds that the PA used these funds to underwrite terrorism. Israel itself was reluctant to assume full responsibility for social services and reestablish the "civil administration" that had functioned during the years of occupation before the creation of the PA in 1994. That would simply add to the existing burden on manpower and budgets stemming from the protracted presence in Palestinian-populated territories. The plight of the Palestinians was thus likely to evoke international pressure for Israel to ease its restrictions on the civilian Palestinian population.

Moreover, even from an operational assessment Determined Path did not achieve complete success. For about three weeks, the campaign seemed to contain Palestinian attacks, and many Israelis began to accept the simple formula, "IDF goes in, terror stops coming out." Security officials insisted that the presence on the ground enabled Israel to disrupt or intercept dozens of planned terrorist attacks. In a related by-product, the inability of Palestinians to resist ongoing Israeli operations and the apparent willingness of the world to tolerate them helped provoke a Palestinian debate about the potential advantages of curbing terrorism and even demilitarizing the conflict. But any sense that Determined Path might have provided a solution to the problem was undermined in July by a new wave of shootings and bombings, not only in the heart of the West Bank, but also in or near Tel Aviv, Jerusalem, Safed, and other Israeli cities.

Following these attacks, some voices were heard, inside and outside the government, calling for even more extreme measures, such as the deportation to Gaza of the relatives of suicide bombers. The long-abandoned practice of blowing up the homes of terrorists was also revived, and it was subsequently claimed that several proposed bombings were rejected by terrorists at the urging of their relatives. Nevertheless, such measures hardly provided a panacea. Specifically, it was increasingly clear that with Israel in effective control of virtually the entire West Bank, military measures had been practically (if not theoretically) exhausted. Thus, in the perceived absence of any valid interlocutor or chance of productive negotiations, momentum grew for a different course of unilateral action: a barrier separating the territories from Israel proper. Proposals for unilateral separation or disengagement had been under discussion for many years and advocated by some public personalities and organizations. The decision made in the spring of 2002 to construct a fence, however, did not provide for the kind of withdrawal from the West Bank and/or Gaza implied in the terms separation or disengagement. Instead, it simply meant the erection of a physical barrier – some combination of wall, fence, no-go zones, sensors, monitoring, and patrols – to prevent unauthorized entry of Palestinians from the territories into Israel proper. Even if the barrier were effective, Israeli civilians (settlers) and military personnel would still be scattered throughout the territories, and the barrier would have little or no effect on the prospects for violence there. Besides, authorization extended to only 80-100 kilometers out of the 360 needed to encircle the West Bank in its pre-1967 dimensions (or more, if the expansion of Jerusalem were to be accommodated), and it was doubtful if the kind of comprehensive effectiveness demanded would actually be achieved.

In short, after more than two years of escalating violence, Israel still had not found the formula it sought to bring about an unconditional end to Palestinian violence. It is true that the number of terrorist attacks did decline quite significantly because of the security services' enhanced ability to preempt or intercept many of them. But not all attempts were forestalled, and continuing efforts, especially by suicide bombers, did produce a considerable number of casualties even after Defensive Shield. At the same time, violence did not force Israel to be more forthcoming politically than it had been before the violence began. In other words, while Israeli security and economic wellbeing had been undermined, this did not translate into the kind of exhaustion or sense of futility that might have led to greater concessions or even to unilateral withdrawal. In that sense, the Palestinians had failed to apply the "Lebanon model" to their own situation.

International and Regional Dimensions

The second ostensible hope of Palestinian strategy – "internationalization" – was also not fulfilled, not because there was no international involvement, rather because it evolved in ways that did not necessarily serve Palestinian national interests and certainly confounded the institutional interests of the PA/PLO. True, there was no lack of sympathetic statements by world leaders, sympathetic demonstrations in the Arab world, and sympathetic coverage in the media – especially in the first few weeks when Israeli security forces confronted Palestinians using stones, Molotov cocktails, and sporadic fire by gunmen mixed in with demonstrators. Israel was harshly criticized for using excessive force in response to these challenges, and the balance of casualties, very much in Israel's favor, was actually a political liability. But that pattern shifted soon after when Palestinians increasingly resorted to live fire, drive-by shootings, and mortar fire, and later even more so with the growing incidence of suicide bombings, Qassam rocket launches, and other attacks against Israeli civilians. PA tolerance of these acts, as well as active complicity, also incurred international disapproval.

A continuous series of diplomatic interventions aimed at ending the violence and reviving the negotiations began with high-level meetings in Paris in early October 2000 that were followed by an international summit at Sharm el-Sheikh in the middle of the month. These and all subsequent efforts foundered on Yassir Arafat's failure to embrace let alone enforce an immediate and unconditional cease-fire, that is, to end the violence without some political achievement that would justify the human and material price paid by his people. Arafat's dwindling credibility with many of his foreign interlocutors compounded the problem. The Sharm el-Sheikh summit did authorize the establishment of a fact-finding committee, headed by former US Senator George Mitchell, but its recommendations, submitted at the end of April 2001, refrained from endorsing the Palestinian demand for an international monitoring or protection force on the ground. A draft United Nations Security Council resolution to approve such a force also failed to pass because of an American veto. The bottom line, therefore, was that no critical international support for the Palestinians was forthcoming. Even the Arab states, which had been unanimous in their rhetorical support and in their decisions to reduce or sever contacts with Israel, failed to deliver the financial assistance they promised at two Arab Summit conferences, much less any kind of material military support. Thus, the vision of an imposed settlement on terms more favorable to the Palestinians remained as elusive as ever.

The manner in which international involvement evolved contrary to Palestinian hopes or expectations is exemplified most vividly in the case of the United States. The inauguration of the Bush administration in early 2001 was eagerly anticipated in some Palestinian and Arab quarters because of a perception that the Clinton administration had been unduly pro-Israel and perhaps because of some expectation that George W. Bush would be willing to apply heavy pressure on Israel in the same way that his father had ten years earlier. But the initial inclination of the new administration was not to apply pressure of any kind on anybody and, instead, to refrain from active involvement in the Israeli-Palestinian conflict. The prevalent feeling was that President Clinton had been too intensely engaged in the micro-management of negotiations, and in any case, the new administration's priority in the Middle East was not peacemaking but resolving the issue of Saddam Hussein.

Yet preferred distance could not translate into complete indifference. During Secretary of State Colin Powell's first trip to the region in February 2001 to sound out sentiment concerning possible American action against Iraq, he was reminded of the centrality of the Israeli-Palestinian issue to most Arabs, and he met with representatives from both sides. Moreover, the administration not only endorsed the conclusions of the Mitchell Committee (a legacy from the Clinton administration) but also sent CIA Director George Tenet to formulate a work-plan that would lead to implementation of the Mitchell recommendations – cease-fire, resumption of security coordination, counterterror and confidence-building measures – and eventual resumption of political negotiations. In other words, the United States was not disengaged, but it did resist calls for the kind of intense, active, detailed intervention demanded by Palestinians, Arab states, and some

Europeans, often with the unstated expectation that intervention would translate into pressure on Israel. The administration's reluctance to pursue that intervention was heightened, especially after major suicide bombings in Tel Aviv and Jerusalem during the summer of 2001, by the inability to secure from Arafat action consistent with his verbal promises to combat terrorism.

But the impetus to wrestle with Israeli-Palestinian violence took on much greater urgency after the September 11 attacks on the World Trade Center and the Pentagon. Hoping to facilitate Arab participation in the global coalition against global terrorism, Powell and Bush began to issue statements more sympathetic to Palestinian national aspirations, and at the United Nations General Assembly held in November, Bush explicitly referred to the vision of an independent state of Palestine (though he pointedly refused to meet with Arafat). As a signal of America's commitment to be more actively involved, Powell appointed a special envoy, retired General Anthony Zinni, and dispatched him to the region with the mission of translating the Tenet work plan into reality. These signals evoked concern on the part of the Israeli government that Arab cooperation with the United States against terrorism might be purchased at Israel's expense, so much so that Sharon, at one point, felt the need to warn publicly against attempts at Munich-style appeasement.

If the United States ever had this sort of diplomacy in mind – and there is no evidence to indicate that it did – any enthusiasm for it quickly faded. Certainly the United States discovered in the course of military operations in Afghanistan that Arab support, at least for that phase of the war against terrorism, was neither necessary nor forthcoming. In addition, Zinni's efforts collided with the reality of ongoing Palestinian terrorism – twenty-five Israelis were killed in a space of twelve hours during his December visit – and the administration's disillusionment with Arafat. For the United States, Arafat's credibility was to be particularly damaged not long after by his denial of involvement in the smuggling of weapons from Iran on the *Karine-A*, a denial that the Americans knew to be false. But already grasping Arafat's failed leadership, the United States not only failed to object but actually expressed understanding for the military actions taken by Israel in December 2001, including the confinement of Arafat to his compound in Ramallah.

Growing American displeasure was expressed in a variety of other ways. During his regional tour in March 2002, Vice President Dick Cheney refused to meet with Arafat. In April, American demands that Israel terminate Operation Defensive Shield were not pressed with any determination, and though Powell was sent to the region to deal with the fighting and its aftermath, it took him a week to get from Washington to Israel. Then came Bush's landmark declaration on the Middle East, delivered at the end of June. In that speech, Bush made the clearest American commitment yet to the principle of Palestinian statehood and expressed the hope that it could be achieved within three years. However, he laid all the hurdles to be overcome at the feet of the Palestinian Authority. Not only did he refrain from criticizing Israeli actions; he explicitly demanded comprehensive reform of Palestinian political, economic, and security institutions. Perhaps most significantly, he urged the Palestinians to choose a new leadership, which was interpreted, by everyone except Arafat himself, to mean the disqualification of Arafat.

If American behavior did not satisfy Palestinian hopes, the response of the Europeans was only slightly less disappointing. In general, European governments, media, and public opinion were consistently more sympathetic to and supportive of the Palestinian cause and the PA than were their American counterparts. European governments, both at the national and European Union-wide levels, routinely issued statements endorsing Palestinian goals and condemning Israeli policies and practices, and Europe continued to provide financial assistance to the PA even when the United States confined its support to Palestinian NGOs. There were also some spontaneous private attempts to organize boycotts of Israel. But apart from a non-binding resolution on the part of the ineffectual European Parliament to review the Israel-EU Association Agreement that regulated trade between the two sides, which in any case was ignored by the member states, no official action of any sort was taken. On the contrary, Europeans increasingly abandoned any pretensions they might once have had of acting as counterweights to the Americans, and sought instead to coordinate policy more closely with the Americans through an ad hoc mechanism established by Secretary Powell in April 2002 known as the Quartet, which also included Russian and UN representation. Indeed, though they objected to the American decision to bypass Arafat, the Europeans soon came around to the idea that the call for thoroughgoing reform of the PA was in order, and even began to assert a central role in promoting that effort. This evolution of cooperation found expression in the elaboration of a Quartet document known as "the roadmap," intended to facilitate the resumption of negotiations by specifying the measures Palestinians and Israelis were required to take within defined time frames in order to facilitate a peace agreement by 2005. But despite persistent pressures to publish this roadmap, pressures that intensified in anticipation of Arab reactions to an Anglo-American campaign in Iraq, the Europeans were unable to overcome American reluctance to make it public. When the war in Iraq began in the spring of 2003, the roadmap still had not been published.

Perhaps the greatest disappointment to the Palestinians, however, came from the Arab world. Since the outbreak of violence in late September 2000, the prospect that it might spill over beyond the confines of Israel/the West Bank/Gaza and destabilize other areas of the Middle East was a major source of concern to regional and international actors. The concern focused on two potential dangers. The first was that expressions of solidarity with the Palestinians by the "Arab street" would somehow get out of control and threaten Arab regimes. The second was that in order to preempt the threat to their stability, some Arab regimes might take actions that would heighten tensions more and perhaps even escalate into an Arab-Israeli war.

These concerns were not entirely without foundation. In the early days of the fighting, mass demonstrations were held throughout the Arab world, especially in Jordan, Egypt, and Morocco. Jordan was particularly vulnerable because of its proximity and its large Palestinian population, and demonstrators there clashed with riot police on more than one occasion. But Egypt too experienced recurring anti-Israel demonstrations, often with an undertone of opposition to the Egyptian government's policy. As a result, Jordan and Egypt expended considerable diplomatic energy in the search of some formula that would bring the violence to an end or at least contain it enough to remove it from television screens.

There were several other reasons for the acute sensitivity to events in the Israeli-Palestinian arena, among them the potential of modern mass communications. While Arab national print and electronic media are unfailingly hostile to Israel and supportive of Palestinian interpretations and demands, they generally refrain from criticizing the policies of national governments. But the proliferation of independent Arab satellite television networks has exposed viewers, if not to more inflammatory scenes than those they already see, then at least to advocates of more vigorous intervention by their own governments.

In addition, the religious dimension of the Palestinian cause was intensified by the Palestinians' own efforts (the very name "al-Aqsa Intifada" was calculated to play on these sentiments) and by the active endorsement of Hizbollah and other Islamist movements. This conflation of nationalism and religion raised the threat that Islamist forces might exploit the alleged "passivity" of national governments to rally anti-government sentiment. Finally, the violence provided an opportunity for Saddam Hussein to present himself as the most radical champion of the Palestinian cause and to strengthen the perception of a common Palestinian-Iraqi struggle against a "Zionist-imperialist" threat to the Arabs. Highly publicized acts of Iraqi support, such as the direct delivery of $25,000 to the family of each Palestinian "martyr" and the mobilization of a huge (phantom) volunteer force to liberate Palestine, were designed, at the very least, to forestall any regional tolerance for an American-led action against Iraq. In that sense, they reflected Saddam's vested interest in prolonging and, if possible, exacerbating the Israeli-Palestinian confrontation. More critically, Iraq's behavior could also embarrass other Arab governments into more vigorous and belligerent action against Israel.

Still, after more than two years of ongoing violence, none of the worst potential consequences actually materialized. In part, this was because concern about these very consequences constrained the behavior of virtually every participant or bystander in the confrontation, except those who had an interest in expanding the conflict – the PA itself and Iraq. Although Israel progressively resorted to higher levels of force, it nevertheless viewed the prospect of regionalization of the violence with considerable apprehension, and this consideration played a role both in its operational policies and in its attempts to maintain open channels of communication with its most important Arab neighbors. Arab governments (especially Egypt) relied on verbal belligerency and demonstrative political acts precisely to preempt or compensate for the absence of direct engagement that might implicate them in a clash with Israel that they much preferred to avoid. Thus, Egypt recalled its ambassador from Israel, Jordan failed to name a replacement for the one who had completed his term, and Qatar, Oman, Tunisia, and Morocco downgraded or suspended diplomatic and commercial links with Israel.

These "anti-Israel" actions, however, were not complemented by active "pro-Palestinian" measures. Arab governments refrained from providing any kind of military support or encouragement to the Palestinian Authority. They even failed to follow through fully on the commitments of financial aid taken at various summit and foreign ministers' meetings since September 2000. Indeed, apprehension about the consequences of regional destabilization acted as something of a double-edged sword from the Palestinian perspective, at least insofar as Jordan and Egypt were concerned (the latter especially following the replacement of Amr Musa as foreign minister by Ahmed Maher). For along with the verbal and diplomatic support those countries offered, they also acted to urge restraint on the Palestinian leadership, both through quiet back channels and by making it crystal clear that under no circumstances would they allow themselves to be dragged into a war by and for others.

In this sense, the governments proved to be more resistant to the mood of "the Arab street" than many observers had initially expected. In fact, even "the street" was less supportive than had been anticipated. There is no doubt that hostility to Israel increased dramatically. This was manifested in a variety of ways, including popular culture. Nevertheless, Palestinians were generally disappointed, not only in Arab governments, but also in the way that Arab publics went about their daily lives, most notably, in their indifference to the Palestinian appeal that "Nakba Day" in 2001 be observed throughout the Arab world.

Perhaps the most surprising and noteworthy development was the evolution of Saudi policy, especially after September 11. Foreign commentators traditionally grouped Saudi Arabia with the Arab "moderates," but Saudi posturing was always self-effacing, and any influence it exercised in favor of moderation was so discreet as to be virtually invisible. After September 11, however, the revelation that so many Saudis had taken part in the terrorist attacks against the United States and that even more were supportive of militant Islam in general and al-Qaeda and Osama Bin Laden (himself a Saudi) in particular, threatened to inflict serious damage on US-Saudi relations. Efforts to forestall such a development included a reevaluation of Saudi public positions on a variety of issues, including the Israeli-Palestinian conflict. The most notable expression of this reevaluation was an interview with *New York Times* journalist Thomas Friedman in February 2002, in which Saudi Crown Prince Abdullah asserted that an Israeli withdrawal to the lines of June 4, 1967, the establishment of an independent Palestinian state with East Jerusalem as its capital, and a just solution to the refugee problem would lead the Arab states to consider the conflict over, sign a peace agreement with Israel, and establish normal relations with it.

There was nothing substantively new in this proposal and nothing that departed from official Palestinian objectives. Indeed, all Arab parties had consistently interpreted UN Security Council Resolution 242 to mean Israeli withdrawal to the pre-Six Day War lines and insisted that a just solution to the refugee problem should involve implementation of UN General Assembly Resolution 194, which they interpreted to mean the "right of return." Also, given the conviction held for decades by many others that only Israel's continued occupation of territories stood in the way of peace, it is not self-evident why Abdullah's restatement of the obvious was considered innovative and generated so much excitement.

But the fact remains that it aroused substantial international interest, probably because while the proposal itself was not new, this sort of Saudi assertiveness – namely, the presumption to speak in the name of and in advance of all other Arabs, including Palestinians – was new. Indeed, this assertiveness extended to an Arab Summit Conference in Beirut at the end of March 2002, which was held despite Egyptian President Mubarak's refusal to attend, Israel's refusal to permit Arafat to attend, and the Lebanese hosts' refusal (undoubtedly with Syrian encouragement) to allow Arafat to address the Summit by video-transmission, despite a threat, which proved to be hollow, by the Palestinian delegation to walk out. Notwithstanding these complications, the Summit essentially endorsed the Saudi position, with some tightening of the provisions concerning the refugee issue.

Yet while Saudi Arabia endorsed the substance of Palestinian demands, it did not embrace Palestinian behavior or Palestinian leadership. For example, Saudi Arabia had long stopped responding both to Arafat's demands that all financial assistance to Palestinians be routed through him and to his complaints when it wasn't. Moreover, when American policy highlighted the issue of Palestinian reform, Saudi Arabia, though itself hardly a paragon of government transparency and accountability, signaled disapproval of Arafat by registering its willingness to cooperate, along with Egypt and Jordan, in the formulation and implementation of Palestinian reform.

Prospects for Palestinian Reform

By mid-2002, the seeming futility of Palestinian violence and the failure of the outside world to come to the Palestinians' defense had unlocked a Pandora's Box of criticism directed against the strategy, performance, and personnel of the

Palestinian Authority. Palestinian casualties were high (more than triple those of Israel), and the Palestinian economy was devastated; according to the World Bank, per capita income in the West Bank and Gaza, which had stood at $1,660 in 2000, had dropped by almost 20% in 2001 (to $1,340) and was expected to fall by another 20% (to $1,070) in 2002. Furthermore, the PA had proven utterly inept, not just of securing Israeli withdrawal or an end to settlement activity, but even of shielding Palestinians from Israel's responses to the very violence intended to promote those ends. As a result, President Bush's June 2002 speech demanding comprehensive reform and new leadership unlocked a floodgate of Palestinian resentment and desire for change that had been simmering near or just below the surface for many years.

Some of this criticism focused on the manner of waging the conflict with Israel. For example, voices questioning the utility of violence that had risen very early on and were then suppressed re-emerged following Operation Defensive Shield. For the first time, a group of political personalities and intellectuals issued a public statement denouncing terrorism against Israeli civilians, and this was followed by broader discussions between Fatah/Tanzim activists, Hamas, Islamic Jihad, and other political forces, both on the ground and in Cairo under Egyptian and European auspices, about the advisability of continuing to use suicide bombers and other forms of terrorism against Israeli civilians. This reassessment of the means employed by Palestinians against Israel was prompted not by considerations of morality but rather by the growing conviction that terror against civilians damaged Palestinian interests. Specifically, it addressed only terrorism within the pre-1967 borders, and by the end of 2002, it had not yet produced any agreement on a decisive shift in Palestinian tactics. Nevertheless, given the general sentiment prevailing among Palestinians, the very fact of an emerging debate represented a serious challenge to the central theme of the current Palestinian cause, and it was almost certainly provoked by the futile, indeed counterproductive, manner in which Arafat had directed, or at least tolerated, the evolution of the campaign.

However, the bulk of the criticism dealt with internal Palestinian affairs. For years, resentment had been building against the authoritarianism and corruption of the PA. Arafat had previously faced down several challenges by the Palestinian Legislative Council (particularly in 1997 and 1998) and had eliminated any signs of judicial independence. In addition, he recreated the patrimonial regime based on personal control of finances and competition among fiefdoms headed by his own appointees with nebulous but overlapping areas of responsibility that had characterized the PLO before the creation of the PA in 1994. Thus, when outside pressure mounted following growing endorsement by other countries of Bush's demand for comprehensive reform, it was echoed by renewed calls for change from within. Indeed, many argued that reform was, first and foremost, a Palestinian need and interest that should be pursued, notwithstanding the instinctive tendency to rally around a leader under American/Israeli attack.

The background to the hope that more open political and economic systems could be promoted was the vigorous Palestinian civil society that had evolved following the rise of Palestinian national consciousness in the mid-1960s, and especially after Israel took control of the West Bank and Gaza in 1967. Palestinians then began to build a myriad of organizations and institutions associated with civil society, both in the occupied territories and abroad. Whether they did this despite the conflict with Israel or because of it – as a necessary substitute for the state they did not have – is not clear. It may well be that the national struggle encouraged voluntarism, and the absence of a Palestinian state facilitated it. True, the authorities under whom Palestinians found themselves operating were not always sympathetic to local voluntarism. Yet the more important fact was that there was no central *Palestinian* authority to compete with those organizations and institutions that stood between the family and the state, no government intent on subordinating, co-opting, or subsuming civil society for the alleged purpose of advancing an overarching national goal. Thus, for almost twenty years after 1967, the Israeli occupation left considerable space for Palestinians to set up and operate a wide range of civil society institutions: municipal councils, chambers of commerce, professional associations, labor unions, universities, student organizations, women's organizations, newspapers, and more.

When the Palestinian Authority was created in 1994 following the Oslo Agreement, it repressed this dynamic civil society and aborted what appeared to be the potential for Palestinian democratization. Even before the creation of the PA, many of these associations had been emptied by the PLO of most functions other than mobilization of support for the Palestinian national movement's exiled leadership. But after 1994 and the creation of a quasi-state, the Palestinian Authority, with direct civil jurisdiction over the bulk of the Palestinian population in the West Bank and Gaza, significantly expanded "the state" from a Palestinian institutional point of view. This did not prevent the continued growth of institutions, organizations, and other groups associated with civil society. By the end of the 1990s, hundreds of such bodies were operating in the West Bank and Gaza, and 65 of them were members of a Palestinian Non-Governmental Network. But ironically, the creation of a Palestinian governmental structure meant the limitation of civil society, specifically because of constrained autonomy for most of these entities.

The reason for the decline in viable civic institutions lies in the character of the political system. In theory, the Palestinian Authority conformed to the structural model of democracy: an elected executive and legislature and an independent judiciary. Indeed, the elections of January 1996, despite some irregularities, were widely perceived to be as free and fair as any that have taken place in the Arab world. In practice, however, Arafat applied the same methods he had used for twenty-five years in the PLO to establish a regime of personal authoritarianism in the PA. The most important of these was the creation of competing bureaucracies, including security bureaucracies, with ill-defined and overlapping areas of responsibility, all headed by loyalists forced to compete for his favourable arbitration. In addition, he retained personal control of PA finances, most of which came from outside sources rather than from taxes. As a result, Arafat could ignore the Palestinian Legislative Council (PLC), which quickly lapsed into impotence. For more than five years, he refused to approve the Basic Law (Constitution) that defined the separation of powers in the PA, and he evaded PLC demands, especially in 1997 and 1998, for government reforms and investigations of widespread corruption. He also forestalled the emergence of intermediate levels of authority by postponing municipal elections, personally appointing mayors, and simultaneously appointing District Governors, while leaving the division of responsibility between districts and municipalities undefined, or in other words, subject to his own determination. At the same time, he crushed any judicial independence by simply ignoring the civilian courts, dismissing judges whose stances he opposed, or transferring proceedings to state security courts operating under military rules.

The Palestinian Authority's governing methods contributed directly to shrinking the space left for civil society. Semi-independent newspapers that had existed before the emergence of the PA were mobilized to applaud the regime or suppressed on grounds of insufficiently sympathetic (or sycophantic) coverage, and the new electronic media - radio and TV - became vehicles for pro-Arafat propaganda and anti-Israel incitement. Dissidents, even non-violent ones, were subjected to arbitrary arrest, imprisonment, and physical maltreatment. In addition, instruments of economic centralization and patronage (licenses, monopolies, exclusive distributorships) encroached on the space left for market forces and the private sector, except for the few in favor with the regime, as did the "informal" collection of taxes from businessmen by various security agencies.

The indirect impact of the creation of the PA on civil society was almost as profound. Before 1994, many Palestinian municipalities, as well as universities and other NGOs, were sustained by direct contributions from foreign donors. After 1994, the bulk of foreign economic assistance was channeled to the PA, i.e., Arafat, and these institutions, apart from those with an Islamist orientation, had to rely on him, financially as well as politically, for their continued operation. This dependence cast doubt on whether many of the civil society institutions could still be accurately described as "non-government organizations."

These developments explain not only why Bush's rhetoric focused almost as much on Palestinian political and economic reform as it did on the need to combat terrorism, but also why the outside pressure for reform found a responsive chord inside Palestinian society. In his desperate situation in mid-2002, therefore, Arafat had little choice but to show some responsiveness to these pressures, yet he chose ways that would forestall the outcome ultimately desired by Bush (and Sharon): his own replacement. He announced a cabinet reshuffling that reduced the number of ministers from thirty-one to twenty-one but, with only five exceptions, it failed to infuse "new blood." Apart from the appointment of a professional economist as minister of finance, there was no evidence of serious financial reform. Nor was anything done to establish judicial independence. Arafat initiated a reorganization of the security agencies, ostensibly to produce clearer lines of authority, but made sure to retain personal control over several of them (the Presidential Guard, Force 17) while placing others, especially the Preventive Security Forces that had previously been led by "insiders" with independent bases of power (Jibril Rajoub in the West Bank and Muhammad Dahlan in Gaza), under the command of an old PLO loyalist from the outside. And he responded to the longstanding demand for municipal elections and new national elections by announcing that they would be held in reverse order in early 2003, lest the anticipated gains of the Islamists at the local level create some momentum that would carry them forward in legislative and presidential elections. Finally, some of the reform measures, including elections, were made contingent on Israeli redeployment to positions held in September 2000 - a consistent Palestinian demand in every proposed stabilization plan, and one that Israel refused to implement without the restoration of security cooperation and determined Palestinian action against terrorism.

Such measures did not directly address Israel's most immediate concerns, terrorism and hostile incitement, although they were presumably connected, in the sense that they could theoretically encourage the emergence of a Palestinian government more willing and better able to deal with terrorism and incitement. More significantly, however, they did not satisfy the demands of Palestinian reformers who still professed support for Arafat but wanted a thorough renovation of the PA (including elevation of Arafat to a ceremonial role) or, failing that, its dismantling and replacement by an entirely different system with a different cast of characters.

By late 2002, Sharon had failed to deliver on his election promises and produce some formula that could credibly advance the cause of peace, security, or both. Nevertheless, his domestic approval ratings remained extremely high, and Israel's relations with the most important factor in its foreign policy, the United States, were on fairly solid ground. The most obvious manifestation of this was the January 2003 general election. With his landslide victory, Sharon became the first incumbent Israeli prime minister since Menahem Begin in 1981 to be re-elected by a convincing margin.

Arafat, by contrast, was under intense pressure both at home and abroad, not only for his failure to promote Palestinian aspirations, but also for his failure to protect the Palestinians from the consequences of that failure, including a dramatic deterioration in relations with the United States. The most obvious manifestation of this was his acceptance in early 2003 of the longstanding demand by Palestinian reformers to nominate an empowered prime minister, a demand now reinforced by American and European pressure as a precondition for publication of the

Quartet's roadmap. The extent to which Arafat had to retreat was evident, in part, from the identity of his nominee – not some anonymous non-entity but Mahmoud Abbas (Abu Mazen), a veteran PLO leader and prominent personality who had publicly expressed highly critical views of how the intifada in particular and Palestinian affairs in general had been managed in recent years. It was also evident from the fact that the PLC, in a rare show of defiance, rejected Arafat's demand to reserve for himself the power to appoint and dismiss ministers and instead assigned that authority to the prime minister.

While Arafat's growing predicament was clear, it was not at all clear how or even if he would extricate himself from this situation. Nor was there any solid foundation for predicting who might succeed him when he departed the scene. Notwithstanding Abu Mazen's appointment, there was no obvious heir-apparent, and the interplay between various Palestinian power centers and social formations (such as "Young Guard" and "Old Guard," "insiders" and "outsiders," West Bank and Gaza, politicians and militants, Islamists and nationalists, and competing clans) was too complex to permit a confident forecast of how the succession struggle would play out or how long it might take. What was clear, however, perhaps for the first time since Arafat took control of the PLO in 1969, was that Palestinians themselves had joined many in the rest of the world in perceiving a widening gap between Arafat's own agenda and the cause of the Palestinian people.

The Israeli-Syrian-Lebanese Triangle

The linkage between the Palestinian-Israeli and Arab-Israeli relationships was stronger at the emotional level than at the operational level, and for the Palestinians, Arab states (with the exception of Iraq) contributed no more to "constructive" internationalization of the confrontation than did the United States or Europe. Thus, there appeared to be nothing in the inherent dynamic of the Israeli-Palestinian confrontation that would lead to a wider regional war. The catalyst for such a war, if there was one, lay elsewhere – on Israel's northern border.

Since its withdrawal from southern Lebanon in May 2000, Israel's declared policy was to hold Syria responsible for any attacks launched by Hizbollah (or others) from Lebanese territory. An indication of what that accountability could mean was provided by the bombing of a Syrian radar installation in Lebanon in mid-April 2001 following a Hizbollah attack on an Israeli outpost on Mount Dov, in an area that is demarcated as part of the Golan Heights but that Lebanese refer to as Shab'a Farms and claim as Lebanese territory that Israel refuses to evacuate.

Hizbollah stressed its solidarity with the Palestinian cause and even declared that some of its operations were meant to strengthen the Palestinian struggle. But after the Israeli air raid in April, Syria imposed restrictions on Hizbollah activities, and some important figures in the Lebanese political system, including Prime

Minister Rafiq Hariri, openly voiced their opposition to the timing or character of Hizbollah attacks. This incident neatly summarized the dilemma facing Hizbollah in the aftermath of Israel's withdrawal.

On the one hand, Hizbollah's political prospects and perhaps even its viability depended on preserving some unique niche in the Lebanese political spectrum after Israel's withdrawal deprived it of its central raison d'etre: armed resistance to the Israeli occupation of the south. To maintain a prominent role, it needed some pretext for continued militancy, and Shab'a Farms provided that pretext. So, too, did identification with the Palestinians, particularly (though not exclusively) with the Islamists among them. Thus, the organization initiated periodic exchanges of ground fire in and around Shab'a Farms and also tried to provoke limited Israeli attacks in other sectors by firing at Israeli aircraft patrolling near the border or in Lebanese airspace; expended anti-aircraft shells sometimes fell into Israeli territory. But it also engaged in a vigorous campaign of anti-Israel propaganda, using its Manar television station and other media to trumpet Palestinian operational successes and denounce repressive Israeli practices. It provided some logistical support to Palestinians, in the form of attempts to smuggle weapons and explosives into Gaza by sea. Finally, it exploited the fate of missing Israeli soldiers and a kidnapped businessman in a crude form of psychological warfare.

On the other hand, Hizbollah was perfectly aware that it could not push too hard lest it alienate its main constituency – Lebanon itself – as well as its major supporters – Syria and Iran. It clearly understood that once the problem of the security zone had been resolved, neither the Lebanese government nor most of the Lebanese public were prepared to risk a major conflict with Israel for the sake of a marginal and ambiguous issue like Shab'a Farms, much less the interests of the Palestinians. Lebanon was particularly sensitive to disruptions to its fragile economic recovery and to the determined efforts of the government to manage a crushing foreign debt burden and attract foreign investment.

Hizbollah also understood that Syria, in no position to confront Israel, was opposed to actions that might lead to uncontrolled escalation, especially in light of signs of growing resistance to Syrian presence by other segments of Lebanese society. It is true that Syrian control was less intrusive and restrictive than it had been before the death of Hafez al-Assad in June 2000. Assad's successor, his son Bashar, had not developed the same self-confidence in dealing with Hizbollah (or other policy actors in the region). He was much more deferential to Hizbollah's Secretary-General, Hassan Nasrallah, and received him personally on several occasions, something his father had never done. But provoking a war with Israel was nevertheless a red line that Hizbollah would not be permitted to cross. Finally, Hizbollah's main benefactor, Iran, was also concerned about the consequences of excessively provocative behavior. To be more precise, reformist elements identified primarily, though not exclusively, with President Khatami and the Foreign Ministry felt that Hizbollah unnecessarily aggravated the Iranian-American relationship, which was a source of growing apprehension, particularly following the post-September 11 war on terror, President Bush's "axis of evil" speech, and evidence of American determination to act forcefully against Iraq.

The various sources of influence coalesced during Operation Defensive Shield in April 2002. As an expression of solidarity with the Palestinians, Hizbollah initiated an intense exchange of fire and Israel responded by warning of severe retaliation against Lebanon and Syria. In this atmosphere of brewing crisis, Secretary Powell, who was already in the region, carried the warning messages directly to Beirut and Damascus, and it was argued that Hizbollah's decision to deescalate was Powell's major (and perhaps only) success of his Middle Eastern mission. Much less attention was paid to the fact that Iranian Foreign Minister Kharrazi was in Lebanon and Syria a week before Powell, presumably delivering the same message and probably securing the outcome that was later attributed to Powell.

This small crisis was resolved, but it illustrated the nature of the ongoing problem. If Hizbollah did not continue to restrain itself or would not be restrained by others, that is, if Israeli deterrence failed, there is a significant risk that retaliation could cause the situation to deteriorate into a Syrian-Israel war, perhaps leading to an even broader conflict in the region. Nonetheless, if that sort of scenario plays out, it would be due to Israeli, Lebanese, Syrian, and Iranian calculations (or miscalculations) that are functionally distinct from the Palestinian arena.

CHAPTER 6

Israeli Society Challenged

Shai Feldman and Yehuda Ben Meir

Israel affects the prospects of peace and war in the Middle East significantly and in complex ways. Operating as a highly dynamic democracy, its government reflects in some measure the Israeli public's preferences and its socio-political proclivities. Hence, understanding how Israel impacts on the odds of peace and war in the region requires an evaluation of its society's characteristics. In particular, it is imperative that Israel's resilience in the face of the difficult security challenges it confronts be assessed.

The portrait provided here of Israel's public mood draws from extensive polling of Israeli public opinion conducted by different organizations, primarily by the Jaffee Center in the framework of its project on Public Opinion and National Security. Those polled in the surveys cited here constituted representative samples of Israel's adult Jewish population. As with any public survey, the results of these polls are open to competing interpretations, and therefore the following analysis should be regarded as merely one way of understanding Israel's political and social leanings.

By the year 2003, Israel was well into its mid fifties. Within the short period of its statehood, it had already experienced the struggle for independence and state formation, waves of mass immigration, five major wars, an extended invasion of Lebanon, a Palestinian popular uprising (the first intifada) and more than two and a half years of sustained violence and terrorism (the second intifada). These developments have left important imprints on Israel's society.

What were these imprints? Regarding Israel's foreign and defense policy agenda, the country's Jewish majority supported strong measures to defend itself against terrorism and other security challenges, while willing to go to great lengths in attempting to end the ongoing conflict with the Palestinians. In this sense, Israel's society was tactically and operationally hawkish, while remaining open to strategic and political compromise. At the same time, the years of violence have made Israelis increasingly pessimistic: although still willing to make the compromises required for peace, they were not convinced that even the most far-reaching concessions would result in an end to the conflict.

This conclusion was strongly supported by data obtained in the annual surveys of the Jaffee Center's project on Public Opinion and National Security. The percentage of respondents who thought most Palestinians wanted peace fell from 64% in 1999 to 52% in 2000, 46% in 2001, and 37% in 2002. In 2002, only 32% thought it was possible to reach a peace agreement with the Palestinians. The percentage of those who believed that an end to the Arab-Israeli conflict would be achieved by reaching peace agreements with the Palestinians and the Arab states declined dramatically from 67% in 1999 to 30% in 2001 to a mere 26% in 2002. Also, support for the Oslo process dropped from 58% in 2001 to 35% in 2002.

Similarly, in a poll conducted in late August 2002 by Tel Aviv University's Tami Steinmetz Center for Peace Research, 71% of the respondents stated that they did not think the Oslo agreements would lead to peace, versus 15% who still believed in the Oslo process. Seventy-two percent of the respondents indicated they did not believe the Palestinians wanted peace, while only 23% thought to the contrary. In a Steinmetz poll conducted in early October 2002, 71% of the respondents supported the proposition that "a majority of the Palestinians" have not come to terms with Israel's existence and want its destruction, while only 18% rejected it. In late February 2003, only 10% believed that Arafat would sign a peace agreement with Israel that would include major concessions on both sides.

Trends in Public Opinion

Resilience

Over the years, Israeli society has proven itself much more resilient – defined here as willing to sustain hardships and costs - than it has been given credit for, even by the country's own political leaders. While it is true that cumulative costs produced the public pressure that compelled the Israeli government to withdraw its forces unilaterally from southern Lebanon in May 2000, a more balanced view must give at least as much weight to the fact that the public tolerated Israel's involvement in Lebanon for almost eighteen years. In retrospect, one can say that the public pressure for unilateral withdrawal did not reflect a lack of basic resilience but rather a growing conviction that the Israel Defense Forces (IDF) presence in Lebanon was futile and had ceased to serve Israel's vital interests. Similarly, during the 1991 Gulf War, the Israeli public sustained Iraqi ballistic missile attacks without pressuring its government to retaliate. The public seems to have been persuaded that retaining close relations with the United States, and avoiding any damage to the US-led coalition confronting Iraq, was more important than satisfying a need for revenge and upholding the principle of instant retaliation.

Over the years 2001-2002, Palestinian violence tested Israeli stamina again. By March 2003, the casualties Israel had suffered since the violence began in September 2000 reached more than 760 dead. For the sake of illustration only, according to the relative size of their respective populations, this figure is equivalent to over 36,000 Americans – more than twelve times the number of US casualties caused by the September 11, 2001 terror attacks and higher than the level of casualties sustained by Israel in any previous period of its history, with the exception of full-fledged conventional wars such as the 1948 War of Independence, the 1967 Six Day War, and the 1973 Yom Kippur War. And yet, this high number of casualties did not propel the Israeli society to pressure its government to make undue concessions or, conversely, force it to adopt draconian measures in the hope of ending the violence.

To date, Israel's society has refrained from producing a mass movement to force its government to bow to Palestinian or other sources of pressure. Objection to military service in the territories, among regular soldiers and reservists, remained a relatively marginal phenomenon. Whatever dissent or resistance did exist was much less vocal than that of the 1990s with regard to Israel's presence in southern Lebanon. In fact, of the 75,000 Israelis active as volunteers in the civil guard or auxiliary police, 30,000 volunteered in 2002.

This widespread consensus mirrored the agreement in the top IDF ranks about Israel's efforts to combat Palestinian terrorism, where debate was not nearly as sharp as the debate among these ranks regarding Israel's involvement in Lebanon. In fact, there was a remarkable degree of consensus within the IDF's general staff regarding military operations as well as overall strategy in response to Palestinian violence. This consensus, coupled with the existence of the national unity government until late 2002, led to strong and sustained public support for the government and its policies. The military and political leadership succeeded in convincing the Israeli public that the struggle against Palestinian terrorism and violence was indeed an existential one, or as it was expressed by Prime Minister Sharon, "a war on our home." Moreover, any cultural manifestations of opposition to Israel's military measures against the Palestinians were far less caustic than in previous periods, for example during the 1969-70 War of Attrition. At that time, Israeli artists, particularly on stage, sharply questioned the validity of the war along the Suez Canal.

By the same token, public pressure for extreme measures against the Palestinians also remained largely circumscribed. Thus, if one of the objectives of PA leader Yassir Arafat during this period was to provoke Israel to take measures that might have helped portray it as "a second Serbia," the objective failed miserably. Moreover, even the Israeli settler community – a constituency that included some of the most ideologically driven individuals – largely refrained from leveling undue pressures on the Israeli government to respond to the conflict more aggressively. This was especially noteworthy given the fact that settlers became the prime targets for Palestinian gunmen during the second intifada. In part the settler community was dissuaded from exerting such pressures by its assessment of the greater Israeli public. Their fear was that calling for increased military activity would alienate them from the vast majority of Israelis who were opposed to greater violence and who would regard the settler community as provoking an unnecessary escalation of the conflict, resulting in more Israeli casualties as well as in a dangerous rift with the United States.

The most vulnerable aspect of the Israeli society's resilience involved the economic dimension of the conflict. At least until early 2003 Israelis proved exceedingly responsive to calls for military reserve service, even when such service was associated with considerable physical danger. This was manifested clearly in mid-2002 during Operations Defensive Shield and Determined Path. However, the same Israelis became far less forgiving once the protracted conflict began to affect their financial situations, either through higher taxes or through the consequences of the deepening economic crisis such as increased unemployment.

In 2001-2002 Israelis became more pessimistic about their country's economic prospects as well as their own personal finances. Unlike the pessimism over a political settlement with the Palestinians, however, the bleak economic outlook was reflected in the assessment of the country's leadership. While Israelis tended to express confidence in their defense leaders, they gave far lower grades to the navigators of their national economy. This conclusion was clearly shown in polls conducted by the Smith Institute in June 2002 and for the leading daily newspaper *Yediot Aharonot* in July 2002, where 71% of the respondents gave Ariel Sharon good marks as prime minister, but only 29% approved of his handling of the economy. Sixty-six percent of the respondents trusted Sharon to lead the country, while only 26% trusted the minister of finance to manage the economy successfully.

In the future, the combined economic effect of the global slowdown, the crisis of confidence affecting the US financial markets, the crisis in the global high-tech sector, and the costs of some two and a half years of violence may become a strategic factor. Thus, it is far from clear that if the violence is prolonged Israelis would be willing to place their economy under a "war footing." Indeed, this potential weakness was identified by the Israeli Left, and in late 2002 some pro-peace groups placed advertisements in the Israeli printed media calling for "an end to the killing and an end to economic stagnation."

The importance of the economic dimension has increased with time. As the IDF and the security services became more successful in combating the various Palestinian terrorist organizations and reducing the incidents of terror attacks in Israel proper to less overwhelming proportions, the Israeli public became more and more preoccupied with the economic situation. In a poll taken by the Smith Institute in mid-February 2003, for the first time since the start of the violence Israelis described the economic crisis as more urgent than the violent conflict with the Palestinians: 36% responded that the former should be the first priority for the new government versus 18% who chose the latter; 46% attributed to the two equal importance. Answering an almost identical question, 45% of respondents in a February 2003 Steinmetz poll viewed revitalizing the economy as the first priority of the new government, versus 42% who viewed a resolution of the conflict with the Palestinians as the number one priority.

The Short Term: Support for Tough Measures

While resisting steps they viewed as extreme, Israelis strongly supported various offensive measures against the Palestinians to arrest the violence. Thus, the 2002 Jaffee Center poll found that 90% of respondents supported the elimination, i.e., targeted killing, of those active in terror, 80% supported the use of fighter aircraft and tanks against the Palestinians, and 73% supported the use of closures and economic sanctions. In a June 2002 Steinmetz poll, 80% of the respondents supported an extended IDF presence in the Palestinian cities as part of Operation Determined Path. Indeed, the June 2002 poll showed that even among those identifying themselves as having voted for the Labor candidate (then PM Barak) in the February 2001 elections, this position was supported by 68% of respondents. In a December 2002 Steinmetz poll, only 15% viewed Sharon's policy toward the Palestinians as "too harsh," while 31% saw it as "too lenient" and 47% as "just right."

Facing unrelenting Palestinian violence and "a war on [their] home," Israelis had two main reasons to favor the wide array of measures taken to stem the violence. The first involved the perceived absence of credible alternatives: in early 2003 Israelis continued to regard the attempts to end the violence through diplomacy as abysmal failures. The second reason was a loss of faith in the Palestinian leadership's willingness to abide by the commitments it had undertaken in the past and the various promises it had made since late 2000 to stop the violence. Consequently, the Israeli public apparently felt that demonstrating to the Palestinian people the costs that their leaders had imposed on them was the only way to induce Arafat to reconsider his tacit if not active support of terrorism, or, preferably, to induce the Palestinians to get rid of Arafat.

Accordingly, the diminished support for the Oslo process among Israelis should be regarded less as reduced willingness to make concessions and more as a reflection of exasperation with Yassir Arafat and despair about a process that relied on the Palestinians' "good behavior." Moreover, the majority of Israelis were not only convinced that Yassir Arafat was no "partner" for peace; they were also persuaded that he never really intended to make peace and that for him the Oslo accords were only an act of deceit. In retrospect, the intense, extended violence provided a context for understanding Arafat's rejection of the far-reaching concessions offered by Barak at Camp David in July 2000 and by President Clinton in the framework of the "bridging proposals" presented in December 2000.

The Long Term: Latent Support for Concessions

The Israeli public's support for forceful measures to combat Palestinian violence did not diminish the long-term trends in Israeli public opinion favoring moderation. Thus, while deeming concessions unwarranted as long as violence persisted and Arafat remained at the Palestinian helm, the Israeli public continued to be committed to the general contours of the Oslo grand-bargain: a divorce between Israel and the Palestinians based on an exchange of territory for peace and security. Accordingly, public opinion polls indicated strong opposition to stopping the peace process, even in the absence of viable evidence that the process was still alive. In the 2002 Jaffee Center poll, only 27% of the respondents supported the suspension of the peace process "even if doing so might lead to war," while 54% opposed such suspension. In the December 2002 Steinmetz poll, 63% of the respondents supported conducting negotiations with the Palestinian Authority versus 31% who were opposed. When asked to project themselves into a situation in which Israel and the Palestinians were to reach an advanced stage in negotiations for peace, 58% said they would support the creation of a Palestinian state versus only 37% who said they would oppose such an outcome.

If anything, the latent support for making far-reaching concessions in exchange for peace and security has only strengthened in recent years. This is due largely to an important development accelerated by the past two and a half years of Palestinian violence: the growing awareness among Jewish Israelis of the demographic factor and the dangers to sustaining Israel's character as a Jewish state. This new sensitivity, added to the growing weariness with a conflict that seemed to have no end, has propelled an increasing number of Israelis to view the West Bank and Gaza less as an asset to Israel's defense against strategic threats and more as a liability to the basic purposes of the state.

In a poll conducted in October 2002 for *Yediot Aharonot*, 60% of the respondents supported initiating negotiations for a peace agreement with the Palestinians, while 39% opposed it. In the same poll, 78% believed that Israel should agree, in the context of a peace agreement with the Palestinians, to dismantle the majority of Jewish settlements in the territories (32% supported the removal of all the settlements while 46% supported the removal of settlements from "densely populated Arab areas"). Only 20% were opposed to the removal of any settlement. A poll conducted for *Yediot Aharonot* in November 2002 among registered members of Sharon's Likud party showed that even among right wing constituents, an astonishing 54% supported the removal of settlements in "densely populated Arab areas," 11% supported the removal of all the settlements, and only 33% opposed the removal of any settlements.

The conceptual shifts, particularly regarding the demographic threat, were reflected clearly in the change of Israelis' approach toward the issue of Jerusalem. During the first three decades that followed the conquering of East Jerusalem during the 1967 war, Jerusalem was viewed primarily through the prism of the commitment to maintain the city's unity as an integral part of Israel's national ethos. In recent years this has been gradually supplanted if not replaced by the growing propensity to view Jerusalem through the prism of demography. Consequently, transferring the Arab neighborhoods of Jerusalem to Palestinian control, although still opposed by a majority, has become less of a taboo, it being seen on the one hand as an inevitable necessity for reaching a viable political solution and on the other hand as the only way to exclude some two hundred thousand Arabs from citizenship in the Jewish state and from participation in its pluralist democracy.

The February 2003 Steinmetz poll found strong support for major and far-reaching Israeli concessions in the context of a permanent settlement, in which the Palestinians would sign a peace treaty ending the conflict, renounce the right of return, recognize the historic connections of the Jewish people to the Temple Mount, and undertake to cease terror. In such a case, 58% (versus 37% opposed) would accept the establishment of a Palestinian state on the basis of the 1967 borders with certain border modifications; 69% versus 26% would support the removal of all the settlements in Gaza and isolated settlements in the West Bank; and 41% (versus 54.5% opposed) would support the transfer of the Arab neighborhood in east Jerusalem to Palestinian sovereignty.

Clearly, however, the support of Jewish Israelis for tough measures to stem Palestinian violence and their complete loss of faith in the present Palestinian leadership implied that the Israelis' support of concessions should be regarded as more latent than concrete. In practice, it meant that the willingness to exercise such flexibility was unlikely to manifest itself until Israel's strategic environment changed – that is, until violence has ended and a new Palestinian leadership, less implicated in terrorism, has emerged. Once these developments resulted in some restoration of Israelis' faith and trust in their Palestinian partner, the willingness to compromise might be transformed from latent to real.

More of a practical indication on the readiness for compromise was represented by the Israeli government's decision in mid-2002 to build a fence mostly along the 1967 lines, and the general public support for the decision. Even among most Likud cabinet and Knesset members resistance to the decision was limited, countering the expectation that they would vehemently oppose such a move since the fence would be interpreted as willingness to withdraw almost to the 1967 lines. The settler community as well responded hesitantly and with relative acquiescence to the decision to construct the security fence. In early 2003, a significant split occurred among the leadership of the settlers when a majority decided to present the government with their position regarding the precise delineation of the security fence – a demarcation that would be further east and farther from the 1967 lines than the one recommended by the IDF, thus including more settlements on the Israeli side. In the minority view, such a proposal nevertheless constituted the abandonment and betrayal of the ideal of "greater

Israel." The move to present an alternative plan for the fence, rather than reject it outright, reflected the settlers' appreciation of mainstream public opinion and their desire to compromise with it, rather than defy it entirely.

Support for Ariel Sharon

As of early 2003, public support for Sharon's handling of Israel's foreign and defense affairs remained very high, between 65 and 75%, depending on the wording of the questions asked in different polls. The apparent reason for the strong backing was that Sharon succeeded in navigating a policy that reflected many general preferences of the Israeli populace. In his public statements, Israel's prime minister echoed the public's assessment of Palestinian violence, and especially the suicide bombings in Israel's population centers, as a comprehensive attack on Israeli society within its own backyard. Throughout the long months of struggle, Sharon also reflected (and cultivated) the aversion that Israelis have developed toward Arafat – a view of the Palestinian leader as deeply embedded in a culture of violence and unwilling to part with his role as a revolutionary.

At the same time, Sharon was recognized for his restraint and his caution to avoid crossing certain boundaries as he managed the struggle against the Palestinians – such as killing Arafat or forcefully deporting him. This, despite pressures exerted to take strong measures by then-IDF Chief of Staff, Lt. Gen. Shaul Mofaz, as well as by some of the country's right wing political leaders, including former minister of internal security Uzi Landau, National Union leader Avigdor Lieberman, and National Religious Party leader Effi Eitam. By avoiding extreme measures and indicating that even Israel's aggressive actions such as Operation Defensive Shield and Operation Determined Path were not intended as a re-conquest of the West Bank and Gaza, Sharon also avoided a rupture of Israel's relations with the United States – an important litmus test for the Israeli public's assessment of its leaders. While adopting a tough stance, Sharon has not hesitated to reiterate that there is strength in restraint and that he will not lead Israel to war.

The care which Sharon took to avoid crossing these lines met another objective strongly favored by the public, namely, the continued participation of the Labor Party in Israel's national unity government. The public preference for a unity government reflected a deep-seated desire that as long as Palestinian attacks continue, Israeli leaders speak with one voice and the efforts to stem the violence not become another arena of partisan quarrels. Consequently, the national unity government survived from February 2001 until November 2002, much longer than most political observers had expected.

At the same time, Sharon also captured the public sentiment by expressing its latent support for far reaching compromises. Thus, he reflected the public's willingness to make "painful concessions" and to accept the eventual emergence of a Palestinian state. Significantly, Sharon refused to abandon these positions even in the face of sharp criticism expressed by members of his party's Central Committee and a frontal attack launched against him on this issue in May 2002 by former prime minister Binyamin Netanyahu. Sharon's steadfastness likely resulted from his judgment that it was more important to express the priorities of the public at large than to uphold indiscriminately his party's ideology.

The Israeli Political Map

Immediately after Ariel Sharon's election as prime minister in February 2001, Israeli legislation separating parliamentary and prime ministerial elections was repealed, restoring the Israeli electoral system to the status it had enjoyed during most of Israel's history: proportional elections to the Knesset followed by the formation of a government requiring the confidence of the majority of Knesset members. This change was expected to increase the representation of the larger parties in the Knesset, since the system employed during 1992-2001 had encouraged split voting: for a small party in the elections to the Knesset and for a candidate of one of the larger parties in the parallel election of the prime minister. With the original system restored, a desire to see an individual elected as prime minister would prompt voting for his/her party. Thus, it was anticipated that the larger parties would ride the tails of their respective candidates for prime minister.

The results of the January 2003 elections provided only partial confirmation for this theory. While Likud enjoyed a dramatic increase in its following, doubling its number of seats, Labor saw a further erosion of its power. Apparently the reversal of the electoral system to its pre-1992 system coincided with a major crisis of leadership in Labor's top ranks and a dramatic decline in the appeal of Labor-held policies, especially in the Israeli-Palestinian realm. Specifically, Labor was associated by voters with the defunct Oslo process. Hence, although the changes in the electoral system could have been expected to favor the larger parties, Labor was far less poised to benefit from this change than Likud.

The decline in Labor's standing could be interpreted as a general weakening of the Israeli political center. But this perception may also prove to be misleading. In recent years Likud has moved more to the center of the political map, as Sharon himself has adopted a position accepting the eventual emergence of a Palestinian state. It is also noteworthy that some members of the Likud leadership, such as Meir Shitreet and Tzipi Livni, both members of the first and second Sharon-led governments, seemed at least as pragmatic as their Labor counterparts. Moreover, platforms of parties to the right of Likud – for example, the National Religious Party led by Effi Eitam, and the National Union, headed by Avigdor Lieberman – increasingly helped define the Likud as a centrist party.

In addition to the fact that the center of the Israeli political map remained firm if not strengthened, the country continued to enjoy a robust parliamentary system capable of mitigating and brokering social cleavages. Accordingly, Israelis refrained from taking to the street issues that constituted important sources of social tension, such as the divide between secular and ultra-orthodox Jews, and the rift between Jews of European origin and those whose families came from Arab countries (Sephardic Jews). Instead, these issues became important determinants of the public's votes in Knesset elections. This was manifested clearly during the late 1980s and during the 1990s, when the drive to advance the socio-economic position of the Sephardic Jews led to the rise of the Shas party.

Israelis have taken to the street on more than one occasion to demonstrate their views on war and peace issues. Noteworthy were the demonstrations in the central squares of Tel Aviv and Jerusalem protesting the massacre in Sabra and Shatila in Lebanon in 1982, rallies demonstrating for and against the Oslo process, and the large scale gatherings following the assassination of Yitzhak Rabin in 1995. In contrast, however, the public has largely refrained from utilizing this form of protest for domestic issues. For example, when in July 2002 the Knesset adopted legislation that institutionalized the exemption of ultra-orthodox students of religious schools from military service (the Tal Law), not a single demonstration was organized to reflect the public's disapproval of a law that legalized unequal burden sharing. This was particularly surprising given that over 2000-2002, continued Palestinian violence compelled the cancellation of all plans to shorten the length of Israel's compulsory military service. Moreover, reserve duty was lengthened, causing some reservists to serve as much as 84 days. These requirements increased the existing disparity in public service between Israeli secular and ultra-orthodox Jews.

At the same time, the dramatic increase in the vote for the Shinui party in the January 2003 elections demonstrated that the Israeli electorate was not indifferent to civil issues. The party's platform centered on issues such as the cancellation of the Tal Law. Thus, the phenomenon observed is that Israelis angered by domestic issues refrained from exercising extra-parliamentary venues for expressing their views. Instead, they channeled their dissent to the electoral process, proving Israel's parliamentary system especially robust.

Civil Society Issues

Jewish-Arab Relations

One of the most significant trends in Israeli society over the past two and a half years of violence was the growing rift between the country's Jewish and Arab citizens. From the Israeli Arabs' perspective, this was not in essence a new phenomenon, but it intensified sharply in the shadow of the Palestinian violence. To them, the rift reflected their perception of being second class citizens – a perception based on many factors, primarily the fact that Israel was established to comprise a Jewish state. The gap in average incomes between Jews and Arabs in Israel, as well as in public investments in the two sectors of the Israeli society, merely reflected the basic purpose and priorities of the Jewish state at the expense of their community.

On the part of Israeli Jews, the worsening of relations with Israeli Arabs resulted from three developments experienced during recent years, all tied directly to the violence of the intifada. The first was the large-scale demonstrations of Israeli Arabs in October 2000, expressing their sympathy for their Palestinian brethren. The intensity of these demonstrations and their violent character shocked most Israelis, many of whom were still optimistic about the prospects of co-existence of Jews and Arabs in Israel. The second development was the prolonged Palestinian-Israeli violence, which placed continuous pressures on Israeli Arabs to affirm their alliance with the Palestinians. Indeed, as sporadic evidence of Israeli-Arab participation in terror acts began to accumulate, the Jewish-Arab divide within Israel increased. Finally, following the outbreak of the intifada, Arab Knesset members themselves fanned the flames of alienation. On more than one occasion, they made statements that could be interpreted as signaling that their primary loyalties lay with the Palestinian cause. For example, in a televised interview given by MK Ahmed Tibi during Operation Defensive Shield in April 2002, he expressed sympathy with the Palestinians resisting Israeli soldiers fighting in the Jenin refugee camp.

These developments seemed to encourage the growing pessimism among Israeli Jews with regard to the prospects of Jewish-Arab coexistence within Israel. In public opinion polls, this was reflected by increased opposition to the inclusion of Arab parties in the governing coalition, growing enthusiasm for the "transfer" (i.e., forceful expulsion) of Israeli Arabs, and new support for excluding Arab population centers such as Umm el-Fahm from Israel's boundaries within an Israeli-Palestinian permanent status agreement. The practical implications of the growing rift included a sharp decline in Jewish-Arab economic interactions and extensive Jewish boycotting of Arab businesses: Jews no longer felt safe – let alone comfortable – shopping in Israeli-Arab towns and villages.

At the same time and on the positive side of the ledger, the developments mentioned earlier may have had a sobering effect on both sides, and significantly, the Israeli Arab riots of October 2000 have not repeated themselves. It is also worthwhile to note that in mid-2002, Operations Defensive Shield and Determined Path, the de-facto reoccupation of almost the entire West Bank, and even the false reports of a Jenin massacre spread by Palestinian leaders in April 2002 did not bring Israeli Arabs into the streets. Indeed, since the bloody riots of October 2000 and as of March 2003, Israeli Arabs did not hold a single large-scale demonstration. It would seem that the majority of Israeli Arabs were chastened by the consequences of the violent clashes of late 2000.

And concomitantly, the Israeli Jewish leadership became more aware of the imperative to meet the genuine needs of Israel's Arab minority. Thus, the very slow but continuous integration of academically trained Arabs into the mainstream of the Israeli economy (in medicine, academia, law, and other advanced professions) continued. It remained to be seen, however, whether these positive developments and the government programs to promote the Israeli Arab sector would translate into actual gains for the community, or if they would fall victim to the growing pressures on the Israeli budget.

Finally, an important test of Arab-Jewish relations in Israel occurred on the eve of the January 2003 general elections. In late December 2002 the Central Elections Committee banned two Arab members of Knesset, Azmi Bishara and Ahmed Tibi, as well as Bishara's party, Balad, from running, thus de facto accepting the argument that Tibi and Bishara had been engaged in incitement against the state. Israeli-Arab leaders viewed this decision as an attempt to strip their community of its participatory rights. A few days later, however, Israel's Supreme Court, acting in its capacity as a Court of Appeals, overturned the Committee's decision, reinstating Tibi and Bashara as candidates and Balad as a legitimate party in elections. The Supreme Court's decision demonstrated that the Israeli political and judicial system enjoyed self-evaluating and self-correcting mechanisms, which in this case effectively prevented a rupture of Jewish-Arab relations.

Civil-Military Relations

In a democracy, involvement in a protracted conflict is fertile ground for civil-military tensions. Therefore, Israel, especially since September 2000, would be a likely candidate for this sort of friction. In Israel, however, it has generally been difficult to define the fault lines between the two categories. If individuals are to be defined as "military" to the extent that military service constituted their formative experience, then judging by the number of former senior military officers at top leadership positions Israel should be considered as having become "militarized."

Yet the Israeli example at the same time supports a competing characterization, namely, individuals assume a posture that society has defined, according to the positions they hold. Thus, once former military officers become civilian leaders they adjust their behavior to their new role. That this may prove a more accurate depiction of the Israeli scene could be observed through the prism of Lt. Gen. (ret.) Ehud Barak, in his dramatic personal transformation from IDF Chief of Staff to the post of prime minister. With this career change, Barak clearly behaved as a civilian leader. Accordingly, he decided to implement a unilateral withdrawal from southern Lebanon despite deep reservations held by many members of the IDF top command. Similarly, in announcing his intention to end the Palestinian-Israeli conflict within a year and a half, Barak overruled the numerous objections by the IDF Chief of Staff and the Director of Military Intelligence. At the time, both leading military figures made public their assessment that a historical conflict could not be resolved within eighteen months.

There is near-complete unanimity among observers of the Israeli scene as to the hierarchy whereby Israel's civilian leaders enjoy supremacy over the military. Thus, not a single senior IDF officer has ever questioned the absolute imperative of the Israeli military to obey the directives issued by Israel's civilian leaders. Indeed, even the severe tensions generated by the past two and a half years of violence have not resulted in any questioning of this basic precept of a democratic government.

Yet at the same time, other more subtle dimensions of the Israeli scene have demonstrated that civil-military relations in Israel have become much more complex than the crude hierarchical depiction of these relations – "it is the prerogative of the civilian leaders to decide and it is the imperative of the military to obey" – would lead one to expect. While the involvement of uniformed officers in Israeli political life was limited, certainly in comparison to the involvement of their predecessors in the 1940s and 1950s, they continued to assume a disproportionate role in interpreting the country's strategic environment, especially in the Palestinian sphere and in evaluating the regional and international "realities." In the absence of civilian bodies entrusted with the important task of producing a national "net assessment," the IDF performed this task by default, despite the fact that legally its Directorate of Military Intelligence is responsible for providing no more than a "national intelligence estimate."

In addition, throughout the 1990s and into the new millennium, the IDF has played an important role in the negotiations held with Syria, Jordan, and the Palestinians. While in the negotiations with the first two the role of the uniformed officers was largely confined to security issues, this was not the case with regard to the negotiations with the Palestinians. True, in the latter example civilian and security issues were far less distinct than in the case of state-to-state negotiations. Still, it seemed that on more than one occasion senior IDF officers took part in negotiating almost purely political issues, including some that were subject to deep ideological debate. A case in point was the involvement in early 2003 of senior IDF officers in formulating the "political initiative" (regarding the Palestinian issue) and Israel's response to the "roadmap" proposed by the Quartet, both prepared in the prime minister's office.

Perhaps predictably, the past two and a half years of violent conflict with the Palestinians created numerous opportunities for heightened tensions between Israel's top military and civilian leaders. Yet the pattern of these tensions was not consistent. On more than one occasion Israeli civilian leaders expressed their exasperation with a military that seemed reluctant to use all the resources at its disposal in order to "triumph" over the Palestinians. In such cases top IDF officers found themselves having to explain to their political superiors the possible strategic damage that might result from a less measured use of force.

In other instances, however, the pattern was quite the opposite, with former IDF Chief of Staff Mofaz strongly advocating more aggressive actions against the Palestinians. For this he was reprimanded by Binyamin Ben Eliezer, then minister of defense, who at one point actually threatened to fire him. On another occasion Mofaz was overheard pressing Prime Minister Sharon to seize an opportunity to forcefully expel PA leader Yassir Arafat from Ramallah into exile outside the territories. At the time, Sharon's sensitivity to the Bush administration's refusal to endorse such a step led him to overrule Mofaz's recommendation. Interestingly, when Mofaz later crossed the civil-military fault lines to become Sharon's minister of defense, he was far less enthusiastic about Arafat's possible expulsion.

As of March 2003, Israel seems to have balanced what at times were conflicting interests of civilian and military leaders. At no point during the second intifada was there a danger of a serious civil-military rift, the significant differences of opinion between the defense minister and the prime minister on the one hand and the chief of staff on the other hand notwithstanding. More than once General Mofaz himself stated that while his opinions and the right to express them were not subject to anyone's authority, he did not question the fact that his actions were in fact subject to the authority of the country's civilian leaders. With a sufficient level of freedom and latitude surrounding the execution of any military operation, the IDF faithfully implemented the decisions and policy of its civilian superiors, specifically those of the prime minister.

Conclusion

The past two and a half years of Palestinian violence have affected the Israeli society at large in different ways, but have not eroded its resilience in any substantive way. Clearly it has become more pessimistic about the prospects of achieving peace with the Palestinians. Specifically, it has become increasingly weary of Palestinian leader Yassir Arafat whom it no longer regards as a viable negotiating partner.

On tactical issues the Israeli public has become distinctly more hawkish, supporting most measures that promise to end or even merely reduce the magnitude of Palestinian violence and its consequences. Strategically, however, this did not diminish the Israeli public's commitment to ending the conflict by separating itself from the Palestinians, notwithstanding the risks and painful concessions this would require. But to date this flexibility remains theoretical: its translation to reality seems contingent on an ending or at least a significant permanent reduction of the violence and the emerging of a viable alternative to Arafat's leadership.

Another effect of the Palestinian violence launched in September 2000 has been the heightened erosion of positive Jewish-Arab relations within Israel. While the violent clashes of October 2000 did not recur, other facets of the damage done to the relationship between the two communities have not been repaired. Most clearly, Jews and Arabs have remained alienated from one another, with very little commercial contact between them.

The intense violence of the past few years has sharpened tensions embedded in civil-military relations, even though the fundamental subordination of Israel's military to its civilian superiors has never been seriously questioned. Specifically, this tension has been well managed and in any case did not seem to exceed the tensions existing within the military itself or internal tensions between the Israeli society and its political leadership

Finally, the Israeli democracy continued to manifest a robust parliamentary system capable of mitigating and brokering social cleavages. It is still too early to tell whether Israeli politics is experiencing a permanent or even semi-permanent realignment. The reversal of its electoral system promised to strengthen the larger parties, an effect achieved by Likud in the 2003 elections. But this change was not sufficient to stop Labor's loss of public sympathy. While Likud's success can be interpreted as a public realignment to the right, such a conclusion should be balanced by the observation that Likud has demonstrated a gradual but consistent movement to the center of Israel's political map.

CHAPTER 7

Israel 2002:
A Strategic-Economic Assessment

Imri Tov

The Israeli economy between 2000 and 2002 was influenced by two sets of factors: the severe escalation of the violent confrontation between Israel and the Palestinians, and external processes of critical importance that lay outside the influence of Israeli decisionmakers. The strategic-economic assessment presented below examines the changes that took place in the state of the economy and the factors that contributed to the significant economic decline in 2002, particularly the influence of the global economy and the connection between the Israeli–Palestinian crisis and economic developments.

Performance of the Israeli Economy 2000–2002

Towards the end of 2000, following a number of years of continuing growth, an unremitting recession began in the Israeli economy that continued to intensify through 2002. This recession was reflected at all levels of the economy and over the course of the year exerted a negative impact on the capital markets, with the banks at their centers. The integrated Melnick Index charts the Israeli economy's development during this period (figure 1).[1] The overall picture is of a protracted

---

[1] The Melnick index, comprised of a number of sub-indices, is an aggregate measure of the behavior of the Israeli economy. The breakdown of the index for the month of September, as published in October 2002, is presented as an example. The data of the September index indicates: a 0.6% decline in the industrial manufacturing index in August, following the 0.2% decline in July; a 1.7% decline in the revenue index of the trade and services sectors in August, which followed the 2.9% decline during the preceding month; a 1.9% rise in the import volume in September, after a 2.9% decline during the month of August, and a 0.4% decline in salaried positions in the business sector in July, after a 0.4% decline in June. Compiled by Prof. Rafi Melnick, Arison School of Business, Interdisciplinary Center, Herzliya.

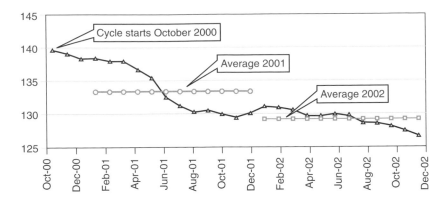

Figure 1. Melnick State of the Economy Index, October 2000-December 2002, 1994=100.

slowdown in activity, measured by industrial manufacturing, revenues of the trade and services sectors, import volume, and unemployment.

During the second half of 2002, a negative effect was recorded in the financial arena as well. This was evident in the higher cost of raising commercial capital overseas and in the increasing reluctance of the local banks to provide credit, leading to some discussion of a possible "credit crunch." Furthermore, the fall of the stock exchanges caused a drop in the values of the clients' securities in the banks, which in turn led to an increase in the volume of bad debts, exposing the banks to direct risk. The rise in risk and uncertainty in the local and overseas capital markets was translated into a curb on new projects, suspension of nonessential activities, and attempts to maintain the status quo in different sectors. The banks, being an important liquidity generator in the economy, became less willing to provide credit and to participate in the risks undertaken by the various economic units.

According to the overall index, the rate of the general slowdown in the economy eased during the second half of 2002. However, the consensus among most observers of the Israeli economy is that there was no significant improvement during this period. At the end of 2002, the economy still had not reached a turning point marking the beginning of the end of the crisis.

Key Macro Variables 2000-2002

Table 1 presents a status report of the country's macro-economic variables. The negative development of these variables was clear, and reflected a drop in the level of economic activity. The standard of living, measured by the rate of the change in personal consumption per capita, also declined. The extent of the economic recession was manifest by the fact that the gross domestic product (GDP) decreased since the end of 2000 by roughly $1400. The accelerated rate of inflation and the rise in unemployment completed the picture of the economy's negative development. The Israeli economy, with an annual growth potential of 5-6%, lost some $11–14 billion of GDP during the twenty-seven months under review.

Table 1. Israeli Economy Performance 2000 – 2002

Indicators	Aggregate rate of change
GDP growth	–1.9
Per capita growth	–5.5
Standard of living	–13.8
Exports	–2.3
Imports	–18.0
Investments	–8.5
Tourism	–12.8

Success of the Economic Policy Objectives

Macro-economic performance must be measured against the backdrop of the objectives that a country's economic policy are meant to achieve (table 2). These objectives are fairly universal but decisionmakers ascribe different quantitative values to each of these parameters, depending on the emphasis they place on the different dimensions of the economy. The picture presented in table 2 points to a recession in all parameters of Israel's economic policy.

Table 2. Evaluation of the Government Policy

The Objective	Desired change	Actual change
Full employment	+	–
Growth (GDP per capita)	+	–
"Improvement"[2] in international accounts	+	no significant change
Internal national debt	–	+
Inflation rate	–	+
Supply of the public's needs "to an appropriate extent"[3]	+	–
"More" equal distribution of income (wealth)	+	–

---

[2] "Improvement" intends to encompass a number of variables simultaneously, including: the economy's international balance of payments, the status of the external debts, and the capital movement in the short and long term. No material change in these variables was recorded, and therefore while as of the close of 2002 the desired growth did not occur, the behavior of the different variables in this group did not appear to be problematic.

[3] The critical public needs are: defense, health, education, physical infrastructures.

Since the decline in the economy's overall development began in late 2000, several troubling trends have emerged: an increase in the number of unemployed; a fall in the GDP back to the level of the mid 1990s; an increase in the internal national debt that once again exceeded 100% of the GDP; and a rise in inflation, which had dropped during the 1990s to 1-3% and reached 6-7% in 2002. The deviation from the targeted level of inflation also caused a rise in uncertainty among economic units. Income gaps grew according to the conventional indices. In government-provided goods and services (defense, health, education, and physical infrastructures) there was a sense that the gap between the aspirations and reality was too wide.

The State of the Economy: Explanatory Factors

Listed here are four sets of factors, discussed more extensively later in the chapter, that explain the Israeli economy's current state.

- Imbalanced growth among the various economic sectors during the 1990s. This imbalance reached its peak in 2000, and determined the economic conditions prevailing in the economy at the beginning of the period under examination.
- The global crisis, which began with the stock market crash in the United States and spread to other markets, led to disillusionment with the "New Economy" and in turn to a decline in the business cycle in the United States. These developments caused a drop in global demand for products and services from Israel as well as financial difficulties, mainly in raising capital.
- The Israeli government's macro-economic policy failure to re-stabilize the ratio between the exchange rates, interest rates, wages, and the internal price index in a fashion allowing the attainment of the objectives listed in table 2. Attempts by the government and the Bank of Israel to apply policy tools in order to stabilize the price ratios at a proper level were carried out in an uncoordinated fashion, without building public confidence. The cumulative effect was a growing sense of insecurity within the public as well as a lack of faith in the government's ability to manage the economy.
- The escalation of the conflict with the Palestinians, which caused a change in the behavior of the economic units, and consequently, both a drop in aggregate demand for goods and services and a change in the structure of assets among economic units. The escalation also caused a temporary supply crisis that affected economic development in the beginning of 2001, deriving from the layoff of tens of thousands of Palestinian workers who could not reach their workplaces in Israel.

The Imbalance of the 1990s

Israel's economy in the year 2000 followed several years of rapid growth that obscured the differing growth rates of the various sectors of the economy. This lack of balance is of critical importance to understanding the state of the economy following the downturn that began in the latter part of that year.

Since the mid 1990s, the Israeli economy has been characterized by the parallel development of two groups of sectors. The first group, the New Economy, revolved around the advanced hi-tech industries and start-up companies, which symbolized a new wave of capabilities, mainly in the field of communication and its offshoots. The business growth in this group skyrocketed, so that by 2000 it became the locomotive of the overall growth in the economy. Likewise, the collapse of this group of industries, following the sharp drop in demand for its products, affected Israel's economic statistics. The second group, the traditional industries, was not only unable to keep up with the hi-tech sector's growth rate: their slowdown began in the 1990s once the extended impact of the immigration from the former Soviet Union on their growth came to an end. The immigration was not replaced by any other external factor or policy stimulator that could have maintained the growth in this sector of the economy.

During the latter part of 2000, following the market crashes in the Western world, the hi-tech sector reverted to standard business-economic logic. As a result, the economy at the end of 2000 combined a traditional sector developing at a slow pace – relative to its overall growth potential – and a hi-tech sector, whose expansion was arrested after a number of years of exceptional growth. Yet even this exceptional growth, which was fed by an extraordinary wave of demand that ended suddenly during the latter part of 2000, succeeded in towing along only a portion of the traditional economy. Indeed, from 1997 until 2000, the GDP grew cumulatively by 9.5%. After deducting the product deriving from the hi-tech industries, the overall growth rate was only about 7% (1.6% per annum). During this period, the gross business sector product grew by more than 11.5%, versus 8.3% after deducting the hi-tech industries product. This indicates that the general slowdown in the Israeli economy, that is, the failure to realize its potential growth rate, began well before the events of 2000.

The state of the investments in real estate highlights the imbalance between the New Economy sectors and the traditional economy. While the total investments in real estate rose between 1997 and 2000, these investments actually diminished by about 8% if the investments of the hi-tech sector in real estate are deducted. The increase in investments in private dwellings was particularly meager, and the recession in this area has continued persistently since 1995. Thus, the residential construction sector, which in previous decades had served as one of the economy's important growth engines, experienced a protracted slowdown. The textile and clothing industries, metals and basic metals, paper, wood and their products, and leather products and footwear experienced a similar downturn. Were it not for the accelerated growth in the hi-tech industries, the overall slowdown in the economy would have been apparent much earlier. Thus, after a number of years of imbalanced growth, with technology-intensive sectors pulling up the rest of the economy, this growth engine stalled and then dragged down the entire economy.

Prolonged Crisis in the International Markets

The US economy has been contending with a slowdown since mid-2000. It then spread to a majority of the world's real and financial markets through the reduction of the global trade volume and a decline in the volume of activity in the associated financial markets. This chain reaction was relatively swift due to the expanded globalization phenomenon and the extensive trade relations between the various markets.

The first wave of the crisis in the US economy occurred during 2000, when the US capital market reacted to signs of a slowdown in the real sectors of the economy (the industrial, agricultural and service sectors), and when a series of stock market crashes arrested a number of years of continuous growth. This in turn was caused by a set of events, chief among them the bursting of the financial bubble induced by the demand for hi-tech products. The result was a series of steep drops in share prices in the various stock markets, creating a negative wealth effect on the entire American economy. The public felt that its assets on the stock exchange had lost value, and reacted accordingly. Three additional causes of the slowdown were a decline in profitability of industrial companies, following a drop in demand for their output; a cyclical contraction that was to be expected after years of consecutive growth; and a continuous rise in oil prices since 2000, which reduced corporate profits and the population's net income.

A recovery of the US economy – anticipated over 2001 and at the beginning of 2002 – did not gain momentum. In some portions of the economy, mainly in the hi-tech sector, the recession apparently had not ended at all. During 2002, it became evident that the attempts to invent a new economy, that is, one not based on conventional economic logic, not only failed, but fostered a gross breach of codes of business conduct and of accepted accounting principles, to the point of widespread fraud. The continuation of the economic slowdown exposed the fraudulence, and in 2002, it became clear that at least some of the profits of the corporate giants such as Enron and WorldCom had been generated by violating norms of business conduct. This second wave of the crisis caused Americans to lose faith in the capital markets, in the management of major corporations, and in the managers and formulators of business policy. This loss of faith, which destabilized the US capital markets, resounded throughout the economic world. Thus, what normally might have been a "U-shaped" process of entering and exiting a depression instead became a "W-shaped" (double "U" or a "double deep") double recession.

The crisis in hi-tech and sophisticated industries was not independent of the general cyclical crisis in the United States, but it did sport its own uniqueness. Specifically, it reflected a disillusionment with the New Economy – a term used to describe the attempt, which subsequently failed, to act on the basis of new economic principles whose fundamental assumption was that there would continue to be unlimited demand for high technologies. Relying on such an assumption, investors could capitalize on projected profits and realize future profits even before they actually materialized. Such assumptions and the immediate realization of estimated future profits were considered completely unreasonable under the codes of conduct of the "old" economic world.

The crisis in the technological industries did not result from bad management or an inadequate technological base. Rather, it resulted from misconceived demand generated by financial illusions and blind faith, in the limitless growth of demand for new technology. This affected the Israeli economy because a significant portion of these technologies were invented by the Israeli hi-tech sector, nourished by fertile imaginations and impressive technological skills, and accompanied by business naiveté and an indefatigable desire to get rich quickly. The cyclical slowdown and the US economy's slide into a recession dragged the entire world, including the Israeli economy, which was dependent on world markets, into a recession across the board, consequently bursting the New Economy bubble.

The global economic crisis caused the Israeli economy to experience a decline in the volume of financial activity and a reduction in the import and export activity of the various economic sectors. This decline had almost no effect on Israel's accounts with the global markets. In fact, no material change was recorded in Israel's external short and long term debt. In its balance of trade, imports and exports dropped simultaneously, and no major gap was created to cause a drain on foreign currency reserves. Hence, these reserves remained at a level providing a substantive safety net, and therefore, despite the overall economic crisis, no action was necessary to grapple with Israel's international business activity. The international financial markets, meanwhile, internalized at least some of the risks they saw in the economic-political state of the Israeli economy, leading them to downgrade de facto the credit rating of most of the economy's business activities (the Israeli banking sector activity was downgraded officially). This lowered rating was expressed in higher costs of raising new funds and in difficulties in obtaining various types of credit lines. On the other hand, politically motivated attempts on the part of international bodies to boycott Israel's economic activity were made only randomly and did not leave any lasting imprint.

Thus, the eventual downgrading of Israel's credit rating and of its banks resulted from a prolonged internal imbalance combining a high internal debt, an uncontrolled budget deficit, and the failure to conduct a policy acceptable to the credit rating agencies. This lack of internal balance was bound to cause a disruption of the relative stability of Israel's international financial activity, if not harsher difficulties for the national economy. Another emblem of the change in international perceptions of the Israeli economy and the level of attributed risk was the slowdown in the transfer of funds from overseas, despite the higher interest rates offered in Israel.

In summary, the global crisis affected the Israeli economy through the reduction in aggregate demand in the Western world, at the heart of which was a sharp drop in individual wealth, which derived from a fall in stock market values. Another external factor was the rise in oil prices, which negatively prejudiced Israel's terms of trade. On the other hand, the Bank of Israel continued to hold foreign currency reserves exceeding $22 billion. Capital exports did not turn into a capital drain that might have endangered the stability of the currency, and as of early 2003, no material change in net capital movements has been observed, despite the concerns about the availability of resources for financing banking activity and/ or about the stability of foreign resident deposits.

The Economic Policy

Notwithstanding that the most important causes of the economic crisis in Israel lay outside the influence of policymakers, sound macro-economic policy would have made it possible to curtail the damage, prevent exacerbation of undesirable processes, and provide relief for the various sectors during the crisis period.

There were a number of reasons for Israel's failure to formulate and manage macro-economic policy. First, there were no adequate governing institutions and rules for planning, allotting, formulating, and managing long term policy. During 2000 and most of 2001, there was a failure to anticipate that the crisis would continue for an extended period of time rather than for a few months only. This was largely due to the absence of mechanisms for assessment, planning, and implementation for the mid and long term. Similarly, there was a failure to define the economic impact of the escalated Palestinian conflict. Even the defense community's evaluation that the violence between Israel and the Palestinians would continue for some time was not adopted as a working assumption in the macro-economic sphere.

The prolonged crisis with the Palestinians created multiplier effects that rippled through the various sectors in the economy until at a critical stage, the capital market and the banking system were affected. Possible signs that the crisis hit these markets surfaced in the financial statements of Israel's banks for the year 2002. Generally, damage to the banking system is likely to be expressed by a lack of resources for financing economic activity and by a rise in the cost of available financing – factors that are liable to paralyze real and financial activity. In Israel, the absence of a mechanism for long term allocation of public resources, together with the absence of decisionmaking institutions for formulating long term policy, created a decisionmaking structure that attended to the short term, and lacked the long range perspectives and mechanisms needed to extricate the economy from the crisis.

One of the negative consequences of the focus on the immediate was the absence of a bridging policy to prevent the collapse of industries and other businesses through governmental intervention in the market mechanism. Long term, direct, intervention in market processes is not desirable. However, short term government assistance in the form of credit guarantees and/or direct assistance can prevent collapse of businesses caught in a temporary crisis, whereas rebuilding such businesses after their total collapse would be more costly to the national economy. Short term support measures must be accompanied by a clear plan for their termination (an "exit strategy") so that they do not remain intact well after the conditions justifying the initial assistance have expired.

A second consequence of the short term perspective was that the Maastricht guidelines have de facto become the unofficial criteria for policymakers and policy-implementers. These guidelines define strict quantitative targets that limit the leeway of policymakers and managers in macro-economic decisions. In Israel's case, these guidelines now determine the permitted ratio of the state budget deficit to the GDP, the "correct" size of the national debt relative to the state's GDP, the limits of the internal and external debts, and the maximum permitted annual inflation rate.

The Maastricht guidelines reflect the importance of economic globalization and the extent to which the world economy now affects Israel's economic policy. Outside economic entities, such as credit rating agencies, banks and financial institutions, and sovereign lenders, view these guidelines as international standards that define the soundness of economic policy. At the same time, the Maastricht guidelines have been exploited more than once by policymakers to convince the population that any deviation from their stipulations would provoke a negative market reaction. Thus, policymakers set budget priorities that allowed compliance with the limit on the budget deficit set by the guidelines, which became an almost exclusive criterion for formulating and implementing macro-economic policy. In turn, this involved hard choices, for example, between additions to the defense or welfare budgets, or reducing the income of the weak strata – after welfare payments reached such dimensions that only by limiting them could the budget be balanced. Due to the social ramifications and political considerations, decisions on welfare cuts were consistently postponed until they could no longer be avoided in run-up to the 2003 budget.

Reliance on the Maastricht guidelines, without mechanisms for formulating and managing long term policy, caused economic distortions that were aggravated as Israel's economic crisis deepened. Rules that define boundaries of permitted economic activity during normal times proved inadequate in a crisis environment. Not surprisingly, leading European Community member states, such as France and Germany, had no choice but to deviate from the Maastricht guidelines in times of severe crisis.

In Israel's case, as adherence to the Maastricht guidelines denied decision-makers the freedom to implement fiscal tools for managing the economy, the responsibility for such management reverted to the Bank of Israel, which activates monetary tools for this purpose. The result, however, is that economic policy becomes subordinated to the priorities of the Bank of Israel – arresting inflation.

A third consequence of the decisionmaking structure was the insufficient coordination between the Bank of Israel, which is responsible for implementing monetary tools, and the Ministry of Finance, which in Israel's case is the central body responsible for utilizing fiscal tools. This lack of coordination caused imbalances between interest rates, exchange rates, wages, and the price index, imbalances that were not handled simultaneously using proper tools. Yet it is doubtful that correcting these imbalances is possible without coordination among the parties responsible for managing economic activity. In the absence of a balance between the four variables, uncertainty within the economic units intensified, damaging the credibility of the economic leadership, and heightened anxiety among those setting the country's rating in the international markets.

Finally, bureaucratic processes curbed the implementation of policy programs and plans, a chronic problem in Israel's public sector. Furthermore, over the past decade, Israel has lacked an economic leadership that commanded public confidence and respect, demonstrated professional skills in the economic realm, and enjoyed the prime minister's full backing.

These ramifications undermined the ability to exercise a policy that would correct, or at least offset, the exogenic influences that affected Israel's economy since 2000. Moreover, the lack of clarity and consistency in government policy sparked volatile conduct within the economic units, which contributed to even greater instability and intensified the uncertainty and risks involved in economic activity.

Escalation of the Israeli-Palestinian Conflict

The escalation of the Israeli-Palestinian conflict influenced the behavior of Israeli economic units. As the level of the violence increased, the impact on the economy became more severe. Beyond the casualties incurred and the direct damages to property, the sense of risk and uncertainty within the economic units increased, altering the economic behavior of the population. Fear among individuals that they or their families would be killed, injured, and/or lose their property increased. Anxieties intensified when the escalation occurred inside residential areas or adjacent to centers of economic and social activity, and peaked with the suicide attacks that evoked the public's feeling that the conflict cannot be resolved politically.

The uncertainty within the private sector created a change in the relative cost of future activity versus present activity, with increased focus on present activity and thoughts of future activities suppressed. Consequently, activities whose yields were expected to materialize only in the future were cut back. From the standpoint of a complete life cycle, individuals became "poorer." That is, the income expected to be received during one's lifetime ("permanent income"), calculated at its present value, was reduced, and this translated into a drop in both present and future economic activity. The behavior of the private sector was characterized by a drop in leisure product consumption and in the suspension and even reduction of real investments, because individuals preferred to accumulate cash rather than real assets. Under such conditions reduced investments were bound to diminish the productive capital stocks of the economy.

The Israeli-Palestinian crisis had other ramifications. The ongoing escalation caused external tourism to come to a near-complete halt, and caused foreign businesspersons to fear traveling to Israel. Israeli investors tried to spread their financial investments among financial institutions abroad. The costs involved in the effort to thwart hostile acts within densely populated areas rose, and the financial burden associated with these efforts was passed on, at least in part, to the individual consumer. The overall impact was a drop in the aggregate demand in the economy, which led to unrealized potential for economic growth. This added to other negative effects of the continuing escalation of violence on the country's GDP.

The reaction in the public sector was the opposite, where public needs grew in two areas: defense and assistance to populations directly affected by the violence. The increase in such public expenditures partially offset the decline in private demand. However, the continuation of the violence did not permit the return to regular economic activity, as risks to person and property remained at a high level. Moreover, as the escalation of the violence continued, the damage to the economy also grew and had a cumulative effect that spread to the different sectors of the economy. By early 2003 it seemed that even the banks and the financial markets and institutions would be hurt severely, making sound economic policy more crucial than ever.

Quantitative Estimate of Escalation Damages

The impact of the escalation in the conflict was evident first and foremost in the damage to the tourism, construction, and agricultural sectors. The continued recession in tourism – a clear result of the uncertainty and the growing personal risk – made it difficult for some hotel chains to survive, leading them to freeze their business or dip into their limited reserve funds. The damage to the agricultural and construction sectors resulted from the disappearance of Palestinian labor due to the closures of the West Bank and Gaza that followed the outbreak of the violence in late 2000. The further escalation of the violence during the following two years intensified the direct damage to these sectors, particularly through a decline in overall demand, and spread to affiliated sectors, mainly construction-related services and industries. Continued fears and economic uncertainty caused additional drops in demand. The slowdown in the economy occurred in all sectors with the exception of defense-related industries, which despite its expansion could not offset the overall downward direction of the economy.

By March 2003 damages caused directly by the violence were estimated at tens of millions of dollars, more than 750 people killed, and thousands wounded. These direct damages acted as catalysts for secondary effects, with enormous cumulative costs. Estimates of the annual damages range between 3% and 7% of GDP.

The behavior of the economy during the present period of violence differed from its performance during previous such periods, with the exception of the 1948-49 War of Independence. During previous conflicts, beginning with the 1956 Sinai Campaign, negative impacts were reversed over time as the violent phase of the conflict was relatively short and the process of recovery was set in motion soon after the damage occurred.

The state of the Israeli economy in early 2003, however, is far different, and therefore does not leave policymakers with many options. The desire to achieve rapid economic growth is understandable but not realistic. The time it will take to extricate the country from the economic slump is liable to be longer than currently expected as the negative forces affecting the economy have yet to change direction. Therefore, preventing a financial crisis seems an absolute priority for government policy.

The year 2002 will be recorded as the worst in Israel's economic history since the beginning of the 1950s. Every index pointed to negative developments that ran counter to Israel's economic goals and added to the cumulative effect of harmful processes that had begun in previous years. If the process of exiting the recession is further delayed, government intervention will become even more important to prevent the collapse of sectors that cannot bridge the crisis period on their own. In this context, the government must activate recovery engines that would accelerate the overall demand.

CHAPTER 8

The Israeli Arabs

Nachman Tal

With the establishment of the State of Israel, there were 156,000 Arabs in the country. In 2002, including Arabs of East Jerusalem and the Golan Heights, Israeli Arabs numbered approximately 1,250,000, compared to 5,400,000 Jews, comprising nearly 20% of Israel's population. Eighty-two percent of the Arab population in 2002 were Muslim, 9% was Christian, and 9% was Druze. The Central Bureau of Statistics projected that by the year 2020 the number of Israeli Arabs would reach 2,100,000, compared to 6,500,000 Jews. If the estimated number of Palestinians in the West Bank and Gaza Strip is added to this figure, then in seventeen years (2020) the population between the Mediterranean Sea and Jordan River will soar to 15,000,000 people, with the Jews comprising only 45% of this figure.

This is why demography has become a burning issue in Israel, one that occupies many government agencies, academic departments, and independent think tanks. The demographic vector is undoubtedly a serious threat to Israel's existence as a Jewish democratic state. It is a long-term issue with ramifications beyond the scope of this study, but nonetheless provides the context for the discussion that follows.

The tumultuous events of October 2000 left an indelible mark on relations between Israeli Arabs and Israel's Jewish citizens and state institutions. In a spontaneous virulent outburst of rioting in Israel's Arab sector, groups of young Arabs took to the streets in Arab villages in northern Israel with an unprecedented intensity of violence. Angry confrontations had occurred before between Israeli Arabs and the State of Israel, such as the "Land Day" events of March 30, 1976, which resulted in the deaths of six Arabs. The riots of October 2000, however, which coincided with the opening shots of the al-Aqsa Intifada, proved to be among the most ferocious internal clashes in the state's history. In a show of violence and civil disobedience to challenge Israeli sovereignty, demonstrators battled with police, blocked roads, and channeled the brunt of their anger against state symbols and institutions, desecrating the Israeli flag and trashing post offices, banks, police stations, traffic lights, and gas stations.

The riots exacted high casualties: thirteen Arabs and one Jew were killed. Beyond the death toll, the delicate fabric of Arab-Jewish relations that had been painstakingly woven in Israel over the years was damaged, as mutual animosity reached boiling temperatures.

The two immediate causes for the outbreak of the rioting were Ariel Sharon's visit to the Temple Mount on September 28, 2000, perceived as a provocation and sacrilege of a Muslim holy place, and the deaths of seven Palestinians killed in the Temple Mount area following Sharon's visit, which ignited tempers and pushed incitement to the streets. These catalysts were boosted by the traditional focal points of friction between the Arab public and the State of Israel that intensified when the October events erupted, aggravating the street sentiment, fueling the riots, and leaving the Arab leadership at a loss to control the mobs.

As Israeli Arabs had increasingly identified with their brethren in the Palestinian territories over the years, the October riots were in part – but not only – an expression of solidarity with the Palestinians. Frustration and despair had been mounting in the Arab public for years based on the feeling of discrimination by the Israeli government and the belief that no Jewish regime would be prepared to practice equality in budget allotments, land holdings, infrastructure development, and housing construction, or deal equitably with the problem of Arab refugees and stateless persons. The Barak government had been a disappointment to the Arab population, when poverty levels rose and unemployment increased, which added to the Arabs' sense of alienation from the state. A generational change in the Arab sector also began to offer different approaches: the leadership was younger and more militant, especially Arab Members of Knesset (MKs) who stoked the flames of incitement and themselves joined in the October street demonstrations. Other factors energizing the riots included the widespread lack of law and order in the Arab sector where civil disobedience and contempt for the Israeli police had become the norm, coupled with a growing tendency to violence. Thus when moderate leaders tried to rein in the crowds, they realized that it was a lost cause.

Even before the bitter taste left by the riots passed, the Israeli Arabs' militant leadership instigated another sharp, radical, and anti-Israeli move by boycotting the elections for prime minister in February 2001. The elections resulted in the downfall of the Barak government and the ascendancy of Ariel Sharon. Only 18% of the Arab voters voted on election day, compared with a 60% turnout in the Jewish sector. The reasons for the Arab boycott were the blame placed on the Israeli government for the deaths of the thirteen Arab citizens the previous October, and the Arab leadership's pronouncement that both candidates, Sharon and Barak, were unworthy of office because of their hostility to Israeli Arabs and the Palestinians. Coming on the heels of the October riots, the pervading atmosphere among the Israeli Arab public at the time of the elections was one of disillusionment and depression.

Approximately one month after the October 2000 events, Prime Minister Ehud Bark ordered a state commission of inquiry to examine what had happened, headed by Supreme Court Justice Theodore Orr. In late August 2002 the Orr Commission finished its public hearings, which included testimony from 377 witnesses. Fourteen people received letters of warning from the commission that they were liable to be hurt by its conclusions. Among those admonished were former Prime Minster Barak, the previous minister of internal security and foreign minister, Shlomo Ben-Ami, and the former police commissioner, Yehuda Wilk. The panel charged that the deteriorating course of events in the Arab sector could have been anticipated and that Prime Minister Barak had failed to prepare the police adequately for the likely consequences of the decline. Letters of warning were also sent to several Arab leaders, charging them with incitement and failure to act to restore quiet.

Over the two and a half years since the disturbances, the Arab sector tried to evaluate what transpired. The majority remained convinced that the protests were justified in light of Israel's discriminatory policy, though some voices claimed that Israeli Arabs had crossed certain red lines and caused an excessively sharp rift in Arab-Jewish relations, demonstrated, for example, by an unofficial Jewish boycott of the Arab commercial sector. The Democratic National Assembly (Balad), the Islamic Movement (IM), and the radical movement Sons of the Villages all justified the violent events and the absence of Arab participation in the 2001 elections for prime minister.

Neither the Israeli government nor the Arab leadership acted sufficiently to heal the breach. The October riots and the abstention from the elections elevated the question of the Arab citizenry's relationship to the state to one of the most crucial issues on Israel's national agenda. The subject became the focus of attention in every quarter - the media, academia, conferences, and seminars – yet little was done to alleviate past ills, and indeed, the focal points of friction between Israeli Arabs and the state continued unresolved.

Growing Friction with the State

The Israeli Arab public's sense of alienation towards the Jewish state, government institutions, and the Jewish population continued in 2002. The Jewish "economic boycott" that began after the violent October 2000 events and was manifested by rare visits to Arab markets, restaurants, and businesses in Arab towns and villages bolstered this feeling. In cities with large percentages of Arab residents, such as Haifa, Acre, and Jaffa, the boycott was milder and the situation less antagonistic. Nevertheless, this economic pressure, together with the existing high levels of poverty and unemployment, exacerbated the economic plight and reinforced the atmosphere of gloom within the Arab sector. Another factor contributing to the sense of alienation was the Orr Commission's hearings, which reawakened the tension and anger as the Arab public recalled the October 2000 events, especially the high number of casualties. The right wing government headed by Ariel Sharon was also inherently inimical to the Arab minority.

An important phenomenon in the Arab sector was the heightened identification and solidarity with the Palestinians in the West Bank and Gaza Strip. The unremitting Israeli-Palestinian violence contributed to this process, especially during and after Operation Defensive Shield in April 2002. In dozens of towns and villages, Israeli Arabs responded by demonstrating in support of the Palestinians, with tens of thousands of people marching in protest against Israeli military activity in the Palestinian territories. Wide coverage was given in the Israeli Arab newspapers to the Palestinians' suffering, and at the same time Israeli Arabs collected money and supplies for their brethren. In a related development, 2002 witnessed a sharp rise in Israeli Arabs' involvement in terrorism.

The increased terrorist activity joined the October riots to aggravate the Jewish public's animosity towards Israeli Arabs. Surveys indicated that the Jewish majority was convinced that Israeli Arabs were untrustworthy citizens who could even be regarded as traitors. A call was voiced for the "transfer" of Israeli Arabs, and many Jewish public figures, researchers, and right-wing politicians publicly supported the transfer of the Arab city of Umm el-Fahm (population 40,000) from Israeli jurisdiction to the Palestinian Authority (PA) in the framework of a negotiated "territorial exchange." The Arab public perceived that the Jewish public and the state authorities were accusing the entire Israeli Arab community of complicity in terror and betrayal despite the small number of Israeli Arabs (a few dozen) actually involved in these acts. This attitude forced the Arab public to defend itself and take countermeasures.

A number of publicized decisions by the Israeli establishment heightened the Israeli Arabs' sense of alienation further. The decisions to indict MK Azmi Bishara and to prohibit Sheikh Ra'id Salah, the leader of IM's radical wing, from traveling abroad were perceived as concerted actions against the Arab sector. The Central Elections Committee's disqualification in January 2003 of Ahmed Tibi and Azmi Bishara, as well as of Bishara's party, to run for the Knesset, added fuel to the fire. These injunctions, restrictions, and bans instilled feelings of a persecuted minority in the Israeli Arab public and bolstered the sense of consistent relegation to an inferior status to increase the hatred and sense of alienation. The subsequent Supreme Court decision to allow Tibi's and Bishara's candidacies lowered the tension somewhat, and resulted in increased support for Bishara's party.

Along with the altercations and confrontations particular to the last two years, the traditional focal points of friction between Israeli Arabs and the state remained intact: civil equality, land rights, the Bedouin of the Negev, the "local absentees" (domestic refugees), illegal construction, and religious property.

Civil Equality

The Israeli Arabs' desire for a share of the state's resources proportionate to their percentage in the population, with an opportunity in various areas of life equal to that of Israeli Jews, has been their main demand over the last several years.

Israeli Arabs insisted on equal budgeting for development in their sector and urged their local councils to correct gross inequities in resources allocations. Hundreds of classrooms were lacking, welfare services were sorely inadequate, and unemployment was on an upward surge. In June 2002 an official report listed twenty-six communities as centers of unemployment (i.e., with over 10% of the inhabitants out of work) - all of them in the Arab sector. Heading the list were three communities in the Galilee - Kafr Manda (17.9%), Dir Hana (15.9%), and Tamra (15.2%) - and Tel Sheva in the Negev (14.9%). In Arab Nazareth and Umm el-Fahm, unemployment registered at 11.2%.

The following data of 2000-2002 testified to the large gaps in the integration of Israeli Arabs in various state professions. Israeli Arabs accounted for only 5 to 6% of all civil servants, although they comprised approximately 20% of the total population. In addition, one-third of Arab civil servants were employed at ad hoc jobs, and over half were on a temporary payroll. Most of the Arab civil servants worked in government hospitals or were employed by the Ministry of Education as teachers or pre-school educators, or were retained by the Ministry of Religious Affairs as Muslim judges (qadis). Out of the 13,000 tenured workers employed by the Israel Electric Company, only six were Arabs.

The poverty report published in November 2002 shocked Israeli public opinion in its announcement that 42% of Arab families subsist below the poverty line, compared to 17.7% of the population at large. Fifty-two percent of Arab children were defined as impoverished, nearly double the 27% figure of the overall population of children.

This gap resulted from decades of government neglect and indifference, and a slate of alternative priorities that have marginalized the Arab populace. Israeli governments consistently avoided dealing with basic problems in all areas of the Arab sector, and ignored the initiation of programs for committing Arab and Israeli Jews to confidence-building measures. No Israeli government showed signs of launching a major, all-inclusive long-term policy for improving the quality of life in the Arab sector, a policy that formally and definitively outlines the rights and obligations of the Arabs to the state. Little wonder, then, that the large gaps created over time between the sectors instilled a sense of distrust in the Arab public. Although nearly every government that came to power designed plans for dealing with the Arab sector, no timetables for their full implementation were ever drafted.

The most recent plan was drawn up during the Barak government and was approved in October 2000 against the background of the tension in the Arab public in the aftermath of the bloody events. The blueprint was termed "The Development Plan for the Arab Sector," but it was popularly referred to as "The Four Billion

Plan" because of the shekel sum allotted for its implementation over the years 2000-2004. Basically, the plan called for conditions in every of area of Arab life to match those in the rest of the country. The program focused on ways to upgrade the infrastructure with more paved roads and improved sewage disposal. Plans called for constructing more educational facilities, adding hundreds of classrooms and class hours, and doubling the number of students in technological programs. For the first time, housing options for thousands of young couples were proposed through low-term grants, loans, and mortgages. Overall unemployment was slated to drop from 10% to 6%.

The heads of the Arab municipal councils agreed to the plan, despite some skepticism as to whether it was sufficient to effect any real narrowing of the social and economic divide. Expectation mounted in the Arab sector once the plan was approved by the Sharon government.

However, despite initial implementation of the program, no actual progress was made in the Arab settlements. Budgetary constraints resulted in several government offices cutting the allocations designated for the Arab sector far more than the slash in the general budget. The following statistics attest to the very gradual implementation of the program in three government ministries between February and April 2002. Additional cuts made in this period (to pay for IDF activity in the territories – and especially Operation Defensive Shield) undoubtedly impaired the plan's implementation even more:

- For development of the housing infrastructure, the Ministry of Housing allotted Arab settlements the sum of 66.5 million shekels (NIS), or 2.6% of the ministry's budget for 2002 (2.75 billion NIS).
- The Health Ministry provided the Arab sector with 1.6 million NIS in 2002 (out of a 227 million NIS budget).
- In 2002 the Ministry of Education began implementing the "Five-Year Plan" in an attempt to address the longstanding education deficiencies in the Arab sector. According to a special bulletin published in November 2001, within the framework of "The Four Billion Plan" the ministry was to allot the Arab sector 50 million NIS in 2001 and the same amount in 2002. In practice, 41 million NIS were apportioned in 2001 and 38 million NIS in 2002. In other words, a deficit of 21 million NIS already accrued in the implementation of the plan.

Economic and social distress intensified in all areas of life due to Israel's general economic crisis. The Arab sector marked the opening of the 2001-2002 school year with protests and strikes because of the over-burdened educational infrastructure. Generally, however, the protests, demonstrations, and strikes in 2002 did not deteriorate into disturbances of the peace and mob violence. Significantly, the annual observance of Land Day passed quietly on in 2002 and 2003.

The Land Issue – the Bedouin in the Negev as a Case Study

The second focal point of friction continued to be the most sensitive one – the unresolved land issue. Indeed, the concept of "land" reflected the main breach between Jews and Arabs in Israel. At the end of the War of Independence, the State of Israel expropriated approximately 4,588,973 million dunams (1.2 million acres) of abandoned Arab lands. By 1950 only 529,428 dunams (130,000 acres) remained in Arab possession. Israeli Arabs viewed the loss of their lands in terms of expulsion and uprooting, and thus the issue survived as an open wound and an ongoing symbol of injustice, discrimination, and exploitation.

The bitterest point of contention over this issue remained among the Bedouin in the Negev. Some background to the problem is pertinent for an understanding of its current importance.

On the eve of the War of Independence there were 60,000 Bedouin in the Negev, the southern part of Israel. By the end of the war only about 9,000 were left; the rest either fled or were expelled. Another 3,000 returned within the framework of the family reunification plan, so that by 1952 the Negev had a Bedouin population of 13,000. As of 2002 there were 130,000 Bedouin there (with another 50,000 in the Galilee). The natural growth rate of the Negev Bedouin was 4.5% per annum, one of the highest in the world and without parallel in Israel. At this rate, the Bedouin population doubled itself every seventeen years. An average Bedouin family consisted of eight to ten people, while in polygamous Bedouin families there were often sixteen to twenty-nine children. Predictably, then, the Bedouin population was overwhelmingly young, with 60% of the people under the age of nineteen. Unemployment ran very high (over 36%), and 60% of the Bedouin children lived below the poverty line.

Notwithstanding numerous social welfare issues, the controversy over land ownership was the focus of the sharpest discord between the state and the Bedouin of the Negev. After the establishment of the state, the Bedouin were concentrated under a military government administration in the area bordered by the Beer Sheva valley and Kibbutz Shoval in the north, and the cities of Beer Sheva in the west, Arad in the east, and Dimona in the south. This region was defined as a "restricted area" with Bedouin dispersed across a 1.5 million dunam area. The state claimed the land for its own, based on the Ottoman Land Law of 1858 whereby unregistered land, termed "dead" (mawat; literally unworthy of cultivation) land, reverts to the state. The Bedouin filed claims for 790,000 dunams in the restricted area between, while the state recognized their rights to 400,000 dunams. The number of landowners was estimated at 20,000, but 25% of the claimants were uninterested in reaching a financial arrangement because of social and political reasons. Many claimants were unable to produce ownership certificates (tabu) for the land, and Israeli governments have consistently postponed a land arrangement on the Jewish people's last and largest land reserves.

In the 1970s Negev land was primarily expropriated for military purposes or industrial areas. The peace agreement with Egypt and the accompanying withdrawal from Sinai called for the confiscation of land in the Tel Malhata region (between Beer Sheva and Arad) and the transfer of 5,000 Bedouin in order to build the Nevatim airbase. Because of Bedouin opposition to vacate land, the Knesset passed the "Peace Law" in 1980 that legalized land expropriation, yet for the first time the government recognized the need to compensate the Bedouin. The idea was that the Tel Malhata arrangement would serve as the basis of a comprehensive resolution of the land conflict in the Negev, but little progress occurred since then. The Bedouin refused to relocate to permanent residences until the overall land issue was solved. As of 2002, therefore, half of the Bedouin population (approximately 65,000) lived in seven recognized towns (Tel Sheva, Rahat, Aro'er, Kuseifa, Segev Shalom, Lakiya, and Hura), and half (65,000) lived in unrecognized settlements south of Beer Sheva. Municipal authorities did not supply unrecognized settlements (estimated at forty-five) basic infrastructure components such as electricity, water, telephones, and roads, but the Bedouin continued to dwell there so as not to sever or risk any connection with their lands. Added to these Bedouin grievances were the education system that was rife with shortcomings, including large distances between homes and schools (sometimes dozens of kilometers); insufficient numbers of classes; dilapidated structures; lack of electricity, water, roads, certified teachers; and the presence of non-Bedouin teachers (37%), who were not accepted by the community.

This painful situation resulted in an upsurge in political and religious radicalization. Studies and surveys consistently pointed to the significant drop in the level of identification with the state among the Bedouin and the growing reluctance to enlist in the IDF. Conspicuous violations of law and order occurred over the last two years such as stoning passing vehicles, erecting roadblocks, and sabotaging pipelines and infrastructure facilities.

In early January 2003, a five year, 1.175 billion NIS plan to address the needs of the Bedouin population in the Negev was presented. The plan, prepared by an inter-ministerial committee in consultation with Negev authorities, included proposals regarding a land arrangement with the Bedouin in the Negev, large budgetary allocations for infrastructure and settlement developments, the establishment of new settlements, and the strengthening of law enforcement measures in an attempt to combat the phenomenon of Bedouin seizure of state land. Two months later, the program had not yet reached the Knesset for approval. While approval was likely, the real test lay in implementation, as many plans before it have remained as plans on paper, even following government approval, with no translation into practice.

No clashes related to land were reported in 2002 between Israeli Arabs and state authorities, excluding one incident that nearly erupted into a serious outbreak but was resolved at the last moment. The issue touched on the paving of the new trans-Israel highway that would entail the confiscation of Arab lands belonging to farmers in the central region of Tira and Taibe. The matter set off a tense dispute between the highway authority and the government on one side, and the land owners together with local and national Arab leaders, on the other. The Arabs' rejection of an agreement stemmed from economic and nationalistic reasons. The dispute delayed progress on the roadwork until the sides reached a compromise based on an equitable compensation of land to the Arab property holders. Yet the absence of violent incidents over the land issue did not auger a turning point, since the problem remained a festering sore, and further confrontations were to be expected.

Another potential volatile dispute concerned unilateral separation from the occupied territories and the creation of a security fence between Israel and the Palestinians in the West Bank. On June 16, 2002, the Israeli government decided to construct the first stage of a 110 kilometer long security fence adjacent to the Green Line on the east, extending from Kfar Salem (Jenin district) in the north to the Tulkarm-Kalkilya region. Property owners in the area where the security fence would be erected received divestiture edicts based on emergency regulations. Israeli Arabs severely criticized the establishment of a security fence because of its implications: expropriation of their land, fear that their property would be divided between the Israeli side and Palestinian side, and concern that family and commercial ties with the West Bank would be hurt. Despite the efforts taken to arrive at understandings and accommodations with Israeli Arabs, the construction of the security fence was liable to turn into a focal point of friction between the two sides.

The Local Absentees (Domestic Refugees)
After the War of Independence and the establishment of the State of Israel, there was a class of people who lost control of their property. They were defined as "absentees," according to various laws dealing with abandoned property. Over the years they were called "local absentees" or domestic refugees. Approximately 20,000 Arabs who remained in the country after the signing of the ceasefire agreements were defined as local absentees (while in 2002 their number was estimated at 150,000-250,000). Local absentees fell into three categories:

1. People not present at their place of residence during the capture of their village by the Israeli army but who were situated in some area controlled at the time by enemy forces that later became part of the State of Israel.
2. People who returned to Israel after the war within the family reunification arrangement or as infiltrators, and were allowed to remain in the country, but in their absence their lands passed into custodianship of the state.

3. People who were removed from their villages during and immediately after the war for reasons of Jewish settlement, development, and security (for example, villagers from Ikrit and Biram near the Lebanese border).

Most of the dispossessed were relocated to Arab settlements near their original villages, yet all attempts to solve their plight by resettling them in their new places of residence have failed. In 1992 the local absentees established the "National Committee for the Protection of the Rights of the Dispossessed" that recently increased its activity under the assumption that the Palestinian Authority would avoid dealing with the issue of uprooted Arabs who were citizens of Israel. The committee held meetings, maintained contact with refugee organizations, and sustained the struggle for the Arabs' right to return to their original villages. Beyond pursuing the specific goals, these activities also inculcated radicalization among tens of thousands of dispossessed Israeli Arabs.

The painful tale of uprooted villagers from Ikrit and Biram, who were removed from their homes in 1948 with the unfulfilled promise that they would be allowed to return soon after, dominated the issue of displaced persons in Israel. Almost all new governments ritually drafted plans for resettling displaced persons in their original villages but were then deterred from setting a precedent for similar demands of thousands of other uprooted Arabs living in Israel. The Ikrit-Biram issue refused to fade away quietly. The conflict was temporarily suspended, following the Supreme Court's decision to accept the Sharon government's plea to grant it time to study the issue.

Starting in the mid-1990s, the National Committee of the Dispossessed made regular visits to abandoned villages in order to strengthen the ties and ensure the upkeep of sites still standing, especially mosques, churches, and cemeteries. The visits have occurred on Israel's Independence Day, which for many Israeli Arabs has become "Disaster Day" (al-Nakba), and have expressed a resurgence of the collective and historical memory of the Nakba – the catastrophe of the loss of the Palestinians' land in the course of the 1948 war. Interestingly, Israel's jubilee anniversary in 1998 sparked a widespread commemoration of the Nakba by Israeli Arabs, especially on the part of the dispossessed. It was as though the Jewish celebration of the fiftieth anniversary of the state reminded the Arab citizens of the fiftieth year of their catastrophe. Since then they have begun commemorating the date annually. Other factors, too, contributed to this awakening: the rise of a new generation of Arab youth (the third generation), which in contrast to the previous one – that of the Nakba – was not witness to the defeat and did not live under the military government. The third generation was unwilling to repress the bitter memory of 1948; it has rejected a celebration of the Zionist state that was created for the Jewish people, and at the expense of the Arab minority. Perhaps predictably, participation in the Nakba events multiplied in 2001 and 2002 because of the anti-Israeli atmosphere following the October 2000 violence.

Much attention has been paid in the media, literature, and arts by Israeli Arabs to the Nakba issue and the heritage, memory, and enshrinement of the 400 Arab villages destroyed in 1948. Voices in the Arab leadership and Arab public bodies have demanded that the State of Israel issue an historical apology for the injustice perpetrated in 1948 and take official responsibility for redressing the personal and collective misery of the Arab victims by enacting legislation to establish an official memorial day for the "Nakba," the Palestinian Disaster.

Illegal Construction

Illegal construction in the Arab sector, a known and ongoing phenomenon for several decades, remained a source of tension with the state's authorities. Over the years tens of thousands of unauthorized buildings were erected. Successive governments avoided enforcing the law and in many instances preferred to look aside rather than apply the legal injunctions for dismantling illegal constructions. As a result, the problem has mushroomed out of all proportion. In the Negev, for example, the Bedouin have built over 24,000 illegal edifices, most of which lie on state lands. In addition to the non-enforcement of the law, failure to come up with an approved master plan for communities in the Arab sector has also contributed to the phenomenon. Without a master plan, construction permits cannot be issued, and the majority of the Arab regional councils did not have approved master plans.

Numerous government committees addressed the dilemma of illegal construction and suggested various solutions, but invariably the recommendations were shelved. On rare occasions the authorities, with police assistance, attempted to implement court injunctions and destroy illegal edifices. In almost every case this led to clashes, threats, and organized protests by the national Arab leadership. In 2002 authorities destroyed a number of illegally built houses in the Negev, in Lod, Ramle, and Majd al-Krum in the north. Except for a violent response by Bedouin in the Negev, the demolitions – under heavy police protection – occurred peacefully. Overall, it was expected that the problem of illegal construction would remain a focal point of severe tension as long as construction laws were not enforced and as long as updated, long-range master plans were not approved

Property of the Muslim Clergy (Waqf)

Another nucleus of friction was created after the 1948 War of Independence when Israel expropriated waqf property and handed it over to the state custodian as abandoned property. In this way the state acquired vast amounts of Arab property that included land sanctified by the waqf, mosques, cemeteries, and holy sites. This kind of property was particularly prominent in the cities with large Arab populations such as Haifa, Acre, Jaffa, Ramle, and Lod.

The Muslim public's main demand was the cancellation of the expropriation – in their eyes a blatantly illegal act – and the return of the holy property to its rightful owners, the Muslim community. The Islamic Movement in Israel led the struggle through an association it established in 1991 called the "al-Aqsa Association for Preserving the Waqf and Islamic Holy Sites." In recent years the al-Aqsa Association engaged in the methodical mapping of Islamic sites in Israel, both existing and destroyed. Association members collected material from various archives, including the Haganah Archives in Tel Aviv and the Ottoman State Archives in Istanbul, and photocopied original manuscripts testifying to the lands and buildings in Israel that were sanctified as waqf property.

The Association marked hundreds of mosques, cemeteries, and graves of holy people throughout the country, and Israeli Arabs have visited these sites and held prayers in abandoned mosques. The organization also claimed that it had knowledge of hundreds of additional holy places not yet located or documented, and it established its own archive center, housing documents and other information. IM representatives ensured the upkeep of waqf sites in Jewish cities. In March 2001 the IM set up the Supreme Muslim Council as an elected Islamic body that it hoped would receive the waqf property from the Israeli government.

A serious point of friction developed in Nazareth over Muslim plans to build the Shahab al-Din mosque on the piazza of the Church of the Annunciation. In November 2001 the Muslims began construction without a permit while accusing the government of delay tactics in deciding the future of the site. The building generated great tension between Muslims and the Jewish authorities as well as between Muslims and Arab Christians, and the Israel Supreme Court decided to halt construction. The Israeli government was under immense pressure from the Vatican, President Bush, and other international parties to prevent the construction of a mosque on a Christian holy site. As a result, on March 3, 2002, the Sharon government overturned the approval issued by the Netanyahu government in April 1996, later upheld by the Barak government, to construct the mosque. On March 6, 2003, the Nazareth District Court directed the waqf to destroy within three days any portion of the mosque that had been built.

Involvement in Terrorist Activity

For over fifty years there were only isolated instances of Israeli Arabs involved in terrorism. Israeli Arabs who might have been ideologically inclined towards terror refrained from this type of activity for two main reasons: first, they realized it would be quickly uncovered; and second, they understood that such activity would evoke a strong reaction by the government that would damage their sector's economic and social gains. However, since the outburst of the al-Aqsa Intifada and the events of October 2000, a steep rise has occurred in both the scope and severity of Israeli Arabs' involvement in terrorism.

The Palestinian terror organizations striving to enlist Israeli Arabs were Hamas, under whose tutelage Israeli Arabs have perpetrated deadly attacks, and Fatah;

Hizbollah of Lebanon also increased its efforts to mobilize Israeli Arabs into its ranks. Israeli Arabs were excellent recruits for terror organizations because of their freedom of movement in the state, their familiarity with most places in Israel, their knowledge of Hebrew, and their social, economic, and professional contacts with Jews. Strong links to the Palestinians in the Palestinian territories because of common ethnic and family ties have fostered some willing participants in pro-Palestinian terror. The al-Aqsa Intifada and the events of October 2000 have joined traditional points of friction to transform the alienation of some Arab Israelis into violent activity. In addition, the preaching of radical Islam to the Arab public, especially in the mosques, incited young Arabs to turn to terrorism.

In the year preceding the outbreak of the second intifada, only eight Israeli Arabs were visibly involved in terror activities. In 2001 the number rose to fifty-six, and in 2002 the number reached a new high of seventy-four. The nature of their involvement was primarily facilitation of terrorist activities, particularly transporting suicide terrorists to their destinations, although there were some cases of Arab Israelis themselves performing terrorist acts. Some of the more glaring examples included:

- The first and as of April 2003 only suicide bombing performed by an Arab Israeli was the attack on September 9, 2001, at the train station near Nahariya, in which three Israelis were killed.
- In November 2002, an Israeli Arab student attempted to hijack an El Al plane en route to Turkey. The attack was foiled by security on board. In his investigation, he claimed he had been influenced by the September 11 attacks.
- Two Israeli Arabs assisted a suicide bomber from Hebron as he prepared for his attack on a bus in Haifa on March 4, 2003, which killed seventeen Israelis.
- Two Israeli Arabs assisted a suicide terrorist from Samaria, selecting his target and transporting him there. On August 4, 2002, the terrorist blew himself up at the Meron Junction aboard a bus, killing nine Israelis and wounding forty-eight.
- On July 17, 2002, an Israeli Arab resident of Jaffa drove two suicide bombers to their destination in Tel Aviv. Five Israelis were killed and forty were wounded in the attack.
- In June 2001 an Arab Israeli drove a suicide terrorist to the Dolphinarium discotheque in Tel Aviv. The attack killed twenty-one young people.

It should be stressed that despite the gravity of the problem, the phenomenon remained marginal. The vast majority of Israeli Arabs had no connection to terror organizations and understood the dangerous implications of such involvement. Nevertheless, some Arab leaders preferred to refrain from a categorical, outright condemnation of Israeli Arab involvement in terrorism.

The Political System of the Israeli Arab Sector

At the start of the twenty-first century, most Arab political leaders were in their forties and fifties, academically educated, and fluent in at least two languages. They developed finely honed rhetorical skills and some were quite charismatic. No women figured in the Arab political leadership. Relative to their predecessors, who were generally more traditionally inclined and pragmatic, the new leaders, especially the Arab MKs, were more militant. Despite the leadership's semblance of unity in the media and Knesset, it was fairly divided along personal, family, and ethnic lines. In fact, disunity has been its trademark for decades. Whenever national election campaigns approached, therefore, public figures, political parties, and Arab institutions desperately rushed to achieve some degree of unity in the ranks and form a single, unified Arab list that could send at least twenty Arab candidates to the Knesset. All efforts thus far have failed and Israeli Arabs consistently went to the polls divided, scattering their votes among a multiplicity of parties.

In the January 2003 elections for the sixteenth Knesset, three of the five Arab parties that contended for seats reached the minimum percentage level to win parliamentary seats. The Communist Hadash party, which had merged with Ahmed Tibi's Arab Movement for Renewal party, retained three seats, but for the first time did not send a Jewish representative to the Knesset, who was fourth on the party's list. Azmi Bishara's Balad party increased its representation from two seats in the previous Knesset, when it had been associated with Tibi's party, to three. Ra'am, the United Arab List, which included the pragmatic faction of the IM, was soundly defeated, losing three of its five seats.

Voter turnout in the Arab sector was approximately 60%, compared with 68% of the general population, and down from 75% in the 1999 Knesset elections. The 2003 elections also showed a continued drop in votes by Arabs for Zionist parties: from 53% in 1992 to 33% in 1996 to 31% in 1999 to 25% for the sixteenth Knesset. The continued decline in support for Zionist parties clearly reflected the growing tension between the Israeli Arab sector and the state. In the sixteenth Knesset, eight Arabs were elected, down from eleven of the fifteenth Knesset (nine from Arab parties, one from labor, and one from Meretz).

The senior internal body of the Israeli Arab sector was known as the "Higher Arab Monitoring Committee of the Arab Population in Israel." This was a large assembly made up of over one hundred members, including Arab MKs, the heads of local councils, Arabs in the Histadrut leadership (Israel's national trade union), union bosses, and political leaders. In order to allow for the committee's efficient operation, a secretariat was elected consisting of twenty-two members.

In July 2001 Shouki Khatib, head of the Yafiya Council (near Nazareth) and a member of the Hadash party, was elected chairman of the Tracking Committee. Under his leadership the committee continued to address most developments in the Arab sector, convening dozens of times and publishing public minutes of the meetings. It regularly denounced the government's policy towards the Arab minority, often in the most strident language. The committee's decisions, such as calling a general strike, were incumbent upon the entire Arab sector. Khatib devoted most of his time to the Israeli Arabs' struggle for equality, especially in the budgets allotted to the local councils, but he also dealt with land disputes, education issues, and infrastructure development. Khatib's policy represented his belief in the integration of Israeli Arabs in all areas of life of the state on the basis of equality. He argued that the struggle must be carried out through negotiations with the authorities within the framework of the law.

Numerous unions and associations, roughly one hundred, were also active in the Arab political system. One such association that characterized the prevalent atmosphere and current activity was "Adalah" (justice). Established in 1996 and headed by progressive Arab lawyers and civil rights activists, Adalah demanded recognition of Israeli Arabs as a national minority and strove to attain their cultural autonomy. The main thrust of its efforts, however, was directed towards the struggle for gaining equality. The association brought appeals to the court with the aim of obligating the state to mete out rights to Israeli Arabs in all spheres of life: education, health, unemployment reduction, and religious affairs.

For example, Adalah appealed to the Supreme Court to allow an Arab family to purchase a home in a Jewish settlement village inside Israel. The Supreme Court's decision in favor of the family created a precedent regarding Arab settlement on Jewish state land. Adalah was also active in the struggle against land expropriation, defense of the local absentees, and representation of the unrecognized settlements in the Negev. On July 25, 2002, the Supreme Court determined that mixed Arab-Jewish cities would be required to erect public signs in Arabic, a verdict in the wake of a plea submitted by Adalah against city municipalities. The verdict related especially to Tel Aviv-Jaffa, Ramle, Nazareth, and Lod., the Acre municipality having previously changed its signs and the Haifa municipality having already pledged to do so. In the plea, Adalah claimed that the present state of affairs where most signs are in Hebrew smacked of discrimination and disrespect to the Arab population, especially since Arabic is one of Israel's official languages. The Court's decision had two salient implications: first, it was an unprecedented legal affirmation of the Israeli Arabs as a national minority; second, it implied that NGOs like Adalah and the "Citizens Rights Association" were achieving important gains in the Arab minority's struggle for greater rights, in comparison to less impressive civic achievements by Arab MKs over the years.

Three Competing Trends

A look at the dominant ideological trends in the Israeli Arab sector revealed three main schools, each vying to shape the Arab sector's approach towards Israel and its Jewish majority: integration, separatism, and religious separatism.

The most widespread approach supported integration into the state, labeled by some researchers as "Israelization." It would be more accurate to refer to it as the struggle for integration. It was the preference of the majority of the Israeli Arab public, the silent majority that acted prudently, weighed potential gain and loss regarding its status in the country, and has come to the conclusion that despite the discrimination and apathy toward the Arab sector by consecutive Israeli governments over the years, it made no sense to forfeit the economic and social achievements that have been earned. A number of organized political bodies represented the integrationist trend. Chief among them were the Israel Communist Party (Maki) and its allies from the Democratic Front for Equality (Hadash). MK Ahmed Tibi and the majority of members of the United Arab List (Ra'am) also supported this trend, although with less intensity than Maki.

Aware of the need for co-existence, the integrationist school claimed that Israeli Arabs must give top priority to the struggle for equality in the allocation of the state's resources. That is, integration meant equal rights and opportunities, not a separation of institutions, and definitely not a separate parliament for Israeli Arabs as the separatist school proposed. Regarding the Israeli-Palestinian conflict, the integrationist trend favored the partition of the area between the Mediterranean and Jordan River into two states dwelling in peaceful coexistence.

Proponents of this school sought the preservation of a distinct Israeli Arab character, partly because they remained acutely aware of the limitations of their ability to change the character and government of Israel. Integration for them did not imply assimilation within the Jewish state. Furthermore, supporters of the integrationist trend, especially Maki-Hadash, saw themselves in a perpetual struggle with the Israeli authorities and with elements in Israeli society that, integration supporters contended, wished to continue discrimination against Israeli Arabs and prevent them from obtaining their rightful share of the state's resources.

This trend, however, suffered a major reversal in the wake of the October riots, and has weakened since. Integration activists, and again, especially members of Maki-Hadash, interpreted the violent police conduct towards Israeli Arabs in October 2000 as an intentional move, representing an attempt to bring about the Arab citizens' de-legitimization in Israeli society, their enfeeblement, the prolongation of their discrimination, and the attempt to transfer them out of Israel into territory of the future Palestinian state. In light of this perspective, Maki-Hadash opposed a full boycott of the 2001 elections and instead advised the Arab public to vote with a blank slip, because a total boycott, they believed, would play into the hands of those forces in the state trying to push Israeli Arabs into a segregated corner. The integrationists feared that in the wake of a widespread election boycott the alienation process would accelerate and thus impede the Israeli Arabs' ability to continue their struggle for equal rights.

For the integrationist school to recover from the setback in the aftermath of the October 2000 events, there must be changes in two directions: first, the willingness and active response by the State of Israel to act in closing the gaps of civil inequality, for integration cannot take place unless there is a willingness to integrate; and second, progress in negotiations with the Palestinians towards a resolution of the conflict based on the establishment of a sovereign Palestinian state alongside Israel.

The second school, the separatist trend, called for a comprehensive redesign of Israel, from a Jewish-Zionist state to a state for all its citizens. This trend was led by MK Azmi Bishara, head of the National Democratic Assembly (Balad). Since October 2000 the approach gained in strength among Israeli Arabs. Separatists claimed that as long as the state's Jewish nature dominated, Israeli Arabs were fated to endure discrimination. Their call for equal rights translated into the demand that the Jewish character of the state be annulled and the Law of Return, which affords automatic citizenship to Jewish immigrants, rescinded; in other words, equality – yes; integration – no. This approach aimed at no less than the de-Zionization of Israel. The separatist trend's main ideas that netted it popular support were the demand for institutional autonomy, including separate representative institutions in all areas, and the recognition of Israeli Arabs as a national minority on the basis of the 1992 International Declaration of Minority Rights.

In March 2001 MK Bishara proposed a law that included these elements of separatism. Separatist activists openly touted the idea of territorial autonomy for Israeli Arabs. A varying idea prominent in the separatist trend was the establishment of Arab cantons in Israel that would have a status similar to those in Switzerland, though the Arab cantons would be allowed to have foreign relations with the Palestinian people in the diaspora and the future Palestinian state. Bishara has also presented proposals to the Knesset regarding the abolishment of national institutions of the state and the Zionist movement, such as the Jewish Agency, the Zionist Organization, the Jewish National Fund, and the World Jewish Congress. He proposed to nullify the Law of Return and neutrally refashion state symbols, the flag, and the national anthem. The separatist school, striving to change the Jewish character of Israel, embodied potential for endangering the fragile relations between the state and its Arab citizens.

In December 2001 Bishara was indicted on charges of organizing visits of Arab Israelis to Syria, defined by the government as an enemy state. In addition, he was charged with expressing legitimacy for Hizbollah activities against Israel during a visit to Syria. The charges have not yet been decided, but both the indictment and the Supreme Court's decision to qualify the party for Knesset elections no doubt strengthened support for Bishara among the Arab community.

The third school that won support among Israeli Arabs was the Islamic trend whose religious separatist approach was under the leadership of the Islamic Movement in Israel. This was a political, social, religious movement that has had an important impact on Israeli Arabs. The IM's goal was to establish an Islamic theocratic state in Palestine, and its ideology was identical to that of its parent movement, the Muslim Brotherhood.

The structure of the IM, and especially its radical wing, facilitated the capacity to commit subversive and terrorist acts mandated by the ideological goal. A strict distinction must be made between open and closed cells (the cell forming the movement's basic unit); by definition the closed cell operated clandestinely. The IM naturally denied the existence of secret cells, and it was possible that many branches operated without them. Nevertheless, Islamic movements in general operated according to the tactics of the Muslim Brotherhood, and therein lay the potential for secret cells. The heads of the IM claimed that the concept of secrecy and education towards secretiveness strengthen internal discipline, loyalty, and obedience to authority.

The main problem concerned the movement's radical wing. The Islamic Movement had split following a bitter debate over practical dealings with Israel as a Jewish state. Specifically, on the eve of the 1996 elections, the question of IM's participation in the elections arose. Abdullah Nimer Darwish, the leader of the movement at the time, declared that IM had to integrate into Israel's political life and take part in Knesset elections while continuing its Islamic preaching and other activities. The rival camp, the radical separatists headed by Sheikh Ra'id Salah, then mayor of Umm el-Fahm, asserted that it was forbidden for IM to participate in the elections because every MK was required to swear allegiance to Israel, the state of the Jewish people. They argued that the oath signified recognition of Israel as a Jewish state and recognition of the Jews' right to continue controlling the land of Palestine, which is holy Islamic land that must be liberated in a jihad. This was the ideological background to the IM schism.

The radical wing made no pretense in hiding its non-recognition of the State of Israel as it promoted the Arab sector's religious, cultural, and social separation. In this way its approach was more extreme than that of Bishara's secular separatist trend. The radical wing's leader, Sheikh Ra'id Salah, defined the Jews and the State of Israel and its institutions as enemies of Islam that have usurped Muslim land and holy Islamic property. In speeches, sermons, religious instruction, and on the pages of the movement's weekly journal "Saut al-Khak wa al-Khouria" ("The Voice of Truth and Freedom") Sheikh Ra'id assailed the state by citing verses from the Koran and Islamic holy writings. At times he has compared the Jews and Israel to Nazi Germany. After the October 2000 events the Ra'id faction set up the "Institute for Humanitarian Aid" with the sheikh at its head. The purpose of the body was to collect funds for the movement, and it succeeded in amassing donations of millions of dollars from Arab-Muslim sources in the Gulf and Saudi Arabia.

This new-found wealth has been invested in three primary areas of activity:

1. Planning alternative economic, social, educational, and health services to those offered by the state. This kind of activity represented a realization of the idea of the autarchic society based on conclusions that Sheikh Ra'id drew from the October 2000 events, and was designed to strengthen the IM's separatist wing.
2. Allocating money for Arabs in Israel and the territories who were hurt in the al-Aqsa Intifada. Special funds were extended to Hamas elements in the territories.
3. Contributing to the al-Aqsa mosque and to Jerusalem. This channel has won top priority in both wings of the IM, and although the radical wing is more active, MK Dehamshe, a member of the pragmatic wing, has also declared, "I am ready to be a martyr for the defense of al-Aqsa."

Sheikh Ra'id conducted a propaganda campaign designed to incite Arab and Muslim public opinion in Israel and abroad against what he called Israel's machinations to sabotage the Temple Mount mosques. Both the radical and the pragmatic factions arranged free transportation throughout the Arab sector to the Temple Mount mosques. Radical supporters have endeavored to maintain the upkeep of the mosques, cleaning and repairing them and even building a new mosque on the Temple Mount. The construction at such a sensitive location ignores the official Israeli restriction against such building and endangers Jewish archeological sites underground. Despite the uproar in the Jewish community, the government has opted not to obstruct the Islamic Movement's activity on the Temple Mount in an attempt to avert further tension with the radicals.

The leaders of the radical factions repeatedly proclaimed that, "the al-Aqsa mosque was in danger," and they echoed this slogan at the IM's annual mass assembly at the Umm el-Fahm soccer stadium. Tens of thousands of people attended the rally held on September 14, 2001 and heard the IM spokesmen threaten that any harm to the al-Aqsa mosque would justify a recourse to violence. At the September 2002 gathering, 50,000 Muslims participated, and the sheikh again called on the Muslims of the world to unite against Israel's attempt to seize and control the mosque. The al-Aqsa-centered activity has won Sheikh Ra'id considerable prestige in the Israeli Arab sector and Muslim world. In a related development, the Israeli authorities issued an injunction forbidding Sheikh Ra'id, for security reasons, to travel abroad. The sheikh appealed to the Supreme Court, claiming that his intention was to enter Jordan and proceed to Mecca in order to perform the religious commandment for pilgrimage. The Court, however, rejected his plea and upheld the order preventing his departure.

Supplemental to IM's religious activity was its connection with terror. In recent years a number of attacks were perpetrated by people emerging from the ranks of the Islamic Movement, especially from Ra'id's radical wing. The most prominent attacks included: the murder of four IDF soldiers near Kibbutz Gilad in 1992; the murder of two Israeli hikers in a forest near Megiddo in August 1999; car bomb explosions in Tiberias and Haifa in September 1999; and the suicide attack by an IM-linked Israeli Arab in Nahariya in September 2001.

Although the terrorists who carried out these attacks may not have been sent to their assignments by the IM, the movement cannot escape its share of the responsibility and complicity. First, the leaders of the radical faction publicly identified with Hamas in their statements at party meetings and their sermons in the mosques. In "The Voice of Truth and Freedom," the heads of the radical wing have expressed their understanding of the motivation behind Hamas' suicide attacks against Israelis. The radical wing also maintained a line of contact with Hamas in the territories.

Second, the radical wing's sermonizing in the mosques, especially on Fridays, was a form of direct and indirect incitement. In many sermons the preachers lauded the value and significance of jihad for liberating Islamic lands from the yoke of the stranger. They repeatedly embellished the saga of Islam's victory against the crusaders under the military leadership of Saladin. Worshippers who absorbed the speakers' charismatic words were encouraged to feel their experience as their own version of infidels threatening Islamic land and consider that the modern crusaders endangering the al-Aqsa mosque were the Israelis.

Israeli law did not consider sermons such as these as incitement. In Egypt and Jordan, on the other hand, the law clearly and definitively prohibited such public expressions, and severe action was taken against imams and preachers who transgressed the regulations of sermonizing. But it is doubtful whether any Israeli government would initiate legislation of this sort.

There have only been rare instances of Israeli Arabs' participation in subversion and terror. However, the persistence of Islamic indoctrination to fomentation and hatred of the Jews and Judaism, the repeated image of the crusaders placing the al-Aqsa mosque in jeopardy, and the shadowy presence of clandestine cells – all of these elements when combined had the potential for unleashing organized separatism, subversion, and terror.

Conclusion

The Arab minority in Israel faces a host of severe problems such as the crisis in land ownership and infrastructure development, gaps in education and health services, the lack of state budgets for local councils, and rising unemployment. These problems emerged with the outcome of the 1948 War of Independence and have been aggravated by the unresolved Israeli-Palestinian conflict and the basic conditions of the Israeli Arab sector. The indifference and negligence displayed by most Israel governments to the problems confronting the Israeli Arabs have intensified their sense of alienation from the state, deepened their feelings of despair, frustration, and bitterness, and then perhaps predictably, strengthened the radical trend.

The events of October 2000 shattered Arab-Israeli relations, already sensitive and fragile at best, and cast doubts on Arab-Jewish coexistence in Israel. The Arabs' boycott of the national elections in February 2001 widened the rift. Since then, neither side – the Israeli government or the Arab leadership – has tried substantively to bridge the gaps. Indeed, the resentment among both Jews and Arabs regarding the status and future of Israeli Arabs has made this task exceedingly problematic and complex. Many Israeli Arabs abandoned their trust in the Israeli authorities and displayed signs of sensitivity and nervousness in light of the public debate in Israel that the Arab sector portends a demographic and strategic threat to the existence of the state. They heard repeated calls to solve the threat by transferring large sections of the Arab population, such as residents of Umm el-Fahm, to PA jurisdiction. They read articles in the Israeli press and listened to statements of certain Israeli leaders testifying that the Israeli public regarded its Arab citizens as untrustworthy neighbors, even as traitors. For its part, the Jewish majority too has grown insecure in light of the Israeli Arabs' demands to be recognized as a national minority, to repeal the Jewish character of the state, and to convert it to a country for all its citizens. The aggregate of these feelings in the two publics coincided with Israel's ongoing battle with the PA, a situation that enflamed the passions of both sides and heightened the feeling of solidarity and identification of Israeli Arabs with their Palestinian brethren in the territories. All of these circumstances have reinforced the Israeli Arabs' sense of alienation from the state.

PART II
MILITARY FORCES

Introductory Note

Readers who have followed the *Middle East Military Balance* since its first edition in 1983 will notice that this volume differs from the previous ones, as indicated by the new name of the publication. The greatest change in this portion of the book is the level of detail presented. For each of the countries reviewed below, only total numbers of main weapon systems are given, without breakdown into further detail. Major changes in the military composition of each country are listed, followed by selected general data and a summary of data regarding arms procurement and sales, foreign military cooperation, military industry, weapons of mass destruction, space assets, and the order-of-battle. The table representing the order-of-battle of each country often gives two numbers for each weapon category. The first number refers to quantities in active service, and the second number, which appears in parentheses, refers to the total inventory. In the wake of the war in Iraq, the material about Iraq has been updated.

The final section includes tables and charts representing the distribution of weapon systems in three distinct regions of the Middle East:

1. Eastern Mediterranean (includes Egypt, Israel, Jordan, Lebanon, Syria, and Turkey)
2. The Gulf (includes Bahrain, Iran, Iraq, Kuwait, Oman, Qatar, Saudi Arabia, and UAE)
3. North Africa and other countries (includes Algeria, Egypt, Libya, Morocco, and Tunisia. To these are added Sudan and Yemen.)

The detailed data formerly published in the *Balance* is now available on line at the Jaffe Center website: http://www.tau.ac.il/jcss/balance/index.html.

Definitions and Criteria

The following criteria refer to the data presented in the tables below, which present only aggregate numbers of major types of weapon systems. These same criteria are used with the data presented on line.

Military Acquisitions and Sales

Data on military acquisitions and sales as well as on security assistance is limited to information pertaining to the past five years. The year in parentheses indicates the most recent information about the data.

Armor

Tanks are divided into two main categories: light tanks (under 25 tons) and main battle tanks (MBTs). High quality MBTs and other MBTs are also differentiated. The criteria for "high quality" are any three of the following attributes:

- A 120mm (or higher) caliber gun
- A power plant of more than 900hp and/or power-to-weight ratio of 19 hp/t or better
- Reactive or modular armor
- A capability to fire barrel launched AT missiles
- An advanced fire control system, with tracking capability

Under this categorization some versions of the T-72 MBT are categorized as "high quality," although they are not necessarily on par with tanks like the M1A1 or the Merkava Mk III.

Armored Fighting Vehicles

AFVs are divided into three categories:

- Armored personnel carriers – armored vehicles designed to carry several infantrymen, armed with light weapons only
- Infantry fighting vehicles – armored vehicles built to carry several infantrymen, armed with heavier weapons, such as guns or missiles
- Reconnaissance vehicles – armored vehicles of various sizes and armament, designed to carry a small crew of weapon operators (but not intended for dismounted infantry fighting)

It should be noted that the dividing lines between categories are not always absolute, and sometimes it is difficult to decide how a certain vehicle should be categorized. For example, heavier reconnaissance vehicles can be categorized as light tanks, especially when they use tracks rather than wheels.

Air Defense

Some militaries in the region have a separate Air Defense arm. In other countries, air defense equipment is divided between the Air Force and the Ground Forces. In this volume all air defense weapon systems are aggregated into one sub-section in each chapter, regardless of the organizational distribution of the weapon systems.

Air defense equipment is categorized as follows:

- Shoulder-launched missiles
- Light SAMs - with a range of up to 12 km, self propelled or towed
- Mobile medium SAMs – self-propelled, with a range of 12-30 km
- Medium to heavy SAMs - stationary or towed systems with a range of 12-30 km, or any system with a range of more than 30 km
- Other systems – AA guns and combined systems

For heavy and medium SAMs, numbers follow the number of independent fire units. For the sake of brevity, the number of batteries for smaller SAMs is calculated (although in these types usually each launcher can operate independently). The same method is used to build up the charts.

Combat Aircraft

Combat aircraft are divided into the following categories:

- Interceptors
- Multi-role (high quality and others)
- Ground attack
- Obsolete

Economic Data

The tables on economic data include data on GDP (in current US dollars) and defense expenditure only. Sources for the economic data are EIU Country Profiles, EIU Quarterly Reports, IMF International Financial Statistical Yearbook, and SIPRI Yearbook.

Data on military/defense expenditure in the Middle East is notoriously elusive. Hence it should be regarded primarily as an indication of procurement trends.

Note on Symbols

The following symbols are used to denote instances where accurate data is not available:

NA   Data not available. This symbol is used in the economic data tables only.
~   The tilda is used in front of a number to denote an imprecise number.
+   The weapon system is known to be in use, but the quantity is not known.

Thanks go to all those who assisted me in preparing this data. I alone, however, am responsible for any inaccuracies.

Yiftah S. Shapir
August 2003

Review of Armed Forces

1. ALGERIA

Major Changes

- Over the past two years, Algeria has improved its security cooperation with the US. After more than a decade of embargo, the US has been willing to discuss sales of military equipment to Algeria.
- At the same time, Russia remains Algeria's major arms supplier. Over the past two years Russia has rescheduled Algeria's debt of $4 billion. It upgraded Algeria's Su-24 combat aircraft, and upgraded two of its frigates and one corvette. Two more frigates will undergo the same upgrade program. Under the same upgrade program, Algeria acquired Kh-35 ship-to-ship missiles.
- Other important arms deals include the acquisition of Russian-made MiG-29 combat aircraft from Belarus.
- Algeria also upgraded its Mi-24 attack helicopters with aid from South Africa and ordered L-39 training aircraft from the Czech Republic.

General Data

Official Name of the State: Democratic and Popular Republic of Algeria
Head of State: President of the High State Council Abd al-Aziz Buteflika
Prime Minister: Ali Benflis
Minister of Defense: Nureddin Zarhouni
Chief of General Staff: Major General Muhammad Lamari
Commander of the Ground Forces: Major General Salih Ahmad Jaid
Commander of the Air Force: Brigadier General Muhammad Ibn Suleiman
Commander of Air Defense Force: Brigadier General Achour Laoudi
Commander of the Navy: Admiral Brahim Dadci

Area: 2,460,500 sq. km.
Population: 31,300,000

Economic Data

		1997	1998	1999	2000	2001
GDP (current prices)	$ bn	47.8	47.4	47.6	53.3	55.1
Defense expenditure	$ bn	1.76	1.91	1.83	1.88	NA

Major Arms Suppliers

Major arms suppliers are Russia, which recently supplied combat aircraft and naval missiles. Russia also upgraded major weapon systems supplied in the past by the Soviet Union. The Czech Republic supplied tanks and training aircraft.

The US is trying to improve its relations with Algeria, and supplied Algeria with C^3I systems and financial aid.

Other suppliers are Belarus, which sold Russian-made combat aircraft; Ukraine, which sold MBTs; and South Africa, which upgraded attack helicopters and sold UAV systems.

Foreign Military Cooperation

Type	Details
Forces deployed abroad	Congo (MONUC), Ethiopia, and Eritrea (UNMEE) (2001)
Joint maneuvers	US maritime SAR and ASW exercises (2002)
Security agreements	France (2000), Libya (2001), Russia (2001), South Africa (2000)

Defense Production

Patrol boats, trucks, and small arms

Weapons of Mass Destruction

NBC Capabilities

Nuclear capability

One 15 MW nuclear reactor, probably upgraded to 40 MW (from PRC) allegedly serves a clandestine nuclear weapons program; one 1 MW nuclear research reactor (from Argentina); basic R&D; signatory to the NPT. Safeguards agreement with the IAEA in force. Signed and ratified the African Nuclear Weapon-Free Zone Treaty (Pelindaba Treaty).

Chemical weapons and protective equipment

No data on CW activities available. Signed and ratified the CWC.

Biological weapons

No data on BW activities available. Not a party to the BWC.

Armed Forces

Order-of-Battle

Year	1997	1999	2000	2001	2002
General data					
Personnel (regular)	124,000	127,000	127,000	127,000	127,000
Ground Forces					
Divisions	5	5	5	5	5
Total number of brigades	26	26	26	26	26
Tanks	930	860	900	900	900
	(1,060)	(1,060)	(1,100)	(1,100)	(1,100)
APCs/AFVs	1,930	1,930	1,930	2,110*	2,110
Artillery (including MRLs)	985	900 (985)	900 (985)	900 (985)	900 (985)
Air Force					
Combat aircraft	205	187* (205)	187 (205)	184 (214)	228 (258)
Transport aircraft	48	39 (45)	39 (45)	41 (46)	41 (46)
Helicopters	116	114	114	133* (142)	131 (140)
Air Defense Forces					
Heavy SAM batteries	11	11	11	11	11
Medium SAM batteries	18	18	18	18	18
Light SAM launchers	40	78*	78	78	78
Navy					
Combat vessels	29	29	26	26	26
Patrol crafts	21	21	21	16	16
Submarines	2	2	2	2	2

* Due to change in estimate

Personnel

	Regular	Reserves	Total
Ground Forces	107,000	150,000	257,000
Air Force	14,000		14,000
Navy	6,000		6,000
Total	**127,000**	**150,000**	**277,000**
Paramilitary			
National Security Force	16,000		16,000
Republican Guards Brigade	1,200		1,200
Gendarmerie	24,000		24,000

2. BAHRAIN

Major Changes

- Following the events of September 11, 2001 and the war against Iraq, Bahrain's importance as a base for US forces increased. Bahrain is now officially a non-NATO ally of the US.
- Last year, the US agreed to sell Bahrain ATACMS tactical ballistic missiles and the Bahraini Air Force received 10 new F-16 Block 40 combat aircraft, capable of carrying AMRAAM air-to-air missiles.

General Data

Official Name of the State: State of Bahrain
Head of State: Amir Shaykh Hamad bin Isa al-Khalifa
Prime Minister: Khalifa ibn Salman al-Khalifa
Minister of Defense: Lieutenant General Khalifa ibn Ahmad al-Khalifa
Commander-in-Chief of the Armed Forces: Salman bin Hamad al-Khalifa
Chief of Staff of the Bahraini Defense Forces: Major General Rashid bin Abdallah al-Khalifa
Commander of the Air Force: Hamad ibn Abdallah al-Khalifa
Commander of the Navy: Lieutenant Commander Yusuf al-Maluallah

Area: 620 sq. km.
Population: 700,000

Economic Data

		1997	1998	1999	2000	2001
GDP (current price)	$ bn	6.4	6.2	6.6	8.0	8.5
Defense expenditure	$ bn	0.289	0.295	0.327	0.321	NA

Major Arms Suppliers

Major arms suppliers are the US, which supplied combat aircraft, helicopters, and tactical ballistic missiles, and the UK, which supplied transport and training aircraft. Bahrain also received air defense systems from Sweden.

Foreign Military Cooperation

Type	Details
Foreign forces	As of mid-March 2003, US and coalition forces were in the process of a buildup in advance of the war in Iraq. Since the outbreak of the war, the forces have been in constant flux.
Forces deployed abroad	Saudi Arabia (part of GCC "Desert Shield" Rapid Deployment Force)
Joint maneuvers	Egypt (2001), GCC countries (2001), Jordan (2001), US (2001)
Security agreements	US, UK, GCC countries

Weapons of Mass Destruction

NBC Capabilities

Nuclear capability
No known nuclear activity. Signatory to the NPT.

Chemical weapons and protective equipment
No known CW activities. Party to the CWC.

Biological weapons
No known BW activities. Party to the BWC.

Future procurement
GID-3 CW detection system (2002)

Ballistic Missiles

Model	Launchers	Missiles	Since	Notes
Future procurement				
ATACMS		30		

Armed Forces

Order-of-Battle

Year	1997	1999	2000	2001	2002
General data					
Personnel (regular)	7,400	7,400	7,400	7,400	7,400
SSM launchers			9	9	9

Order-of-Battle (continued)

Year	1997	1999	2000	2001	2002
Ground Forces					
Total number of brigades	3	3	3	3	3
Number of battalions	7	7	7	7	7
Tanks	110	180	180	180	180
APCs/AFVs	217 (237)	277 (297)	277 (297)	277 (297)	277 (297)
Artillery (including MRLs)	44 (50)	48 (50)	48 (50)	48 (50)	48 (50)
Air Force					
Combat aircraft	24	24	34	34	34
Transport aircraft	2	2	2	2	2
Helicopters	41	41	39 (41)	39 (41)	40
Air Defense Forces					
Heavy SAM batteries	1	1	1	1	1
Medium SAM batteries	2	2	2	2	2
Light SAM launchers	40	40	40	40	40
Navy					
Combat vessels	11	11	11	11	11
Patrol boats	19	21	21	21	21

Personnel

	Regular	Reserves	Total
Ground Forces	6,000		6,000
Air Force	1,500		1,500
Navy	700		700
Total	**8,200**		**8,200**
Paramilitary			
Coast Guard and National Guard	2,000		2,000

3. EGYPT

Major Changes

- Egyptian industry is now assembling 200 more M1A1 Abrahms MBTs, which will reinforce the 555 tanks already in service. The project will continue until 2007.
- The Egyptian artillery ordered 26 MLRS launchers with the new extended range (ER) rockets.
- Missile forces allegedly received 24 No-Dong missiles from North Korea, and Egypt is likely engaged in a project to assemble or manufacture these missiles indigenously.
- The Air Force received 24 new F-16Ds in the framework of the Peace Vector VI deal. The Air Force also decided to upgrade its 35 Apache AH-64A to the AH-64D standard, although Egypt will not receive the Longbow radar. The Air Force will upgrade its 5 Hawkeye AEW aircraft and will get another aircraft from the US.
- The Air Defense force acquired 18 new early warning radars from the US, and it is now absorbing its first refurbished and upgraded S-125 (SA-3) SAMs that were transformed to a self- propelled configuration by Ukraine.
- The Navy ordered 2 new Moray class submarines, and 4 Ambassador Mk III missile patrol boats. The Navy is also absorbing 6 used Tiger missile patrol boats from Germany.

General Data

Official Name of the State: The Arab Republic of Egypt
Head of State: President Muhammad Husni Mubarak
Prime Minister: Atef Muhammad Ebeid
Minister of Defense and Military Production: Field Marshal Muhammad Hussayn Tantawi
Chief of General Staff: Lieutenant General Hamdi Wahaba
Commander of the Air Force: Major Gen. Magdi Galal Sha'rawi
Commander of the Navy: Vice Admiral Ahmad Saber Salim

Area: 1,000,258 sq. km. (dispute with Sudan over "Halaib triangle" area)
Population: 65,300,000

Economic Data

		1997	1998	1999	2000	2001
GDP (current price)	$ bn	75.6	82.7	89.1	92.4	84.8
Defense expenditure *	$ bn	2.23	2.35	2.39	2.39	2.19

* Published defense expenditure data apparently does not include $1.3 bn annual foreign military assistance from US.

Major Arms Suppliers

Major arms suppliers are the US (MBTs, MLRS, combat aircraft, attack helicopters, radars, combat vessels, advanced air force and naval armament), Germany (missile patrol boats), North Korea (ballistic missiles), PRC (training aircraft), Netherlands (AIFVs), Ukraine (upgrading SAMs and tanks), Belarus (upgrading SAMs), Russia (upgrading SAMs).

Major Arms Transfers

Bosnia (tanks, artillery)

Foreign Military Cooperation

Type	Details
Foreign forces	US forces as of December 2001 include some 665 soldiers; MFO's soldiers as follows: Australia (25), Canada (29), Colombia (358), Fiji (338), France (15), Hungary (41), Italy (75), New Zealand (26), Norway (4), Uruguay (60)
Forces deployed abroad	Bosnia (UNMIBH); Georgia (UNOMIG)
Joint maneuvers	France, GCC countries (2001), Germany (2001), Greece (2001), Italy (2002), Jordan (2001), Netherlands, Spain (2001), UK (2001), US (2001)
Facilities	US forces' use of airfields at Cairo West, Qena, Inshas, Hurghada

Defense Production

Ballistic missiles, assembly of US MBTs, artillery pieces. Upgrading of AFVs. Assembly of basic training aircraft. Small patrol boats. Electronics and optronic equipment.

Weapons of Mass Destruction

NBC Capabilities

Nuclear capability

22 MW research reactor from Argentina, completed 1997; 2 MW research reactor from the Soviet Union, in operation since 1961. Party to the NPT. Safeguards agreement with the IAEA in force. Signed, but not ratified the African Nuclear Weapon-Free Zone Treaty (Pelindaba Treaty).

Chemical weapons and protective equipment

Alleged continued research and possible production of chemical warfare agents. Alleged stockpile of chemical agents (mustard and nerve agents). Personal protective equipment;

Soviet-type decontamination units; Fuchs (Fox) ABC detection vehicles (12), SPW-40 P2Ch ABC detection vehicle (small quantity). Refused to sign the CWC.

Biological weapons

Suspected biological warfare program; no details available. Not a party to the BWC.

Ballistic Missiles

Model	Launchers	Missiles	Since	Notes
SS-1 (Scud B/ Scud C)	24	100	1973	Possibly some upgraded
Future procurement				
Scud C/ Project-T		90		Locally produced
Vector				Unconfirmed
No-Dong		24		Alleged

Armed Forces

Order-of-Battle

Year	1997	1999	2000	2001	2002
General data					
Personnel (regular)	421,000	450,000	450,000	450,000	450,000
SSM launchers	9	24	24	24	24
Ground Forces					
Divisions	12	12	12	12	12
Total number of brigades	53	49	49	49	49
Tanks	2,662	~2,750	~3,000	~3,000	~3,000
	(3,162)	(3,505)	(3,505)	(3,585)	(3,585)
APCs/AFVs	3,025	~3,400	~3,400	~3,400	~3,400
	(4,995)	(~5,300)	(~5,300)	(~5,300)	(~5,300)
Artillery (including MRLs)	3,158	~3,550	~3,530	~3,530	~3,530
			(~3,570)	(~3,570)	(~3,570)
Air Force					
Combat aircraft	505	481 (494)	481 (494)	481 (494)	505 (518)
Transport aircraft	35	44*	44	44	44
Helicopters	223	~225	~225	~225	~225
Air Defense Forces					
Heavy SAM batteries	105	109*	109	109	109
Medium SAM batteries	48	44	44	44	44
Light SAM launchers	50	50	105	105	105

Order-of-Battle (continued)

Year	1997	1999	2000	2001	2002
Navy					
Submarines	6	4	4	4	4
Combat vessels	64	65	64	64	62
Patrol crafts	83	104	104	104	104

* Due to change in estimate

Personnel

	Regular	Reserves	Total
Ground Forces	320,000	150,000	470,000
Air Force	30,000	20,000	50,000
Air Defense	80,000	70,000	150,000
Navy	20,000	14,000	34,000
Total	**450,000**	**254,000**	**704,000**
Paramilitary			
Coast Guard	2,000		
Frontier Corps	6,000		
Central Security Forces	325,000		
National Guard	60,000		
Border Guard	12,000		

4. IRAN

Major Changes

- Iran renewed its negotiations with Russia for large weapons deals, but they have not yet materialized.
- The Shehab-3 medium range ballistic missile (MRBM) is assessed as entering its early operational status. It is assessed that Iran has some 20 missiles. Iran performed a test of the Fateh-110 ballistic missile, a medium range (200 km), high accuracy solid fuel ballistic missile.
- Iran admitted that it is building one facility for enriching uranium and another for the production of "heavy water" (deuterium oxide). Iran announced that it is developing an indigenous fuel cycle, has begun mining uranium ores domestically, and is capable of producing "yellow cake."
- The first Iran-140 transport aircraft assembled under a joint program with the Ukraine performed its maiden flight. Though intended for commercial use, Iran plans to develop two versions for military use.
- As in previous years, the Iranian industry revealed this year a line of new weapons systems. These include new trainer aircraft named Tazarve and Shafagh, new guided munitions for combat aircraft, a new SAM called Shahab Thakeb, SP guns (Thunder-1 and Thunder-2). The Iranian industry announced its plans to move the Azarakhsh combat aircraft and the Shabaviz helicopters programs into serial production.
- The Iranian Armed Forces received 21 out of 30 Mi-171 utility helicopters. The rest are scheduled to be delivered by mid-2003.
- The Iranian Navy received China Cat fast patrol boats from the PRC as well as C-701 ship-borne missiles. The Iranian Navy also received 15 small patrol boats from North Korea.

General Data

Official Name of the State: Islamic Republic of Iran
Supreme Religious and Political National Leader (Rahbar): Ayatollah Ali Hoseini Khamenei
Head of State (formally subordinate to National Leader): President Hojatolislam Seyyed Mohammed Khatami
Minister of Defense: Rear Admiral Ali Shamkhani
Commander-in-Chief of the Armed Forces: Major General Mohammad Salimi
Head of the Armed Forces General Command Headquarters: Major General Hasan Firuzabadi
Chief of the Joint Staff of the Armed Forces: Brigadier General Abdol Ali Pourshasb
Commander of the Ground Forces: Brigadier General Nasser Mohammadi-Far
Commander of the Air Force: Brigadier General Mohammed Daneshpour
Commander of the Navy: Rear Admiral Abbas Mohtaj

Commander-in-Chief of the Islamic Revolutionary Guards Corps (IRGC): Major General Yahya Rahim Safavi
Chief of the Joint Staff of the IRGC: Rear Admiral Ali Akbar Ahmadian
Commander of the IRGC Ground Forces: Brigadier General Aziz Ja'afri
Commander of the IRGC Air Wing: Brigadier General Ahmad Kazemi
Commander of the IRGC Naval Wing: Rear Admiral Ali Morteza Saffari

Area: 1,647,240 sq. km. (not including Abu Musa Island and two Tunb islands; control disputed)
Population: est. 64,500,000

Economic Data

		1997	1998	1999	2000	2001
GDP (current prices)	$ bn	93.7	60.2	54.2	70.3	83.9
Defense expenditure	$ bn	2.86	1.93	1.64	2.71	4.07

Major Arms Suppliers

Major arms suppliers are Russia, which supplied submarines, MBTs, helicopters, transport aircraft, and AD systems. The PRC supplied fast missile patrol boats, transport aircraft, cruise missiles, AD systems. North Korea supplied and assisted Iran in the production of SSMs.

Other suppliers include Ukraine, which supplied tanks and transport aircraft, Romania, which supplied AD systems, and France, which supplied trainer aircraft.

Major Arms Transfers

Iran supplied armament and financial aid to Hizbollah in Lebanon. Arms supplies included MRLs, long range rockets, ATGMs, and shoulder launched SAMs.

Some Palestinian organizations received aid that included ATGMs and mortars.

Iran cooperated with Syria in the development of ballistic missiles and allegedly in the production of chemical weapons.

Foreign Military Cooperation

Type	Details
Forces deployed abroad	300 IRGC troops in Lebanon
Joint maneuvers	India (1998), Italy, Kuwait (proposed naval maneuvers), Oman (observers 1999), Pakistan (naval maneuvers 1997)

Defense Production

SSMs, tanks, armored combat vehicles, self-propelled guns, towed guns, artillery rockets, anti-tank missiles, attack helicopters, transport aircraft, trainer aircraft, helicopters, patrol crafts, midget submarines, UAVs, air defense systems, cruise missiles, guided bombs, radars, fire-control systems.

Some of the weapons systems may be copies of foreign types and not indigenously developed. In addition, some may be only prototypes, which were displayed for propaganda purposes and are not in production.

Weapons of Mass Destruction

NBC Capabilities

Nuclear capability
One 5 MW research reactor acquired from the US in the 1960s (in Tehran) and one small 27 kW miniature neutron source reactor (in Isfahan). One 1,000 MW VVER power reactor under construction, under a contract with Russia, in Bushehr; uranium enrichment facility; suspected nuclear weapons program. Party to the NPT. Safeguards agreement with the IAEA in force.

Chemical weapons and protective equipment
Iran admitted in 1999 that it had possessed chemical weapons in the past. Party to the CWC, but nevertheless suspected of still producing and stockpiling mustard, sarin, soman, tabun, VX, and other chemical agents. Alleged delivery systems include aerial bombs, artillery shells, and SSM warheads. PRC and Russian firms and individuals allegedly provide assistance in CW technology and precursors. Personal protective equipment and munitions decontamination units for part of the armed forces.

Biological weapons
Suspected biological warfare program; no details available. Party to the BWC.

Ballistic Missiles

Model	Launchers	Missiles	Notes
SS-1 (Scud B/ Scud C)	~20	300 Scud B, 100 Scud C	
Shehab-3	~5	~20	
CSS-8	16		
Total	**~41**		
Future procurement			
Fateh-110			Under development
Shehab-4/ Kosar			Under development

Military Forces

Space Assets

A communication satellite, Zohreh, is to be launched in 2003 by Russian SLV. Additional six satellites are projected for both civilian and military use.

Armed Forces

Order-of-Battle

Year	1997	1999	2000	2001	2002
General data					
Personnel (regular)	~520,000	~520,000	~520,000	~520,000	~520,000
SSM launchers	~30	~30	~30	~40	~40
Ground Forces					
Divisions	32	32	32	32	32
Total number of brigades	87	87	87	87	87
Tanks	1,500	1,520	~1,500	~1,700*	~1,700
APCs/AFVs	1,200	1,235	1,240	~1,570*	~1,570
Artillery (including MRLs)	2,640	2,640	~2,700	~2,700	~2,700
	(2,930)	(2,930)	(~3,000)	(~3,000)	(~3,000)
Air Force					
Combat aircraft	226 (318)	205 (297)	205 (333)	209 (337)	207 (335)
Transport aircraft	93 (114)	91 (112)	92 (111)	105 (123)	105 (124)
Helicopters	310 (553)	293 (555)	300 (560)	325 (560)	345 (580)
Air Defense Forces					
Heavy SAM batteries	30-35	30–35	30–35	29*	29
Medium SAM batteries	+	+	+	+	+
Light SAM launchers	95	95	95	95	95
Navy					
Combat vessels	33	31	29	29	29
Patrol craft	136	139	~120	~110	~110
Submarines	3	3	3	3	3

* Due to change in estimate

Personnel

	Regular	Reserves	Total
Ground Forces	~350,000	350,000	~700,000
Air Force	18,000		18,000
Air Defense	12,000		12,000
Navy	~18,000		~18,000
IRGC – Ground Forces	100,000		100,000
IRGC – Navy	20,000		20,000
Total	**~518,000**	**350,000**	**~868,000**
Paramilitary			
Baseej		2,000,000	2,000,000

5. IRAQ

Major Changes

- The Iraqi armed forces were completely eliminated in the war. All units have been disbanded, large quantities of materiel have been destroyed, and no information about the present state of this military materiel is available. We prefer, however, to leave the tables of military equipment in this publication as we believe that what remains will be the basis of the new Iraqi armed forces to be organized by the US administration.
- A large occupation force is still present in Iraq.
- Although the Iraqi arsenal of Weapons of Mass Destruction was one of the purported justifications for the war against Iraq, to date no such weapons have been uncovered.

General Data

Official Name of the State: The Republic of Iraq
Head of American Civil Administration: Paul Bremer
Head of State:
Prime Minister:
Minister of Defense:
Chief of Staff of Ground Forces:
Commander of the Air Force:
Commander of the Navy:

Area:. 432,162 sq. km.
Population: 23,600,000 est.

Economic Data

		1997	1998	1999	2000	2001
GDP (current prices)	$bn	15.3	18.1	23.7	31.8	27.9

Note: economic data on Iraq is scarce and unreliable.

Major Arms Suppliers

Since 1991 Iraq has not received any major arms supplies.

Small scale suppliers include Belarus, Russia, Yugoslavia, the Czech Republic, and Ukraine, all of which supplied air defense and radar related equipment.

Defense Production

Following the 2003 War the Iraqi defense industry has not functioned, and it probably will not regain any considerable production capability in the foreseeable future.

Since the 1991 Gulf War Iraq produced ballistic missiles, UAVs (or converted combat aircraft to weapon-carrying UAVs), and upgraded its air defense systems.

Weapons of Mass Destruction

NBC Capabilities

Nuclear capability

Since the 1991 Gulf War, all known Iraqi facilities were destroyed by the UN's and IAEA's facility-destruction and monitoring teams. Renewed inspections after the 2003 war did not reveal any renewal of the nuclear weapon program. Party to the NPT.

Chemical weapons and protective equipment

Inspections by American teams following the 2003 war did not reveal any evidence for renewed production of chemical agents or weapons. Chemical agents produced in the past included mustard (sulfur mustard and purified mustard), sarin, tabun, soman, VX, hydrogen cyanide (unconfirmed); large quantities of chemical agents were destroyed by UN missions, but some may have remained. Delivery systems: SSM warheads, L-29 converted UAVs, artillery shells, mortar bombs, MRL rockets, aerial bombs, and land mines. Personal protective equipment; Soviet-type unit decontamination equipment. Not a party to the CWC.

Biological weapons

Inspections by American teams following the 2003 war did not reveal any evidence for renewed production of biological agents or weapons. Biological agents produced in the past included anthrax, aphlatoxin, botulinum and typhoid. Iraq claims that they were destroyed, but stocks were largely unaffected by UN inspectors' activity. Experiments were also carried out with other agents. Delivery systems: SSM warheads, aerial bombs, and airborne spraying-tanks for combat aircraft, helicopters, and UAVs. Party to the BWC.

Ballistic Missiles

Since the 1991 Gulf War Iraq has been producing the al-Soumoud and the al-Ababil short range ballistic missiles. In addition Iraq was suspected of hiding some al-Hussein missiles. Since the 2003 war the ballistic missile capability has been eliminated and probably will not be renewed in the foreseeable future.

Armed Forces

Order-of-Battle

Year	1999	2000	2001	2002	2003
General data					
Personnel (regular)	432,500	432,500	432,500	432,500	0
SSM launchers*	5	5	5	10	0
Ground Forces					
Divisions	23	23	23	23	0
Tanks	2,000	2,000	2,000	2,000	0
	(2,300)	(2,400)	(2,400)	(2,400)	
APCs/AFVs	2,000	2,000	2,000	2,000	0
	(2,900)	(2,900)	(2,900)	(2,900)	
Artillery (including MRLs)	2,050	2,100	2,100	2,100	0
Air Force					
Combat aircraft	215	215	200	120	0
	(333)	(333)	(333)	(333)	
Transport aircraft	+	+	+	+	0
Helicopters	370 (460)	360 (460)	360 (460)	370 (460)	0
Air Defense Forces					
Heavy SAM batteries	60	60	60	60	0
Medium SAM batteries	NA	NA	10	10	0
Light SAM launchers	130	130	130	130	0
Navy					
Combat vessels	2	0	0	1	0
Patrol crafts	0	0	0	1	0

* Number does not include unguided rocket launchers.

Personnel

Future Iraqi Armed Forces of approximately 150,000 is planned by American civil administration.

Foreign Military Personnel

Approximately 150,000 US troops and 30,000 UK troops.

6. ISRAEL

Major Changes

- The Israeli Army is organizing another divisional HQ to command its forces in the Judea and Samaria areas. While the Army is still absorbing its Merkava Mk III MBTs, the new Merkava Mk IV has been presented and will soon begin to enter service.
- The first Gulfstream V aircraft ordered by the Air Force arrived in Israel, where they will be equipped with electronic equipment for SIGINT missions. The Israel Air Force chose to implement its option on the F-16I and ordered 52 additional aircraft. While the first F-16I (Sufa) are scheduled to arrive in 2003, aircraft from the second group will be supplied between 2005 and 2008.
- Israel Air Force acquired its first advanced JDAM precision guided munitions.
- The Air Force also received its first GROB-120B (Snunit) trainer aircraft. They will be operated by a private company.
- The Air Force deployed the second Arrow BMD battery.
- Israel launched its new reconnaissance satellite, Ofeq 5, to replace the aging Ofeq 3. Besides the military Ofeq series, Israel operates the EROS 1A, which is the first of a projected system of eight civilian reconnaissance satellites. The EROS 1B is scheduled to be launched in 2003.
- The Israeli Navy ordered 8 new patrol boats - 6 Super Devora Mk II and 2 Shaldag. The first of these is scheduled to be supplied in 2003.

General Data

Official Name of the State: State of Israel
Head of State: President Moshe Katsav
Prime Minister: Ariel Sharon
Minister of Defense: Shaul Mofaz
Chief of General Staff: Lieutenant General Moshe Ya'alon
Commander of the Air Force: Major General Dan Halutz
Commander of Army HQ: Major General Yiftah Ron Tal
Commander of the Navy: Rear Admiral Yedidia Ya'ari

Area: 22,145 sq. km., including East Jerusalem and its vicinity, and the Golan Heights.
Population: 6,400,000

Economic Data

		1997	1998	1999	2000	2001
GDP (current price)	$ bn	102.1	102.8	103.1	113.9	111.8
Defense expenditure	$ bn	8.57	8.53	8.21	8.92	8.85

Major Arms Suppliers

The US is the major arms supplier. It supplies combat aircraft, training aircraft, attack helicopters, helicopters, missile corvettes, tank transporters, SAMs, JDAMs, naval SSMs, MLRS, ATGMs, AMRAAM, SP artillery, and other systems.

Other suppliers include Germany, which supplied Dolphin submarines, training aircraft, NBC detection vehicles, CW protection gear, and Seahake heavy torpedoes. South Africa supplied patrol boats, the Netherlands supplied CW protection gear and assistance in building patrol boats, France supplied training aircraft and CW detectors, and Canada supplied helicopter simulators.

Major Arms Transfers

India* is the major Israeli arms receiver. It procured from Israel UAVs, radars, patrol boats, naval SAMs, anti-radar drones, communication equipment, and surveillance systems.

The US procured AGMs, AAMs, digital mapping systems, airborne search and rescue systems, tactical air-launched decoys, flight simulators, mortars, central computers for AFVs, and mine clearing systems. Turkey received AGMs, debriefing systems, aircraft simulators, radars, ECMs, anti radar missiles, search and rescue systems, and debriefing systems.

Other recipients include Angola (aircraft for ELINT and surveillance, transport helicopters), Argentina* (radars and reconnaissance systems), Australia (ESMs, APCs radars, night vision equipment, guns for patrol boats), Belgium (UAVs, debriefing systems), Brazil* (combat aircraft, avionics suit), Canada (ESMs, OWSs), Chile* (patrol boats, AAMs, AAGs, missiles for patrol boats), Cyprus (torpedo boats, radars, flack jackets, communication systems), Ecuador* (combat aircraft), Eritrea* (patrol boats), Finland (UAVs, ATGMs, communication equipment), France (SAR systems, debriefing systems), Greece (EW systems, patrol boats), Italy (laser guided bombs, SAR system, Litening pods, debriefing systems, simulators), Netherlands (ATGMs, C^2 systems, debriefing systems), Nicaragua (patrol boats), Philippines (mini-UAVs), Poland (ATGMs), Portugal (ESMs, debriefing systems), Romania (OWS-25 systems, ground radar systems), Singapore* (debriefing systems, UAVs, ATGMs, reconnaissance satellite), South Korea* (EW systems, AGMs, anti-radar drones, night vision systems, debriefing systems, radars, satellite reconnaissance equipment), Spain* (radars), Sri Lanka* (attack aircraft, MFPBs, UAVs, radars, ESMs, patrol boats), Sweden* (radars), Taiwan* (submarines), Thailand (mini-UAVs, search and rescue systems), UK (ESMs, debriefing systems), Venezuela (radars, Litening pods, SAMs, ESMs).

* According to foreign publications, as cited by Israeli publications.

Foreign Military Cooperation

Type	Details
Foreign forces	Pre-positioning of $200 million worth of stockpiled US military equipment, four Patriot batteries from the US and Germany, as part of coalition preparations for a war with Iraq (2003)
Cooperation in military training	US and Turkish use of Israeli airfields and airspace for training (2000); Israeli use of Turkish airspace and airfields for training (2001)
Joint maneuvers	Jordan — SAR (1998), Turkey — SAR and joint air force maneuvers (2001), US (2001)

Defense Production

Major systems produced by Israel include: Merkava MBTs, THEL system, SP AAGs, ATRLs, simulators, Arrow ATBM, ALCMs, AAMs, AGMs, CBUs, TV and guided bombs, radars, UAVs and mini-UAVs, LCTs, MFPBs, PBs, SSMs, ELINT equipment, ESM, EW jammers, command and control systems, night vision devices, satellite launchers, imaging satellites, communications satellites.

Weapons of Mass Destruction

NBC Capabilities

Nuclear capabilities
Two nuclear research reactors; alleged stockpile of nuclear weapons.* Not a party to the NPT.

Chemical weapons and protective equipment
Personal protective equipment; Unit decontamination equipment. Fuchs (Fox) NBC detection vehicles (8 vehicles); SPW-40 P2Ch NBC detection vehicles (50 vehicles); AP-2C CW detectors. Signed but not yet ratified the CWC.

Biological weapons capabilities
Not a party to the BWC.

* According to foreign publications, as cited by Israeli publications.

Ballistic Missiles

Model	Launchers	Missiles	Since	Notes
MGM-52C (Lance)	12		1976	
Jericho Mk 1/2/3 SSM*	+			
Total	+			

* According to foreign publications, as cited by Israeli publications.

Space Assets

Model	Type	Notes
Satellites		
Amos	Communication	Civilian
Ofeq series	Reconnaissance	Currently deployed Ofeq-5
Eros	Reconnaissance	Civilian derivative of Ofeq
Bezeq	Communication	Civilian
Future procurement		
Military communication satellite		

Armed Forces

Order-of-Battle

Year	1997	1999	2000	2001	2002
General data					
Personnel (regular)	187,000	186,500	186,500	186,500	186,500
SSM launchers	+	+	+	+	+
Ground Forces					
Divisions	16	16	16	16	16
Total number of brigades	77	77	76	76	76
Tanks	3,900	3,895	3,930	3,930	3,930
APCs/AFVs	8,010	8,040	8,040	8,040	8,000
Artillery (including MRLs)	1,312	1,348	1,348	1,348	1,348
	(1,912)	(1,948)	(1,948)	(1,948)	
Air Force					
Combat aircraft	613 (780)	624 (801)	628 (800)	533 (798)	538 (798)
Transport aircraft	83 (93)	77 (87)	77 (87)	64 (87)	64 (79)
Helicopters	278 (288)	289 (299)	287 (297)	232 (297)	239 (302)
Air Defense Forces					
Heavy SAM batteries	21	22	22	22	23
Light SAM launchers	50	~70	~70	~70	~70

Order-of-Battle (continued)

Year	1997	1999	2000	2001	2002
Navy					
Submarines	4	4	6	6	5
Combat vessels	21	21	20	20	17
Patrol craft	35	35	32	32	33

Personnel

	Regular	Reserves	Total
Ground Forces	141,000	380,000	521,000
Air Force	36,000	55,000	91,000
Navy	9,500	10,000	19,500
Total	**186,500**	**445,000**	**631,500**
Paramilitary			
Border Police	7,650		7,650

7. JORDAN

Major Changes

- The Jordanian Armed Forces have a new Chief of the General Staff, as well as a new commander of the Air Force.
- The Jordanian Armed Forces continued their planned joint maneuvers with US forces, though the government of King Abdullah stressed that these maneuvers were unconnected to the US attack against Iraq. Nevertheless, some US and UK forces were operating in Iraq from bases in Jordan.
- The Jordanian Army received the last Challenger I MBTs of 288 MBTs ordered from the UK in 2000. As soon as the order was completed, Jordan announced that it had ordered 114 additional Challenger I MBTs. Challenger I will replace the Tariq (Centurion) MBTs. Jordan launched a project to upgrade at least 100 of its M60 MBTs with a new gun, new engines, and new fire-control systems.
- The ground forces acquired modern TOW 2A ATGMs, as well as man-portable Javelin ATGMs.
- The Jordanian Air Force acquired 16 Firefly training aircraft. They will replace the aging Bulldogs of the air academy.

General Data

Official Name of the State: The Hashemite Kingdom of Jordan
Head of State: King Abdullah bin Hussein al-Hashimi
Prime Minister: Ali Abu al-Ragheb
Minister of Defense: Ali Abu al-Ragheb
Inspector General of the Armed Forces: Major General Abd Khalaf al-Najada
Chief of the Joint Staff of the Armed Forces: Lieutenant General Khalid Sarayrah
Commander of the Air Force: Major General Prince Faisal bin Hussein
Commander of the Navy: Commodore Ali Mahmoud al-Khasawna

Area: 90,700 sq. km.
Population: 5,200,000

Economic Data

		1997	1998	1999	2000	2001
GDP (current prices)	$ bn	7.2	7.9	8.1	8.5	9.0
Defense expenditure	$ bn	0.65	0.71	0.75	0.79	0.79

Major Arms Suppliers

Major arms suppliers include the US, which supplied combat aircraft, MBTs, self-propelled artillery, anti-tank missiles, and radars, and the UK, which supplied MBTs and training aircraft and upgraded light tanks.

Other suppliers include Ukraine (APCs), Belgium (APCs), France (helicopters), Turkey (transport aircraft), and Canada (upgrading of transport aircraft).

Major Arms Transfers

Jordan sold used combat aircraft to the Philippines and light armored vehicles to Qatar and UAE.

Foreign Military Cooperation

Type	Details
Cooperation in military training	Turkey (use of facilities and airspace for training of pilots) (1998)
Foreign forces	US (pre-positioning of military equipment 2002). Some US and UK forces
Forces deployed abroad	Small contingency force in Afghanistan, Congo (MONUC), East Timor (UNTAET), Ethiopia and Eritrea (UNMEE); observers in Georgia (UNOMIG) and Tajikistan
Joint maneuvers	Egypt, Israel (SAR 1998), France, Oman, Qatar, Turkey, UAE, UK, US
Security agreements	Saudi Arabia, Turkey, US

Defense Production

Upgrading of tanks, APCs, conversion of IFVs, night vision equipment

Weapons of Mass Destruction

NBC Capabilities

Nuclear capability
No known capability. Party to the NPT.

Chemical weapons and protective equipment
No known CW activities. Personal protective and decontamination equipment. Party to the CWC.

Biological weapons
No known BW capability. Party to the BWC.

Armed Forces

Order-of-Battle

Year	1997	1999	2000	2001	2002
General data					
Personnel (regular)	94,200	94,200	94,200	94,200	100,700
Ground Forces					
Divisions	4	4	4	4	4
Total number of brigades	14	14	14	14	14
Tanks	834	~900	~900	~920	~990
	(1,226)	(~1,200)	(~1,200)	(~1,270)	(~1,442)
APCs/AFVs	1,475	1,475	1,500	1,500	1,606
	(1,575)	(1,575)	(1,600)	(1,750)	(1,806)
Artillery (including MRLs)	770	788*	788	838	838
	(795)	(813)	(813)	(863)	(863)
Air Force					
Combat aircraft	91	101	100	91 (100)	91 (100)
Transport aircraft	11 (13)	12 (14)	14 (16)	12	14
Helicopters	68	68	68	74	74
Air Defense Forces					
Heavy SAM batteries	14	14	14	14	14
Medium SAM batteries	50	50	50	50	50
Light SAM launchers	50	50	50	50	50
Navy					
Patrol crafts	10	10	13	13	10

* Due to change in estimate

Personnel

	Regular	Reserves	Total
Ground Forces	88,000	60,000	148,000
Air Force	12,000		12,000
Navy	700		700
Total	**100,700**	**60,000**	**160,700**
Paramilitary			
General Security Forces (including Desert Patrol)	25,000		
Popular Army		200,000-250,000	

Note: The Popular Army is not regarded as a fighting force.

8. KUWAIT

Major Changes

- The Kuwaiti Armed Forces have a new Chief of the General Staff.
- In the past year, Kuwait has become a major deployment area for US forces preparing for the war against Iraq, though most of these forces have already left.
- The US administration approved a Kuwaiti request to acquire Apache AH-64D helicopters, some of which will be equipped with the Longbow radar. The administration also approved the sale of AMRAAM AIM-120B advanced AA missiles for the Kuwaiti F-18 combat aircraft.

General Data

Official Name of the State: State of Kuwait
Head of State: Jabir al-Ahmad al-Jabir al-Sabah
Prime Minister: Sabah al-Ahmad al-Sabah
Minister of Defense: Jabir Mubarak al-Hamad al-Sabah
Chief of General Staff: Major General Fahd Ahmad al-Amir
Commander of the Air Force and Air Defense Forces: Brigadier General Sabir al-Suwaidan
Commander of the Navy: Commodore Ahmad Yousuf al-Mualla

Area: 17,820 sq. km. (including 2,590 sq. km. of the Neutral Zone)
Population: 2,300,000

Economic Data

		1997	1998	1999	2000	2001
GDP (current price)	$ bn	29.9	25.4	29.2	35.8	32.8
Defense expenditure	$ bn	2.45	2.27	2.43	3.08	NA

Major Arms Suppliers

US (attack helicopters, ATGMs, fire control radar, AAMs, LASS air defense system, communication systems, maintenance aid, contracting and upgrading air bases), France (helicopters, MFPBs, SAMs, anti-ship missiles), UK (C⁴I, APCs, SAMs, anti-ship missiles), Germany (NBC reconnaissance vehicles), Egypt (air defense missiles).

Major Arms Transfers

Brazil (combat aircraft)

Foreign Military Cooperation

Type	Details
Foreign forces	As of mid-March 2003, US and coalition forces were in the process of a buildup in advance of the war in Iraq. With the outbreak of the war, the forces were in constant flux.
Joint maneuvers	US (amphibious, command post and naval exercises) (2002); UK (marines); GCC countries (2001); Germany (2002); France; Egypt (2001); Jordan (2001); Iran (1998)
Security agreements	Belarus (2001); France, GCC countries; Iran (2002); Italy; PRC; Russia; South Africa (2002); UK, US

Weapons of Mass Destruction

NBC Capabilities

Nuclear capability
No known nuclear activity. Party to the NPT.

Chemical weapons and protective equipment
Fuchs (Fox) ABC detection vehicle (11). No known CW activities. Personal protective equipment; unit decontamination equipment. Party to the CWC.

Biological weapons
No known BW activities. Party to the BWC.

Armed Forces

Order-of-Battle

Year	1997	1999	2000	2001	2002
General data					
Personnel (regular)	15,500	19,500*	19,500	19,500	15,500
Ground Forces					
Number of brigades	6	6	6	6	7
Number of battalions	1	1	1	1	1
Tanks	318 (455)	318 (483)	318 (483)	318 (483)	318 (483)
APCs/AFVs	455 (515)	436 (715)	~490 (755)	~530 (797) *	~530 (797)
Artillery (including MRLs)	75 (128)	75 (128)	~70 (~125)	~100 (~150)	~100 (~130)

Order-of-Battle (continued)

Year	1997	1999	2000	2001	2002
Air Force					
Combat aircraft	40 (59)	40 (59)	40 (59)	40 (59)	40 (59)
Transport aircraft	5	5	5	5	5
Helicopters	24–27	24–27	~25	23 (28)	25 (30)
Air Defense Forces					
Heavy SAM batteries	12	12	12	12	12
Navy					
Combat vessels	4	6	10	10	10
Patrol craft	54	51	69*	69	69

* Due to change in estimate

Personnel

	Regular	Reserves	Total
Ground Forces	11,000	24,000	35,000
Air Force	2,500		2,500
Navy	2,000		2,000
Total	15,500	24,000	39,500
Paramilitary			
National Guard	5,000		5,000
Civil Defense	2,000		2,000

9. LEBANON

Major Changes

- No major change was recorded in the Lebanese order-of-battle.
- The Lebanese Army will not receive the AMX-30 MBTs that were offered a few years ago by Saudi Arabia.
- Lebanon is also the home base for the Hizbollah militia, which operates a large number of MRLs, including Iranian-made, long range Fajr-3 and Fajr-5 rockets.

General Data

Official Name of the State: Republic of Lebanon
Head of State: President Emile Lahoud
Prime Minister: Rafiq al-Hariri
Minister of Defense: Khalil Hrawi
Commander-in-Chief of the Armed Forces: Lieutenant General Michel Sulayman
Chief of General Staff: Brigadier General Fady Abu-Shakra
Commander of the Air Force: Brigadier General George Shaban
Commander of the Navy: Rear Admiral George Malouf

Area: 10,452 sq. km.
Population: 3,600,000

Economic Data

		1997	1998	1999	2000	2001
GDP (current prices)	$ bn	15.0	16.6	16.8	16.4	16.2
Defense expenditure	$ bn	0.44	0.46	0.57	0.58	0.93

Major Arms Suppliers

Lebanon has not received any major arms systems since 1998, when it received helicopters and APCs from the US.

Other suppliers are Norway and the Czech Republic, which supplied mine clearing equipment. Iran and Syria supplied artillery rockets and other equipment to the Hizbollah militias.

Foreign Military Cooperation

Type	Details
Foreign forces	Syria (25,000 in Beka', Tripoli area, and Beirut); Palestinian organizations; 300 Iranian Islamic Revolution Guards Corps (IRGC), several instructors with Hizbollah non-governmental militia in the Syrian-held Beka', UNIFIL force in south Lebanon (3,600 from France, Ghana, Italy, India, Poland, and Ukraine); Pakistan (300 troops in de-mining operations); UAE (30 army engineers in de-mining operations)

Weapons of Mass Destruction

NBC Capabilities

Nuclear capability
No nuclear capability. Party to the NPT.

Chemical weapons and protective equipment
No known CW activity. Not a party to the CWC.

Biological weapons
No known BW activities. Party to the BWC.

Armed Forces

Order-of-Battle

	1997	1999	2000	2001	2002
General data					
Personnel (regular)	51,400	51,400	51,400	51,400	61,400
Ground Forces					
Number of brigades	17	13*	13	13	13
Tanks	320 (350)	280* (350)	280 (350)	280 (350)	280 (350)
APCs/AFVs	730	730	1,235*	1,235	1,235
	(875)	(875)	(1,380)	(1,380)	(1,380)
Artillery (including MRLs)	328 (331)	~330*	~330	~335	~335
Air Force					
Combat aircraft	(16)	(16)	(16)	(6)	(6)
Transport aircraft	(2)	(2)	(1)	(1)	(1)
Helicopters	16 (34)	16 (34)	16 (38)	16 (38)	16 (38)
Navy					
Patrol crafts	39 (43)	39 (41)	32 (35)	32 (35)	20*

* Due to change in estimate.

Personnel

	Regular	Reserves	Total
Ground Forces	60,000		60,000
Air Force	1,000		1,000
Navy	400		400
Total	**61,400**		**61,400**
Paramilitary			
Gendarmerie/ internal security	13,000		13,000

10. LIBYA

Major Changes

- Libya received some 50 No-Dong MRBMs from North Korea.

General Data

Official Name of the State: The Great Socialist People's Libyan Arab Jamahiriya
Head of State: Colonel Muammar al-Qaddafi
Prime Minister: Mubarak Abdallah al-Shamikh (official title: Secretary-General of the General People's Committee)
Minister of Defense: Colonel Abu-Bakr Yunis Jaber
Inspector General of the Armed Forces: Colonel Mustapha al-Kharrubi
Commander-in-Chief of the Armed Forces: Colonel Abu-Bakr Yunis Jaber
Chief of Staff: Brigadier General Ahmed Abdallah Awn
Commander of the Air Force and Air Defense Forces: Brigadier General Ali Riffi al-Sharif

Area: 1,759,540 sq. km.
Population: 5,400,000

Economic Data

		1997	1998	1999	2000	2001
GDP (current price)	$ bn	34.2	32.4	28.3	34.1	27.1
Defense expenditure	$ bn	NA	NA	NA	NA	NA

Major Arms Suppliers

Libya did not procure major arms systems in the past decade.

Arms suppliers include Ukraine, which supplied transport aircraft and SSMs, and North Korea, which supplied SSMs. Other assistance for Libya's weapons program was received from the PRC, Iran, Russia, Ukraine, and private companies in Western Europe.

Foreign Military Cooperation

Type	Details
Forces deployed abroad	As of the end of 2001, about 200 Libyan soldiers were stationed in the Central African Republic.
Security agreements	Algeria, Tunisia

Defense Production

Libya produces toxic chemical agents and SSMs.

Weapons of Mass Destruction

NBC Capabilities

Nuclear capabilities
5 MW Soviet-made research reactor at Tadjoura; basic R&D. Party to the NPT. Safeguards agreement with the IAEA in force. Signed but not ratified the African Nuclear Weapon-Free Zone Treaty (Pelindaba Treaty).

Chemical weapons and protective equipment
CW production facilities, stockpile of chemical agents, nerve gas, and mustard gas. Personal protective equipment; Soviet-type decontamination units. Not a party to the CWC.

Biological weapons
Alleged production of toxins and other biological weapons (unconfirmed). Party to the BWC.

Ballistic Missiles

Model	Launchers	Missiles	Since	Notes
Scud B/C	80	500	1976/1999	In storage
No-Dong	+	+	2000	Allegedly in process of delivery
Total	~80			
Future procurement				
No-Dong	7	50		Allegedly in process of delivery

Armed Forces

Order-of-Battle

Year	1997	1999	2000	2001	2002
General data					
Personnel	76,000	76,000	76,000	76,000	76,000
SSM launchers	110	128	80*	~80	~80
Ground Forces					
Number of brigades	5	1*	1	1	1
Number of battalions	46	46	46	46	46
Tanks	950	600-700*	~650	~650	~650
	(2,700)	(2,210)	(2,210)	(2,210)	(2,210)

Order-of-Battle (continued)

Year	1997	1999	2000	2001	2002
APCs/AFVs	2,750	~2,750	~2,750	~2,750	~2,750
	(2,970)	(2,970)	(2,970)	(2,970)	(2,970)
Artillery (including MRLs)	2,245	2,220	~2,270	~2,320	~2,320
	(2,325)	(2,300)	(~2,350)	(~2,400)	(~2,400)
Air Force					
Combat aircraft	~360 (483)	~360 (443)	~360 (443)	~360 (443)	~340 (443)
Transport aircraft	85 (90)	85 (90)	85 (90)	85 (90)	85 (90)
Helicopters	164 (212)	127 (204)	127 (204)	127 (204)	127 (204)
Air Defense Forces					
Heavy SAM batteries	~30	~30	~30	~30	~30
Medium SAM batteries	~10	~10	~10	~10	~10
Light SAM launchers	55	55	55	55	55
Navy					
Submarines	4	0(4)	0(4)	0(4)	0(2)
Combat vessels	34	34	24	24	20
Patrol craft	2	2	0	0	0

* Due to change in estimate

Personnel

	Regular	Reserves	Total
Ground Forces	50,000		50,000
Air Force and Air Defense	18,000		18,000
Navy	8,000		8,000
Total	**76,000**		**76,000**
Paramilitary			
People's Militia		40,000	40,000
Revolutionary Guards	3,000		3,000
(part of the People's Militia)			
Islamic Pan African Legion	2,500		2,500
(part of the People's Militia)			

11. MOROCCO

Major Changes

- The Moroccan Army is absorbing its 48 refurbished T-72 MBTs from Belarus and 32 M106 (107mm SP mortars) from US Army draw-down that it received during 2000.

General Data

Official Name of the State: Kingdom of Morocco
Head of State: King Mohammed VI
Prime Minister: Driss Jettou
Minister of Defense: King Mohammed VI
Secretary General of National Defense Administration: Abdel Rahaman Sbai
Commander-in-Chief of the Armed Forces: King Mohammed VI
Inspector General of the Armed Forces: General Abd al-Kader Loubarisi
Commander of the Air Force: Ali Abd al-Aziz al-Omrani
Commander of the Navy: Captain Muhammad al-Tariqi

Area: 622,012 sq. km., including the former Spanish Sahara
Population: 29,200,000

Economic Data

		1997	1998	1999	2000	2001
GDP (current prices)	$ bn	33.4	35.8	35.3	33.3	32.8
Defense expenditure	$ bn	1.31	1.32	1.42	1.38	1.39

Major Arms Suppliers

Major arms suppliers include France (patrol boats), Belarus (tanks), US (training aircraft, APCs), UK (upgrading of artillery guns)

Foreign Military Cooperation

Type	Details
Forces deployed abroad	Small contingency force in Bosnia and Croatia (1998), Congo (MONUC)
Joint maneuvers	France, US
Security agreements	Tunisia

Weapons of Mass Destruction

NBC Capabilities

Nuclear capability
No nuclear capability. Party to the NPT. Request for nuclear research reactor approved by US government.

Chemical weapons and protective equipment
No known CW activity. Party to the CWC.

Biological weapons
No known BW activities. Signed but not ratified the BWC.

Armed Forces

Order-of-Battle

Year	1997	1999	2000	2001	2002
General data					
Personnel (regular)	145,500	145,500	145,500	145,500	145,500
Ground Forces					
Number of brigades	7	6	6	6	6
Tanks	364	379	540*	588	640
APCs/AFVs	1,200	1,074	1,120*	1,120	1,120
	(1,537)	(1,374)	(1,420)	(1,420)	(1,420)
Artillery (including MRLs)	970	967	1,027*	1,060	1,060
	(1,020)	(1,017)			
Air Force					
Combat aircraft	72	72	72	59 (72)	59 (72)
Transport aircraft	45	43	43	41 (43)	41 (43)
Helicopters	129	130	130	121 (131)	121 (131)
Air Defense Forces					
Light SAM launchers	37	37	37	37	37
Navy					
Combat vessels	13	13	13	13	13
Patrol crafts	49	48	52	52	52

* Due to change in estimate

Personnel

	Regular	Reserves	Total
Ground Forces	125,000	150,000	275,000
Air Force	13,500		13,500
Navy and Marines	7,000		7,000
Total	**145,500**	**150,000**	**295,500**
Paramilitary			
Gendarmerie Royale	10,000		10,000
Force Auxiliere	25,000		25,000
Mobile Intervention Corps	5,000		5,000

12. OMAN

Major Changes

- In late 2001 Oman hosted one of the largest joint maneuvers in the region. Some 24,000 troops from the UK participated in the "Swift Sword" joint maneuvers.
- Following the events of September 11, 2001, Oman became a base in the Persian Gulf for US military activities against both Afghanistan and Iraq. The US is building a large base in al-Masanah, 120 km. from Muskat.
- The Omani Army is absorbing the 20 Challenger II MBTs that it received in 2001. The army also received 80 Piranha ACVs from the UK. These will be fitted in Oman and enter service during 2003. They will join the 80 Piranhas already in service since 1995.
- The Omani Air Force announced its decision to acquire 12 F-16 C/D combat aircraft. They will be delivered beginning in 2005. Oman will acquire, with these advanced aircraft, advanced armament, including LANTIRN target acquisition pods, AMRAAM AAMs, Harpoon anti-ship missiles, and JDAM precision guided munitions.
- The Omani Air Force will acquire 16 Super Lynx helicopters from the UK.

General Data

Official Name of the State: Sultanate of Oman
Head of State: Sultan Qabus ibn Said al-Said
Prime Minister: Sultan Qabus ibn Said al-Said
Minister of Defense Affairs: Badr bin Saud bin Harib al-Busaidi
Chief of General Staff: Lieutenant General Khamis bin Humaid bin Salim al-Kalabani
Commander of the Ground Forces: Major General Ahmad bin Harith bin Naser al-Nabhani
Commander of the Air Force: Major General Mohammad Ibn Mahfoodh al-Ardhi
Commander of the Navy: Rear Admiral Said Shiab bin Tareq al-Said

Area: 212,000 sq. km.
Population: 2,460,000

Economic Data

		1997	1998	1999	2000	2001
GDP (current price)	$ bn	15.84	14.08	15.71	19.73	19.94
Defense expenditure	$ bn	0.268	0.237	0.240	0.284	0.391

Major Arms Suppliers

Major arms suppliers include the US, which supplied combat aircraft, sea launch missiles, AAMs, early warning network, and aerial reconnaissance systems; and the UK, which supplied MBTs, missile corvettes, APCs, and air defense radars.

Other suppliers include Switzerland (training aircraft), Spain (patrol boats), Pakistan (training aircraft), Italy (helicopters), Netherlands (surveillance radar), and France (air defense systems).

Foreign Military Cooperation

Type	Details
Foreign forces	As of mid-March 2003, US and coalition forces were in the process of a buildup in advance of the war in Iraq. Since the outbreak of the war, the forces have been in constant flux.
Joint maneuvers	Egypt (2001), GCC countries (2001), India (2002), Jordan (2001), Pakistan (2002), UK (2001), US (2001)
Security agreements	GCC countries, Iran, Turkey (2001), US, India (2002)

Weapons of Mass Destruction

NBC Capabilities

Nuclear capability
No known nuclear activity. Signatory to the NPT.

Chemical weapons and protective equipment
No known CW activities. Party to the CWC.

Biological weapons
No known BW activities. Party to the BWC.

Armed Forces

Order-of-Battle

Year	1997	1999	2000	2001	2002
General data					
Personnel (regular)	34,000	34,000	34,000	34,000	34,000
Ground Forces					
Number of brigades	4	4	4	4	4
Total number of battalions	18	18	18	18	18
Tanks	178	131 (181)	131 (181)	151 (201)	151 (201)
APCs/AFVs	135 (166)	135 (166)	~135 (~165)	~225* (~335)	~225 (~335)
Artillery	148 (154)	148 (154)	148 (154)	148 (154)	148 (154)

Order-of-Battle (continued)

Year	1997	1999	2000	2001	2002
Air Force					
Combat aircraft	31 (47)	31 (47)	31	29 (30)	29 (30)
Transport aircraft	38 (42)	38 (42)	38 (42)	41 (45)	41 (45)
Helicopters	37	37	35	41	41
Air Defense Forces					
Light SAM launchers	58	58	58	58	58
Navy					
Combat vessels	9	9	9	9	9
Patrol craft	23	23	22	22	17

*Due to change in estimate

Personnel

	Regular	Reserves	Total
Ground Forces	25,000		25,000
Air Force	5,000		5,000
Navy	4,000		4,000
Total	**34,000**		**34,000**
Paramilitary			
Tribal force (Firqat)	3,500		3,500
Police/border police (operating aircraft, helicopters, and PBs)	7,000		7,000
Royal Household (including Royal Guard, Royal Yachts, and Royal Flight)	6,500		6,500

13. PALESTINIAN AUTHORITY

Major Changes

- Since the outbreak of the violence in September 2000, the Palestinian forces have operated several types of weapons, including mortars and LAW anti-tank missiles. They have acquired 107mm MRLs and allegedly also Strela (SA-7) shoulder launched SAMs and some ATGMs (though these have not yet been used).
- Their existing inventory of BRDM armored vehicles suffered damage and decreased in size.
- Some of the Palestinian forces are using indigenously produced mortars, Qassam artillery rockets, and some anti-tank rockets.

General Data

Official Name: Palestinian National Authority (PA)
Chairman: Yassir Arafat
Prime Minister: Mahmoud Abbas (Abu Mazen)
Minister of Internal Security: Mohammed Dahlan
Chief of Security Forces in Gaza: General Abd al-Rizak al-Majaida
Chief of Security Forces in West Bank: General al-Haj Ismail Jaber

Area: 400 sq. km. (Gaza), 5,800 sq. km. (West Bank). By the terms of the Interim Agreement, the West Bank is divided into three areas, designated A, B, and C. The PA has civilian responsibility for Palestinians in all three areas, exclusive internal security responsibility for Area A (18.2%), and shared security responsibility for Area B (24.8%). Israel maintains full security responsibility for the remaining 57% (area C).
Population: Gaza: 1,120,000 est.; West Bank: 2,000,000 est.

Economic Data

		1997	1998	1999	2000	2001
GDP (current price)	$ bn	3.959	4.230	4.288	4.360	4.093
Security expenditure	$ bn	0.250	0.300	0.500	NA	NA

Major Arms Suppliers

The Palestinian forces smuggle arms from Egypt and Lebanon. Sources of these weapons are not always known.

In 2001, Iran tried to send a shipload of arms, which was intercepted by Israel in January 2002.

Defense Production

Palestinians forces produce Qassam rockets, mortars, and explosive charges. Palestinian forces announced that they had managed to produce ATGMs, but these are probably unguided rockets.

Security Forces

Order-of-Battle

Year	1997	1999	2000	2001	2002
General data					
Personnel (regular)	~34,000	~34,000	~36,000	~45,000	~45,000
Ground Forces					
Regiments				6	6
APCs/AFVs	45	45	45	~40	+
Artillery					+
Aerial Police					
Helicopters	2 (4)	2 (4)	2 (4)	2 (4)	0
Coastal Police					
Patrol craft	7	13	10	13	0

Personnel

	Gaza	West Bank	Total	Notes
General Security Service branches				
Public Security	+	+	14,000	Also referred to as the National Security Force
Coastal Police	+	+	1,000	
Aerial Police	+	+	+	Rudimentary unit operating VIP helicopters
Civil Police	+	+	10,000	The Blue Police – a law enforcement agency; operates the 700-strong rapid deployment special police
Preventive Security Force	+	+	5,000	Plainclothes internal security force
General Intelligence	+	+	3,000	Intelligence gathering organization
Military Intelligence	+	+	+	Unrecognized preventive security force; includes the Military Police.

Personnel (continued)

	Gaza	West Bank	Total	Notes
Civil Defense	+	+	+	Emergency and rescue service
Additional security forces				
Presidential Security	+	+	3,000	Elite unit responsible for Arafat's security
Special Security Force	+	+	+	Unrecognized intelligence organization
Total	~25,000	~20,000	~45,000	

Note: More than two years of armed conflict between the PA and Israel have changed the situation described by this table. Most of the fighting was done by "unofficial organizations" like the Tanzim and Hamas. At present, there is no data concerning the status of the organizations listed above. Some of them ceased to exist, and some may reappear as strong organizations, depending on the personal status of their leaders. Thus, we prefer to display statistics as they were at the end of 2000. The Palestinian security services included several organizations under the "Palestinian Directorate of Police Force" recognized in the Cairo and Washington agreements. In addition, there were some organizations that reported directly to Arafat. Some of the security organizations (particularly the "Blue Police") had little or no military significance. They are mentioned here because of the unusual organizational structure, and because it is difficult to estimate the size of the total forces that do have military significance.

14. QATAR

Major Changes

- Qatar has become a major base for US activities in the Persian Gulf and against Iraq. The command post of the central command was relocated in Qatar. The US is operating a large new air base in al-Udeid, in addition to the large logistics base in al-Sahiliya.
- No major changes were occurred in the Qatari order-of-battle.

General Data

Official Name of the State: State of Qatar
Head of State: Shaykh Hamad ibn Khalifa al-Thani
Prime Minister: Abdallah Ibn Khalifa al-Thani
Minister of Defense: Shaykh Hamad ibn Khalifa al-Thani
Commander-in-Chief of the Armed Forces: Shaykh Hamad ibn Khalifa al-Thani
Chief of General Staff: Brigadier General Hamad ibn Ali al-Attiyah
Commander of the Ground Forces: Colonel Saif Ali al-Hajiri
Commander of the Air Force: General Ali Saeed al-Hawal al-Marri
Commander of the Navy: Captain Said al-Suwaydi

Area: 11,437 sq. km.
Population: 600,000

Economic Data

		1997	1998	1999	2000	2001
GDP (current prices)	$ bn	11.3	10.3	12.4	16.5	16.2
Defense expenditure	$ bn	NA	NA	NA	NA	NA

Major Arms Suppliers

France is the major arms supplier to Qatar. It supplied combat aircraft and MBTs.

The US built major installations, including a large air base and storage facilities. These installations are currently used by US forces.

Foreign Military Cooperation

Type	Details
Forces deployed abroad	Troops part of GCC "Peninsula Shield" rapid deployment force in Saudi Arabia
Foreign forces	As of mid-March 2003, US and coalition forces were in the process of a buildup in advance of the war in Iraq. Since the outbreak of the war, the forces have been in constant flux.
Joint maneuvers	France (2002), GCC countries (2002), Italy (2000), UK, US (2002), Yemen
Security agreements	Bahrain, France (1994), GCC defense pact (2000), Italy (2001), Iran, Kuwait, Oman (1999), Saudi Arabia

Weapons of Mass Destruction

NBC Capabilities

Nuclear capability
No known nuclear activity. Party to the NPT.

Chemical weapons and protective equipment
No known CW activities. Party to the CWC.

Biological weapons
No known BW activities. Party to the BWC.

Armed Forces

Order-of-Battle

Year	1997	1999	2000	2001	2002
General data					
Personnel (regular)	11,800	11,800	11,800	11,800	11,800
Ground Forces					
Number of brigades	1	1	2	2	2
Number of regiments	1	1			
Total number of battalions	10	10	11	11	11
Tanks	24	44	44	44	44
APCs/AFVs	230 (310)	222 (302)	~260 (338)	~260 (338)	~260 (338)
Artillery (including MRLs)	56	56	56	56	56
Air Force					
Combat aircraft	9	14	18	18	18
Transport aircraft	8	8	8	7 (8)	7 (8)
Helicopters	32	31	31	30 (31)	30 (31)

Order-of-Battle (continued)

Year	1997	1999	2000	2001	2002
Air Defense Forces					
Light SAM launchers	48	48	48	51	51
Navy					
Combat vessels	7	7	7	7	7
Patrol crafts	44	36	26	26	13

* Due to change in estimate

Personnel

	Regular	Reserves	Total
Ground Forces	8,500		8,500
Air Force	1,500		1,500
Navy (including Marine Police)	1,800		1,800
Total	**11,800**		**11,800**
Paramilitary			
Armed Police	8,000		8,000

15. SAUDI ARABIA

Major Changes

- Saudi Arabia has been a major base for US forces in past decades. Though it still remains a major base for US forces, the US has been transferring many of its operations to other Persian Gulf states.
- Saudi Arabia's economic situation ruled out further arms procurements. A potential acquisition of French Leclerc MBTs was cancelled.
- Saudi Arabia launched its third satellite using a Russian Start-1 launcher from Kazakhstan. The satellite will be used for civilian purposes.
- The Saudi Navy commissioned its first F-3000 LaFayette Frigate. The other two ships are scheduled to be commissioned in mid 2003 and in 2004.

General Data

Official Name of the State: The Kingdom of Saudi Arabia
Head of State: King Fahd ibn Abd al-Aziz al-Saud
Prime Minister: King Fahd ibn Abd al-Aziz al-Saud
First Deputy Prime Minister and Heir Apparent: Crown Prince Abdallah ibn Abd al-Aziz al-Saud
Defense and Aviation Minister: Prince Sultan ibn Abd al-Aziz al-Saud
Chief of General Staff: General Salih ibn Ali al-Muhaya
Commander of the Ground Forces: Lieutenant General Husein al-Qubeel
Commander of the National Guard: Crown Prince Abdallah ibn Abd al-Aziz al-Saud
Commander of the Air Force: Lieutenant General Muhammad ibn Abd al-Aziz al-Hunaydi
Commander of the Air Defense Forces: Lieutenant General Majid ibn Talhab al-Qutaybi
Commander of the Navy: Vice Admiral Fahd ibn Abdallah

Area: 2,331,000 sq. km.
Population: 21,000,000

Economic Data

		1997	1998	1999	2000	2001
GDP (current price)	$ bn	146.4	146.0	161.2	188.7	186.5
Defense expenditure	$ bn	17.6	20.8	17.6	20.0	25.86

Major Arms Suppliers

The major arms suppliers to Saudi Arabia are the US and France. The US supplied combat aircraft, AAMs, surveillance radars, anti-tank missiles, and early warning networks. France supplied combat vessels.

Other suppliers include Germany (helicopters), Italy (helicopters), UK (hovercraft, ARM missiles), and Canada (APCs, IFVs).

Foreign Military Cooperation

Type	Details
Foreign forces	GCC "Peninsula Shield" rapid deployment force: 7,000–10,000 men at Hafr al-Batin; mostly Saudis, and from other GCC countries
	As of mid-March 2003, US and coalition forces were in the process of a buildup in advance of the war in Iraq. Since the outbreak of the war, the forces have been in constant flux.
Joint maneuvers	Egypt (2001), France, GCC countries (2001), Jordan (2001), Pakistan (2001), UK, US (2001)

Defense Production

APCs, radar subsystems, parts of EW equipment.

Weapons of Mass Destruction

NBC Capabilities

Nuclear capability
No known nuclear activity. Party to the NPT.

Chemical weapons and protective equipment
No known CW activities. Personal protective equipment; decontamination units; US-made CAM chemical detection systems; Fuchs (Fox) NBC detection vehicles. Party to the CWC.

Biological weapons
No known BW activities. Party to the BWC.

Ballistic Missiles

Model	Launchers	Missiles	Since	Notes
CSS-2	8–12	30–50	1988	Number of launchers unconfirmed

Space assets

Model	Type	Notes
Satellites		
Saudisat 1A/1B/1C	Remote sensing and space research	2 satellites (10 kg each) were launched in September 2000 by a Russian military rocket and are orbiting 650 km above earth. The third satellite was launched in December 2002.
Arabsat	Communication	

Armed Forces

Order-of-Battle

Year	1997	1999	2000	2001	2002
General data					
Personnel (regular)	165,000	165,000	171,500	171,500	171,500
SSM launchers	8–12	8–12	8–12	8–12	8–12
Ground Forces					
Number of brigades	18	20	20	20	20
Tanks	865	865	750	750	750
	(1,015)	(1,015)	(1,015)	(1,015)	(1,015)
APCs/AFVs	5,220	~5,310	~5,300	~4,500	~4,630
		(~5,440)	(~5,440)	(~5,300)	(~5,430)
Artillery (incl. MRLs)	~410	~410	~410	~410	~410
	(~580)	(~780)	(~780)	(~780)	(~780)
Air Force					
Combat aircraft	321	~345	~355	~360 (~365)	~345
Transport aircraft	61	61	61	42 (55)	42 (55)
Helicopters	175	160	160	214 (216)	214 (216)
Air Defense Forces					
Heavy SAM batteries	22	22	22	25	25
Medium SAM batteries	16	16	16	21	21
Navy					
Combat vessels	24	24	24	24	25
Patrol craft	92	80	74	74	64

Personnel

	Regular	Reserves	Total
Ground Forces	75,000		75,000
Air Force	20,000		20,000
Air Defense	4,000		4,000
Navy (including a marine unit)	13,500		13,500
National Guard	57,000	20,000	77,000
Royal Guard	2,000		2,000
Total	**171,500**	**20,000**	**191,500**
Paramilitary			
Mujahidun (affiliated with National Guard)		30,000	30,000
Coast Guard	4,500		4,500
Frontier Corps	10,500		10,500

16. SUDAN

Major Changes

- The Sudanese Air Force acquired 12 MiG-29 combat aircraft from Russia. Their operational status is not yet known. Sudan also received 8 Mi-24 attack helicopters from Russia and two Mi-8 from Lithuania.

General Data

Official Name of the State: The Republic of Sudan
Head of State: President Omar Hassan Ahmad al-Bashir
Defense Minister: Major General Bakri Hassan Sallah
Chief of General Staff: General Abbas Arabi
Commander of the Air Force: Major General Ali Mahjoub Mardi
Commander of the Navy: Commodore Abbas al-Said Othman

Area: 2,504,530 sq. km.
Population: 31,800,000

Economic Data

		1997	1998	1999	2000	2001
GDP (current price)	$ bn	10.64	10.27	10.04	12.93	14.09
Defense expenditure	$ bn	0.10	0.21	0.24	0.33	NA

Major Arms Suppliers

Major arms sales to Sudan come from Russia, which supplied combat aircraft.

Previously Sudan received arms from Iran, which allegedly supplied tanks, aircraft, other vehicles, and EW equipment.

Other suppliers included Belarus (combat aircraft), Lithuania (helicopters), and Poland (tanks).

Foreign Military Cooperation

Type	Details
Foreign forces	PRC (alleged presence of forces for the defense of Chinese-operated oil fields) (2001)
Forces deployed abroad	Central African Republic (2002)
Security agreements	Syria (2000), Egypt (2001), Russia (2002)

Weapons of Mass Destruction

NBC Capabilities

Nuclear capability
No known nuclear activity. Party to the NPT.

Chemical weapons and protective equipment
Alleged CW from Iran (unsubstantiated); alleged production of CW (unsubstantiated); personal protective equipment; unit decontamination equipment. Party to the CWC.

Biological weapons
No known BW activities. Party to the BWC.

Armed Forces

Order-of-Battle

Year	1997	1999	2000	2001	2002
General data					
Personnel (regular)	84,500	103,000*	103,000	103,000	104,000
Ground Forces					
Divisions	9	9	9	9	9
Total number of brigades	58	61	61	61	61
Tanks	~320	~320	~350	~350	~350
APCs/AFVs	~560	~560	~560	~560	~545
	(~700)	(~700)	(~700)	(~700)	(~745)
Artillery (including MRLs)	753 (765)	~760 (~770)	~760 (~770)	~760 (~770)	~770 (~785)
Air Force					
Combat aircraft	~35 (~55)	~35 (~55)	~35 (~55)	~35 (~55)	~35 (~55)
Transport aircraft	26	26	25	24	24
Helicopters	~55 (67)	~60 (69)	~60 (69)	57 (73)	59 (71)
Air Defense Forces					
Heavy SAM batteries	5	5	5	20	20
Navy					
Patrol craft	22	22	18	18	18

* Due to change in estimate

Personnel

	Regular	Reserves	Total
Ground Forces	100,000		100,000
Air Force	3,000		3,000
Navy	1,000		1,000
Total	**104,000**		**104,000**
Paramilitary			
People's Defense Forces	15,000	85,000	100,000
Border Guard	2,500		2,500

17. SYRIA

Major Changes

- President Bashar Assad appointed a new Chief of the General Staff for the Syrian Armed Forces.
- Syria tested its first Scud D ballistic missile (with a range of 700 km). It is estimated that some of these missiles can be considered operational.

General Data

Official Name of the State: The Arab Republic of Syria
Head of State: President Bashar al-Assad
Prime Minister: Mohammed Mustafa Miro
Minister of Defense: Lieutenant General Mustafa al-Tlass
Chief of General Staff: Major General Hassan Turkamani
Commander of the Air Force: Major General Kamal Makhafut
Commander of the Navy: Vice Admiral Wa'il Nasser

Area: 185,180 sq. km.
Population: 17,100,000

Economic Data

		1997	1998	1999	2000	2001
GDP (current prices)	$ bn	16.8	17.1	17.7	19.4	19.8
Defense expenditure	$ bn	0.93	1.0	1.0	1.07	1.12

Major Arms Suppliers

Russia was the major supplier, and it remains the major potential supplier. In the past, it supplied Syria with all its major armament systems. Recent arms deals included combat aircraft and ATGMs.

Other suppliers include Iran (ballistic missile technology), North Korea (ballistic missiles), PRC (ballistic missiles), Ukraine (upgrading of tanks, radars), and Armenia (upgrading of tanks)

Major Arms Transfers

Lebanon (artillery rockets)

Foreign Military Cooperation

Type	Details
Forces deployed abroad	25,000 in Beka', northern Lebanon (Tripoli area), and Beirut

Defense Production

Ballistic missiles, artillery rockets, upgrading of tanks

Weapons of Mass Destruction

NBC Capabilities

Nuclear capability
Basic research. Alleged deal with Russia for a 24 MW reactor. Deals with PRC for a 27 kW reactor and with Argentina for a 3 MW research reactor are probably cancelled. Party to the NPT. Safeguards agreement with the IAEA in force.

Chemical weapons and protective equipment
Stockpiles of nerve gas, including sarin, mustard, and VX. Delivery vehicles include chemical warheads for SSMs and aerial bombs. Personal protective equipment; Soviet-type unit decontamination equipment. Not a party to the CWC.

Biological weapons
Biological weapons and toxins (unconfirmed). Signed but not ratified the BWC.

Ballistic Missiles

Model	Launchers	Missiles	Since	Notes
SS-1 (Scud B)	18	200	1974	
SS-1 (Scud C)	8	80	1992	
SS-21 (Scarab)	18		1983	
Scud D	+		2002	
Total	~44			

Armed Forces

Order-of-Battle

Year	1997	1999	2000	2001	2002
General data					
Personnel (regular)	380,000	380,000	380,000	380,000	380,000
SSM launchers	44	44	44	44	~45
Ground Forces					
Divisions	12	12	12	12	12
Total number of brigades	67	67	67	67	67
Tanks	3,700	3,700	3,700	3,700	3,700
	(4,800)	(4,800)	(4,800)	(4,800)	(4,800)
APCs/AFVs	4,980	4,980	~5,000	~5,000	5,060
Artillery (including MRLs)	2,575	2,575	~2,600	~2,600	~2,600
	(2,975)	(2,975)	(~3,000)	(~3,000)	(~3,000)
Air Force					
Combat aircraft	520	520	520	490	490
Transport aircraft	23 (25)	23 (25)	23 (25)	23 (25)	23
Helicopters	295	295	295	285	225*
Air Defense Forces					
Heavy SAM batteries	108	108	108	108	108
Medium SAM batteries	65	65	64	64	64
Light SAM launchers	55	55	55	55	55
Navy					
Submarines	0 (3)	0 (3)	0 (3)	0 (3)	
Combat vessels	25 (30)	24 (27)	14*	14	14
Patrol craft	8	8	8	8	8

*Due to change in estimate

Personnel

	Regular	Reserves	Total
Ground Forces	306,000	100,000	406,000
Air Force	30,000	10,000	40,000
Air Defense	40,000	20,000	60,000
Navy	4,000	2,500	6,500
Total	**380,000**	**132,500**	**512,500**
Paramilitary			
Gendarmerie	8,000		8,000
Workers' Militia		400,000	400,000

18. TUNISIA

Major Changes

• No major change was recorded in the Tunisian order-of-battle.

General Data

Official Name of the State: The Republic of Tunisia
Head of State: President Zayn al-Abedine Bin Ali
Prime Minister: Mohamed Ghannouchi
Minister of Defense: Dali Jazi
Secretary of State for National Defense: Chokri Ayachi
Commander of the Ground Forces: Brigadier General Rashid Amar
Commander of the Air Force: Major General Rida Hamuda Atar
Commander of the Navy: Commodore Brahim Barak

Area: 164,206 sq. km.
Population: 9,700,000

Economic Data

		1997	1998	1999	2000	2001
GDP (current prices)	$ bn	18.9	19.8	20.8	19.5	20.0
Defense expenditure	$ bn	0.36	0.37	0.36	0.32	0.32

Major Arms Suppliers

Tunisia had no major arms deals in the past decade. Minor acquisitions were from France (APCs), US (transport aircraft), and Italy (transport aircraft).

Foreign Military Cooperation

Type	Details
Forces deployed abroad	Bosnia and Herzegovina (UNMIBH), Congo (MONUC)
Joint maneuvers	France, US, Spain (unconfirmed)
Security cooperation	Egypt (2001), Greece (2001), Libya (2001), Morocco (2000)

Defense Production

Patrol boats

Weapons of Mass Destruction

NBC Capabilities

Nuclear capability
No known nuclear activity. Signatory to the NPT.

Chemical weapons and protective equipment
No known CW activities. Party to the CWC.

Biological weapons
No known BW activities. Party to the BWC.

Armed Forces

Order-of-Battle

Year	1997	1999	2000	2001	2002
General data					
Personnel (regular)	35,500	35,500	35,500	35,500	35,500
Ground Forces					
Number of brigades	5	5	5	5	5
Tanks	139 (144)	139 (144)	139 (144)	139 (144)	139 (144)
APCs/AFVs	316	316	316	316	326
Artillery (including MRLs)	205 (215)	205 (215)	205 (215)	205 (215)	205
Air Force					
Combat aircraft	12	12	12	18	18
Transport aircraft	10 (11)	10 (11)	10 (11)	9 (11)	15 (17)
Helicopters	40	40	44	51	49
Air Defense Forces					
Light SAM launchers	73	73	83	83	83
Navy					
Combat vessels	11	11	9	9	9
Patrol crafts	36	36	37	37	35

Personnel

	Regular	Reserves	Total
Ground Forces	27,000		27,000
Air Force	4,000		4,000
Navy	4,500		4,500
Total	**35,500**		**35,500**
Paramilitary			
Gendarmerie	2,000		2,000
National Guard	7,000		7,000

19. TURKEY

Major Changes

- Turkey began to renew some of its procurement programs, which were cancelled or postponed following the economic crisis of March 2001. Turkey expects massive aid from the US as compensation for its role in the war against Iraq.
- The Turkish land forces did not renew their proposed requirement for new advanced MBTs but signed a contract with Israel to upgrade 170 M60 MBTs – out of some 900 fit for this upgrade. The land forces are absorbing a second batch of 551 ACVs from the Turkish industry.
- An ongoing project is the renewal of the Turkish artillery with 300 Firtina 155mm self-propelled guns and 400 Panther 155mm towed howitzers, all indigenously assembled.
- Another important acquisition is the Harpy anti- radar drone received from Israel.
- The Air Force received almost all of its upgraded Phantom F-4 combat aircraft. The upgrade project is scheduled to end by mid 2003. Another upgrade project involves the aging F-5 aircraft, which are being upgraded and will be used for training.
- The Air Force is absorbing its new command and control system, which includes 14 TRS-22XX radars from France.
- The naval aviation is absorbing 8 S-70 Seahawk helicopters. Further acquisitions of these helicopters are expected.
- The Turkish Navy received the last of 6 used A-69 corvettes from France. These are acquired as "gap fillers" until the new Mil Gem corvettes will be supplied. The Turkish Navy also received its seventh Oliver Hazard Perry Frigate from the US Navy. Two more Oliver Hazard Perry frigates are to be supplied. The first of 4 Gur class submarines was launched.
- The Coast Guard received 5 of 10 proposed Seaguard patrol boats.

General Data

Official Name of the State: Republic of Turkey
Head of State: President Ahmet Necdet Sezer
Prime Minister: Recep Tayyip Erdogan
Minister of National Defense: Vecdi Gonul
Chief of General Staff: General Hilmi Ozkok
Commander of the Ground Forces: General Aytac Yalman
Commander of the Air Force: General Cumhur Asparuk
Commander of the Navy: Admiral Bülent Alpkaya

Area: 780,580 sq. km.
Population: 66,500,000

Economic Data

		1997	1998	1999	2000	2001
GDP (current prices)	$ bn	189.9	200.3	184.9	199.3	148.0
Defense expenditure	$ bn	7.8	8.8	9.95	10.0	7.36

Major Arms Suppliers

Turkey's major arms suppliers are the US, France, and Germany. The US supplied combat vessels, combat aircraft, helicopters, early-warning aircraft, AD missiles, anti-tank missiles, and radars. France supplied combat vessels, helicopters, training aircraft, and cruise missiles. Germany supplied submarines and combat vessels.

Other suppliers include Israel (upgrading of combat aircraft, upgrading of tanks, upgrading of helicopters, anti-radiation drones), South Korea (self-propelled artillery guns), Italy (helicopters, radars), Norway (cruise missiles), Spain (transport aircraft), and the UK (AD missiles).

Major Arms Transfers

Turkey sold armament systems to several countries, including Malaysia (IFVs), UAE (IFVs), Israel (APCs), Jordan (transport aircraft), Azerbaijan (patrol boats, APCs), Croatia (transport aircraft), Georgia (patrol boats, helicopters), Kazakhstan (patrol boats, APCs), and Macedonia (combat aircraft).

Foreign Military Cooperation

Type	Details
Foreign forces	Italy, UK, US (2,000 troops)
Forces deployed abroad	Afghanistan; Albania; Bosnia (UNMIBH); Cyprus (30,000 troops); East Timor (UNTAET); Georgia (UNOMIG); northern Iraq (1,000 troops); Iraq/Kuwait (UNIKOM); Italy (F-16 aircraft, part of KFOR); Kosovo (150 troops in KFOR); Israel (TIPH); Macedonia (140 troops)
Cooperation in training	Albania, Azerbaijan, Israel (mutual use of airspace and training facilities), Jordan (mutual use of airspace and training facilities; joint training of infantry), Georgia, PRC
Joint maneuvers	Albania (naval – 2000), Bulgaria (part of multinational peacekeeping brigade – 2001), Georgia (naval), Israel (2001), Jordan, Macedonia (part of multinational peacekeeping brigade – 2000), NATO member states (2000), Pakistan, Poland, Romania (part of multinational peacekeeping brigade – 2000), US (2001)
Security agreements	Croatia (2001), France, Georgia (2001), Kazakhstan (2000), Latvia, Oman (2001)

Defense Production

Turkey has a large and diversified defense industry. Its aerospace industry produces or assembles combat aircraft, helicopters, and transport and training aircraft. Its naval industry produces or assembles submarines, combat vessels, and patrol boats. Land based systems produced include ACVs, self-propelled guns, and AD systems. Other munitions produced include artillery rockets and anti-tank missiles. The electronic industry produces radars, electronic warfare systems, and fire-control systems.

Weapons of Mass Destruction

NBC Capabilities

Nuclear capability

One 5 MW TR-2 research reactor at Cekmerce and one 250 kW ITV-TRR research reactor at Istanbul. Turkey intends to order a 1,000 MW reactor. As a member of NATO, nuclear weapons were deployed in Turkey in the past and may be deployed again. Party to the NPT. Safeguards agreement with the IAEA in force.

Chemical weapons and protective equipment

Personal protective suits; portable chemical detectors; Fox detection vehicles. Party to the CWC.

Biological weapons

No known BW activity. Party to the BWC.

Ballistic Missiles

Model	Launchers	Missiles	Since	Notes
ATACMS	12	72	1997	Using MLRS launchers
Future procurement				
J project			2001	Under development

Space Assets

Model	Type	Notes
Satellites		
Turksat-2A	Communication	Both civilian and military
Satellite imagery		
Ofeq 5	Reconnaissance	Sharing of satellite imagery from Israeli satellite

Armed Forces

Order-of-Battle

Year	1997	1999	2000	2001	2002
General data					
Personnel (regular)	639,000	633,000	633,000	610,000	515,000
SSM launchers	12	12	12	12	12
Ground Forces					
Divisions	5	5	5	5	3
Total number of brigades	67	67	67	67	63
Tanks	4,115	4,115	4,205	2,600	2,600
	(4,190)	(4,190)	(4,280)	(4,255)	(4,255)
APCs/AFVs	4,743	4,520	5,460	5,460	5,460
Artillery (including MRLs)	4,113	4,312	~4,350	~4,350	~4,355
	(4,412)	(4,611)	(~4,650)	(~4,650)	(~4,655)
Air Force					
Combat aircraft	461	416	485	~445 (465)	~390 (410)
Transport aircraft	87	87	92	90 (94)	93 (97)
Helicopters	381	381	395	407	461
Air Defense Forces					
Heavy SAM batteries	24	24	24	24	24
Light SAM launchers	86	86	86	86	86
Navy					
Combat vessels	75	51	65	78	83
Patrol crafts	96	88	108	103	113
Submarines	17	16	15	14	13

Personnel

	Regular	Reserves	Total
Ground Forces	402,000	259,000	661,000
Air Force	60,000	65,000	125,000
Navy	53,000	55,000	108,000
Total	**515,000**	**379,000**	**894,000**
Paramilitary			
Coast Guard	2,200		2,200
Gendarmerie/ National Guard	180,000	50,000	230,000

20. UNITED ARAB EMIRATES (UAE)

Major Changes

- Inauguration of the GCC joint communication network, which is part of the GCC joint early warning system. Delivery of Leclerc MBTs was resumed after a dispute with the manufacturer was resolved.
- The Emiri Army is absorbing its newly upgraded 155mm M109 and G6 guns. It is also absorbing the last of the ACVs from Turkey and new Terrier light APCs from Germany.
- The Emiri Air Force concluded the deal to acquire 80 F-16 block 60 combat aircraft (which will be delivered between 2004 and 2008). The Air Force signed a contract for upgrading its 30 Apache AH-64 attack helicopters and another contract for upgrading its Puma SA-330 helicopters.
- The Emiri Navy began the process of upgrading its TNC-45 MFPBs.

General Data

Official Name of the State: United Arab Emirates
Head of State: Shaykh Zayid ibn Sultan al-Nuhayan, Emir of Abu Dhabi
Prime Minister: Shaykh Maktum ibn Rashid al-Maktum, Emir of Dubai
Minister of Defense: Muhammad ibn Rashid al-Maktum
Chief of General Staff: HRH Lieutenant General Muhammad ibn Zayid al-Nuhayan
Commander of the Air Force and
Air Defense Forces: Brigadir General Khalid bin Abdullah al-Buainnain
Commander of the Navy: Brigadir General Suhail Shaheen al-Murar

Area:. 82,900 sq. km. (estimate)
Population: 3,100,000 (estimate)

Note: The UAE consists of seven principalities: Abu Dhabi, Dubai, Ras al-Khaima, Sharja, Umm al-Qaiwain, Fujaira, and Ajman

Economic Data

		1997	1998	1999	2000	2001
GDP (current price)	$ bn	44.6	46.5	57.9	70.2	67.6
Defense expenditure	$ bn	1.64	1.64	1.64	1.64	1.64

Major Arms Suppliers

The US and France are UAE's major arms suppliers. The US supplied combat aircraft, attack helicopters, AAMs, naval SAMs, anti-ship missiles, command and control aircraft, and advanced air launched munitions. France supplied combat aircraft, helicopters, MBTs, SAMs, ARVs, torpedos, anti-ship missiles, and C^{3}I systems

Other suppliers include Netherlands (frigates, surveillance radars), Germany (training aircraft, APCs, tank transporters, ABC detection vehicles), Indonesia (maritime patrol aircraft), Romania (upgrading of helicopters), Russia (procurement and upgrading of IFVs, air defense systems), Spain (patrol aircraft), UK (AGMs, sonar), and South Africa (EW systems).

Foreign Military Cooperation

Type	Details
Foreign forces	As of mid-March 2003, US and coalition forces were in the process of a buildup in advance of the war in Iraq. Since the outbreak of the war, the forces have been in constant flux.
Forces deployed abroad	In Saudi Arabia (part of GCC "Peninsula Shield" rapid deployment force). In early 2003, UAE sent forces to Kuwait in preparation for the war with Iraq.
Joint maneuvers	Egypt (2001), France (2002), GCC countries (2002), Jordan (2001), US (2001), Turkey (2002)
Security agreements	France (2000), Germany, Slovak Republic (1999)

Defense Production

UAE's industry produces patrol boats, corvettes, amphibious landing craft, and assembles UAVs and mini-UAVs and target drones.

Weapons of Mass Destruction

NBC Capabilities

Nuclear capability
No known nuclear activity. Signatory to the NPT.

Chemical weapons and protective equipment
No known CW activities. Personal protective equipment; unit decontamination equipment. Signed and ratified the CWC.

Biological weapons
No known BW activities. Signed but not ratified the BWC.

Ballistic Missiles

Model	Launchers	Missiles	Since	Notes
Scud B	6		1991	Owned by Dubai; unconfirmed

Space assets

Model	Type	Notes
Satellites		
Thuraya-1	communication	Geosynchronous, civilian satellite

Armed Forces

Order-of-Battle

Year	1997	1999	2000	2001	2002
General data					
Personnel (regular)	46,500	46,500	46,500	46,500	65,500
SSM launchers	6	6	6	6	6
Ground forces					
Number of brigades	9	8	8	8	8
Tanks	~370	~330	~430	~400	532
	(~430)	(~430)	(~470)*	(~470)	(604)
APCs/AFVs	~960	~960	~1,250	~1,250	~1,190
	(~1,120)	(~1,120)	(~1,400)	(~1,410)	(~1,350)
Artillery (including MRLs)	411	411	399	399	399
	(434)	(434)	(422)	(422)	(422)
Air Force					
Combat aircraft	54 (66)	54 (66)	54 (66)	54 (66)	54 (66)
Transport aircraft	31 (34)	31 (34)	31 (34)	33 (36)	33 (36)
Helicopters	93 (95)	93 (95)	100 (102)	91 (103)	102 (114)
Air Defense Forces					
Heavy SAM batteries	~7	~7	5	5	5
Medium SAM batteries	6	6	6	6	6
Light SAM launchers	113	113	~115	~115	~115
Navy					
Combat vessels	12	12	12	12	12
Patrol craft	119	105	110	112	112

* Due to change in estimate

Personnel

	Regular	Reserves	Total
Ground Forces	59,000		59,000
Air Force	4,500		4,500
Navy	2,000		2,000
Total	**65,500**		**65,500**
Paramilitary			
Coast Guard			+
Frontier Corps			+

21. YEMEN

Major Changes

- Yemen is working to improve its defense relations with the US, and the US is scheduled to train Yemeni personnel in counterterrorism activities. The US will help Yemen establish its Coast Guard. At the same time, Yemen continues to acquire weapon systems from other sources, mainly Russia.
- Yemen received 14 new MiG-29 combat aircraft so far, and 10 more are to be supplied.
- The Yemeni land forces are absorbing the T-72 MBTs from Russia and some 100 upgraded T-55 MBTs from the Czech Republic, all of which were received in 2000.
- The Navy acquired 4 landing craft from Poland.

General Data

Official Name of the State: Republic of Yemen
Head of State: President Ali Abdallah Salih
Prime Minister: Abd al-Qadir Ba Jamal
Minister of Defense: Brig. General Abdallah Ali Alaywa
Chief of General Staff: Brig. General Abdallah Ali Alaywah
Commander of the Air Force: Colonel Muhammad Salih al-Ahmar
Commander of the Navy: Admiral Abdallah al-Mujawar

Area: 527,970 sq. km.
Population: 19,000,000

Economic Data

		1997	1998	1999	2000	2001
GDP (current price)	$ bn	6.6	5.9	6.7	8.4	8.4
Defense expenditure	$ bn	0.42	0.4	0.37	0.4	0.46

Major Arms Suppliers

Russia is Yemen's major arms supplier. It supplied combat aircraft and MBTs.

Other suppliers include North Korea (SSMs), Poland (landing craft), Czech Republic (training aircraft, tanks), and the US (C³ systems, patrol boats).

Foreign Military Cooperation

Type	Details
Foreign forces	Some 200 U.S soldiers (2002)
Security agreements	Turkey (2002)

Weapons of Mass Destruction

NBC Capabilities

Nuclear capability
No known nuclear activity. Signatory to the NPT.

Chemical weapons and protective equipment
No known CW activities. Signed and ratified the CWC.

Biological weapons
No known BW activities. Party to the BWC.

Ballistic Missiles

Model	Launchers	Missiles	Since	Notes
SS-1 (Scud B)	6			New missiles received from North Korea, possibly Scud C
SS-21 (Scarab)	4		1988	
Total	10			

Note: Serviceability of missiles and launchers unknown.

Armed Forces

Note: Since the 1994 civil war, all figures are rough estimates.

Order-of-Battle

Year	1997	1999	2000	2001	2002
General data					
Personnel (regular)	~65,000	~65,000	~65,000	~65,000	~65,000
SSM launchers	10	10	10	10	10
Ground Forces					
Number of brigades	33	33	33	33	33
Tanks	575	575	605	~715	~715
	(1,040)	(1,040)	(1,070)	(~1,180)	(~1,180)

Order-of-Battle (Continued)

Year	1997	1999	2000	2001	2002
APCs/AFVs	480	~480	~480	~480	~495
	(1,165)	(~1,170)	(~1,200)	(~1,200)	(~1,210)
Artillery (including MRLs)	~670	~670	~670	~670	~675
	(~1,020)	(~990)*	(~1,000)	(~1,000)	(~1,025)
Air Force					
Combat aircraft	~55 (~150)	~50 (~150)	~50 (~150)	~55 (~180)	~65 (~190)
Transport aircraft	18 (23)	18 (23)	18 (23)	20 (30)	20 (30)
Helicopters	27 (67)	27 (67)	26 (66)	26 (70)	26 (70)
Air Defense Forces					
Heavy SAM batteries	25	25	25	25	25
Medium SAM batteries	+	+	+	+	+
Light SAM launchers	120	120	120	120	120
Navy					
Combat vessels	11	11	10	10	10
Patrol craft	7	3	9	9	8

* Due to change in estimate.

Personnel

	Regular	Reserves	Total
Ground Forces	~60,000	200,000	~260,000
Air Force	3,000		3,000
Navy	2,000		2,000
Total	**~65,000**	**200,000**	**~265,000**
Paramilitary			
Central Security Force	50,000		50,000

Note: The military forces are a combination of personnel from the former Yemen Arab Republic and the People's Democratic Republic of Yemen; no information regarding reorganization is available.

Tables and Charts

The Middle East Military Balance at a Glance

State	Personnel			Ground Forces			
	Regular	Reserves	Total	Tanks	Fighting vehicles (APCs/ AFVs)	Artillery	Ballistic missile launchers (SSM)s
Eastern Mediterranean							
Egypt	450,000	254,000	704,000	~3,000	~3,400	~3,530	24
Israel	186,500	445,000	631,500	3,930	8,000	1,348	+
Jordan	100,700	60,000	160,700	~990	1,606	838	
Lebanon	61,400		61,400	280	1,235	~335	
Syria	380,000	132,500	512,500	3,700	~5,060	~2,600	~45
Turkey	515,000	379,000	894,000	2,600	5,460	~4,355	12
Persian Gulf							
Bahrain	8,200		8,200	180	277	48	9
Iran	~520,000	350,000	870,000	~1,700	~1,570	~2,700	~40
Iraq	0	0	0	0	0	0	0
Kuwait	15,500	24,000	39,500	318	~530	~100	
Oman	34,000		34,000	151	~225	148	
Qatar	11,800		11,800	44	~260	56	
Saudi Arabia	171,500	20,000	191,500	750	~4,630	~410	12
UAE	65,500		65,500	~532	~1,190	399	6
North Africa and others							
Algeria	127,000	150,000	277,000	900	2,110	900	
Libya	76,000		76,000	~650	~2,750	~2,320	~80
Morocco	145,500	150,000	295,500	640	1,120	1,060	
Sudan	104,000		104,000	~350	~545	~770	
Tunisia	35,500		35,500	139	326	205	
Yemen	65,000	200,000	265,000	~715	~495	~675	10

The Middle East Military Balance at a Glance (continued)

Air Force			Air Defense				Navy	
Combat aircraft	Transport aircraft	Helicopters	Heavy batteries	Medium batteries	Light launchers	Submarines	Combat vessels	Patrol craft
Eastern Mediterranean								
505	44	~225	109	44	105	4	62	104
538	64	239	22		~70	5	17	33
91	14	74	14	50	50			10
	16						20	
490	23	225	108	64	55		14	8
390	93	461	24		86	13	83	113
Persian Gulf								
34	2	40	1	2	40		11	21
207	105	345	29		95	3	29	~110
0	0	0	0	0	0	0	0	0
40	5	25	12				10	69
29	41	41			58		9	17
18	7	30			51		7	13
~345	42	214	25	21			25	64
54	33	102	5	6	~115		12	112
North Africa and others								
228	41	131	11	18	78	2	26	16
~340	85	127	~30	~10	55		20	
59	41	121			37		13	52
~35	24	59	20					18
18	15	49			83		9	35
~65	20	26	25		120		10	8

Weapons of Mass Destruction

State	Chemical	Biological	Nuclear	SSM Launchers		
				Up to 150 km	150–600 km	600–3,000 km
Eastern Mediteranean						
Egypt	alleged weapons stockpiles	R&D	R&D		24	+
Israel	R&D	R&D	alleged weapons stockpiles*	12		+*
Syria	weapons stockpiles	alleged weapons program	R&D	18	26	1
Turkey	none	none	R&D	12		
Persian Gulf						
Bahrain	none	none	none		9	
Iran	weapons stockpiles	alleged weapons program	alleged weapons program	16	20	5
Iraq	weapons stockpiles	weapons stockpiles	weapons program		10	
Saudi Arabia	none	none	none			12
UAE	none	none	none		6	
North Africa and others						
Algeria	none	none	R&D			
Libya	weapons stockpiles	alleged weapons program	R&D		80	+
Sudan	alleged weapons program	none	none			

* According to foreign publications, as cited by Israeli publications.

Space Assets

State	Imagery ground stations	Communication satellites	Research Satellites	Reconnaissance satellites	SLVs
Eastern Mediteranean					
Egypt	+	+			
Israel		+	+	+	+
Syria	+				
Turkey		+			
The Persian Gulf					
Saudi Arabia	+	+	+		
UAE	+	+			
North Africa and others					
Algeria			+		

The Eastern Mediterranean Military Forces

Eastern Mediterranean – Personnel

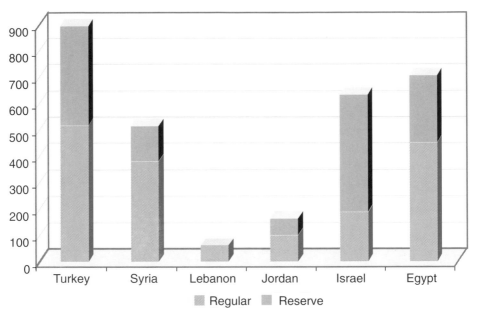

Eastern Mediterranean – Armor

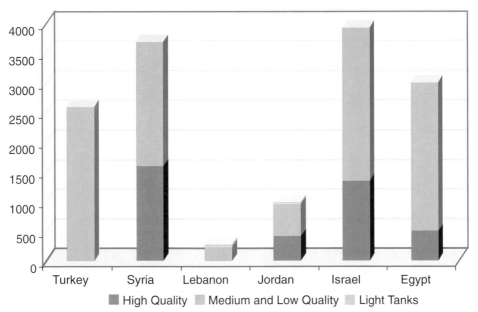

The Eastern Mediterranean Military Forces (continued)

Eastern Mediterranean – ACVs

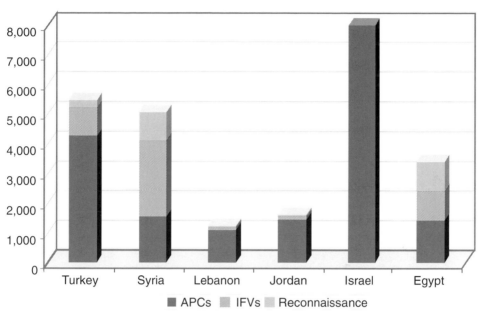

Eastern Mediterranean – Artillery

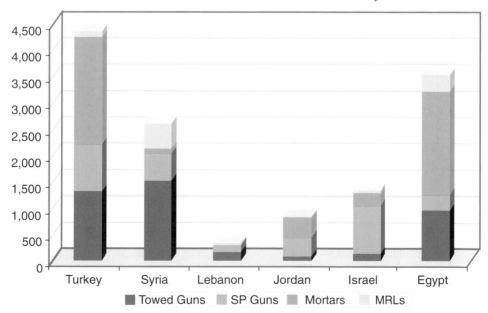

The Eastern Mediterranean Military Forces (continued)

Eastern Mediterranean – Combat Aircraft

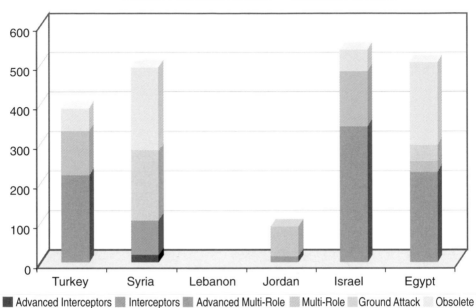

Eastern Mediterranean – Helicopters

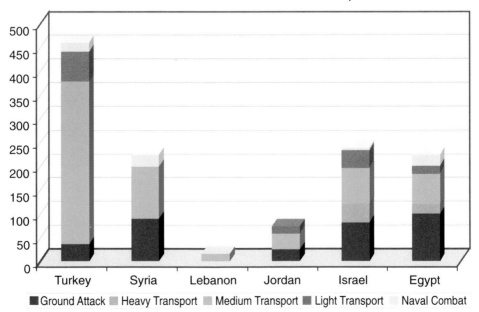

The Eastern Mediterranean Military Forces (continued)

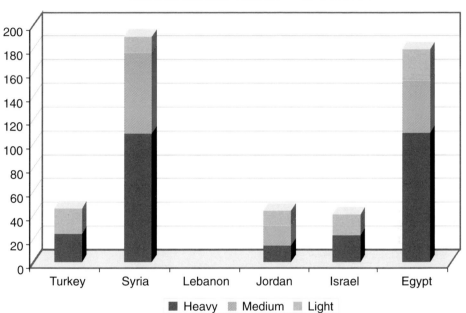

Eastern Mediterranean – Air Defense

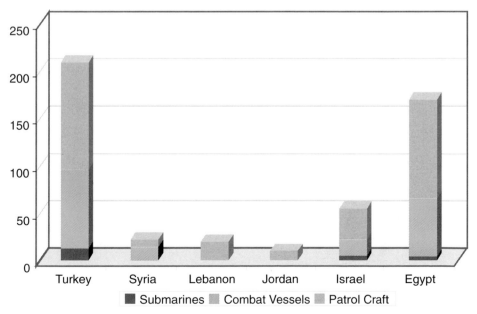

Eastern Mediterranean – Naval Vessels

The Persian Gulf Military Forces

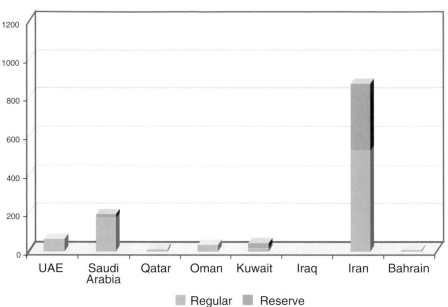

The Gulf – Personnel

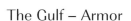

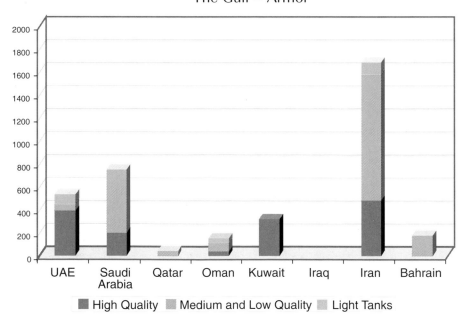

The Gulf – Armor

The Persian Gulf Military Forces (continued)

The Gulf – ACVs

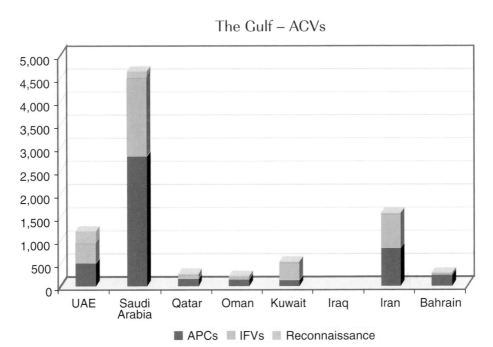

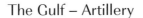

The Gulf – Artillery

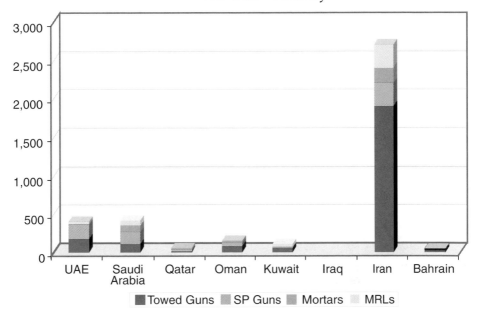

The Persian Gulf Military Forces (continued)

The Gulf – Combat Aircraft

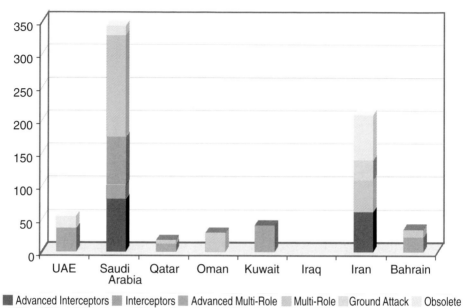

The Gulf – Helicopters

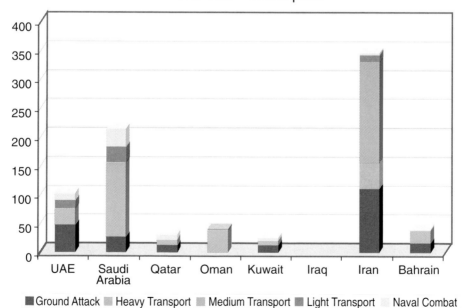

The Persian Gulf Military Forces (continued)

The Gulf – Air Defense

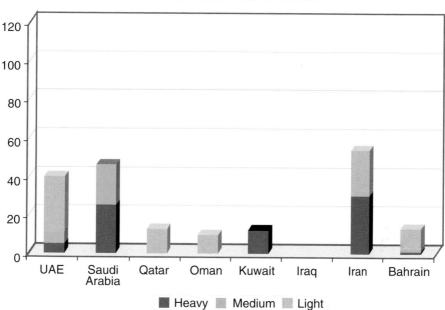

The Gulf – Naval Vessels

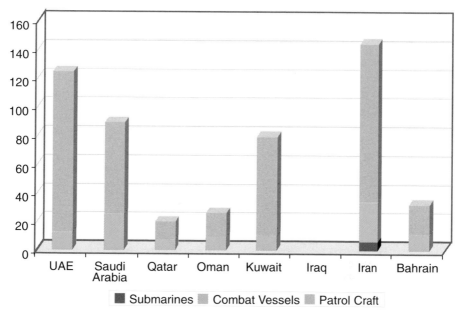

The North African Military Forces

North Africa – Personnel

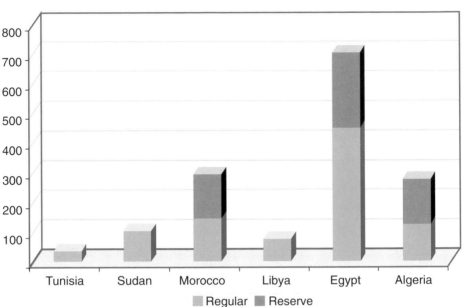

Regular   Reserve

North Africa – Armor

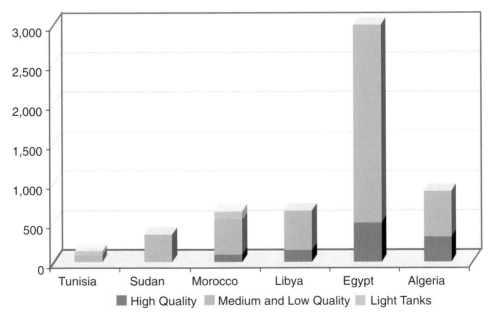

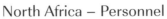
High Quality   Medium and Low Quality   Light Tanks

The North African Military Forces (continued)

North Africa – ACVs

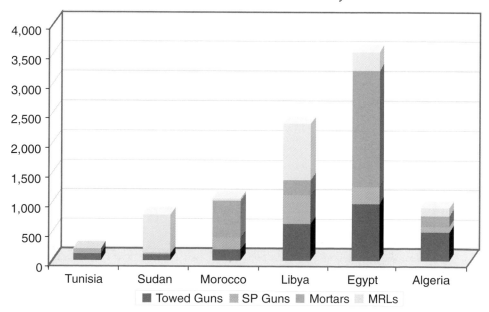

North Africa – Artillery

The North African Military Forces (continued)

North Africa – Combat Aircraft

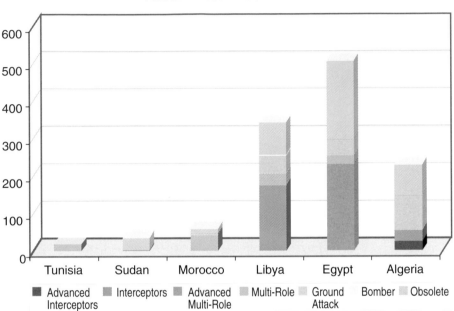

Legend: Advanced Interceptors | Interceptors | Advanced Multi-Role | Multi-Role | Ground Attack | Bomber | Obsolete

North Africa – Helicopters

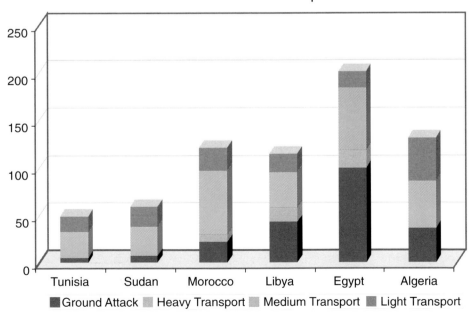

Legend: Ground Attack | Heavy Transport | Medium Transport | Light Transport

The North African Military Forces (continued)

North Africa – Air Defense

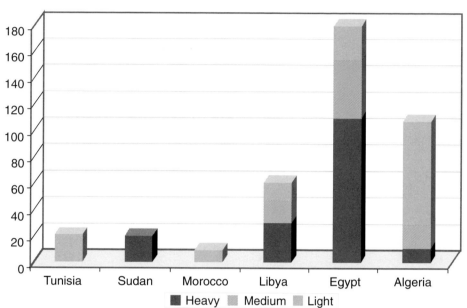

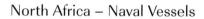

North Africa – Naval Vessels

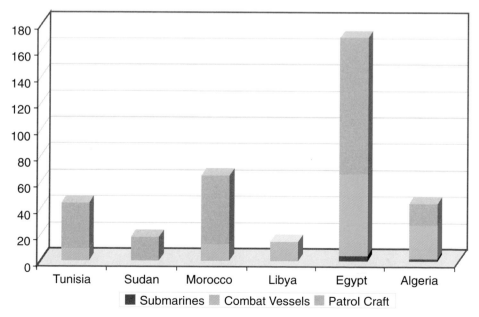

Contributors

Editors

Ephraim Kam, Deputy Head of the Jaffee Center, served as a Colonel in the Research Division of IDF Military Intelligence until 1993, when he joined the Jaffee Center. Positions he held in the IDF included Assistant Director of the Research Division for Evaluation and Senior Instructor at the IDF's National Defense College. He specializes in security problems of the Middle East, strategic intelligence, and Israel's national security issues. He earned his Ph.D. in political science at Harvard University. His book, *Surprise Attack: The Victim's Perspective,* was published by Harvard University Press and was awarded the 1988 prize for best book on intelligence matters from the National Intelligence Study Center, Washington, D.C.

Yiftah S. Shapir joined the Jaffee Center in 1993 as an associate of the Center's Project on Security and Arms Control in the Middle East, where he followed the proliferation of weapons of mass destruction in the Middle East. Since 1996, he has been responsible for the quantitative section of the *Middle East Military Balance.* Before joining the Center, Shapir served as an officer in the Israeli Air Force. He holds a B.Sc. in physics and chemistry from the Hebrew University, and an MBA from Tel Aviv University.

Other Contributors

Yehuda Ben Meir, a psychologist and an attorney, served as an Assistant Professor and Chairman of the Department of Psychology at Bar Ilan University. He served in the Knesset from 1971 to 1984 and as Deputy Minister of Foreign Affairs in the Begin and Shamir governments, from 1981 to 1984. His affiliation with JCSS began in 1984. He is the author of *Civil Military Relations in Israel* and *National Security Decisionmaking: The Israeli Case.*

Shlomo Brom joined the Jaffee Center as a Senior Research Associate in November 1998 after a long career in the IDF. His most senior post in the IDF was Head of the Strategic Planning Division in the Planning Branch of the General Staff. Brigadier General Brom participated actively in peace negotiations with the Palestinians, Jordan, and Syria. In 2000 Brom was named Deputy to the National Security

Advisor, returning to JCSS at the end of his post. He authored *Israel and South Lebanon: In the Absence of a Peace Treaty with Syria*, and edited *The Middle East Military Balance 1999-2000* and *The Middle East Military Balance 2001-2002*.

Shai Feldman was appointed Head of the Jaffee Center in 1997, prior to which he was a Senior Research Associate since the Center's establishment. He is a member of the UN Secretary-General's Advisory Board on Disarmament Matters, the Scientific Advisory Committee of the Stockholm International Peace Research Institute (SIPRI), and other organizations. Dr. Feldman has written extensively on nuclear weapons proliferation and arms control in the Middle East, US policy in the region, American-Israeli relations, and the Middle East peace process.

Mark A. Heller is Principal Research Associate at the Jaffee Center and editor of *Tel Aviv Notes*. He has been affiliated with the Jaffee Center since 1979 and has taught international relations at Tel Aviv University and at leading universities in the US. Dr. Heller has written extensively on Middle Eastern political and strategic issues. He is also currently a member of the Steering Committee of EuroMeSCo, the Euro-Mediterranean consortium of foreign policy research institutes.

Anat Kurz is a Senior Research Associate who has headed the Jaffee Center's Project on Low-Intensity Conflict since 1989. She has published widely on insurgency related issues, and edited *Contemporary Trends in World Terrorism*. Among her recent publications are the co-authored *Islamic Terror and Israel: Hizballah, Palestinian Islamic Jihad, and Hamas* and *Hamas: Radical Islam in a National Struggle*. Her current research focuses on the institutionalization of popular struggles.

Nachman Tal joined the Jaffee Center in 1996 following his retirement from the General Security Service. He was a member of the Israeli delegation to the Madrid Conference in October 1991, took part in the negotiations with the Palestinian–Jordanian delegation in 1992, and was a member of the Israeli delegation to the peace talks with the Jordanians that culminated in the peace agreement signed in October 1994. He is the author of *Islamic Fundamentalism: The Case of Egypt and Jordan*.

Imri Tov was a senior economist at the Bank of Israel, and from 1988 to 2000 served as the economic advisor to the Israeli defense establishment. He teaches defense economics at Tel Aviv University, and he assumed his position as a Senior Research Associate at the Jaffee Center in 2000. He is the author of *The Price of Defense Power* and editor of *Defense and Israel's National Economy: Exploring Issues in Security Production*.